Born and raised in South Australia's famous wine-growing region the Barossa Valley, Andrew Ramsey began working life as a bank teller before realising he was far more comfortable with words than numbers. He worked as a daily newspaper journalist in Adelaide and Melbourne for twenty years, with the final decade spent as a touring cricket writer for *The Australian*, accompanying the Australian cricket team on numerous international tours. He has covered some of the most memorable series of the recent past, including Australia's famous 1999 World Cup win and the historic 2005 Ashes series in England, and has also found himself uncomfortably close to numerous crowd riots, bomb threats and travel disasters.

Andrew has also written about cricket for international publications, such as *The Times*, *The Guardian* and the *Sunday Telegraph* (UK), *The Hindu*, *Hindustan Times* and *Mid Day* (India), and *Wisden Cricketers' Almanack*. He has made semi-regular appearances on radio and television in Australia, England, and in the Caribbean. Since leaving journalism, he has worked as a political speech writer and at universities. He lives in Adelaide, South Australia.

THE
WRONG LINE
Andrew Ramsey

ABC
Books

The ABC 'Wave' device is a trademark of the
Australian Broadcasting Corporation and is used
under licence by HarperCollins*Publishers* Australia.

First published in Australia in 2012
by HarperCollins*Publishers* Australia Pty Limited
ABN 36 009 913 517
harpercollins.com.au

HarperCollins*Publishers*
Level 13, 201 Elizabeth Street, Sydney NSW 2000, Australia
31 View Road, Glenfield, Auckland 0627, New Zealand
A 53, Sector 57, Noida, UP, India
77–85 Fulham Palace Road, London W6 8JB, United Kingdom
2 Bloor Street East, 20th floor, Toronto, Ontario M4W 1A8, Canada
10 East 53rd Street, New York NY 10022, USA

National Library of Australia Cataloguing-in-Publication entry:

Ramsey, Andrew James.
The wrong line / Andrew James Ramsey.
978 0 7333 3165 7 (pbk.)
Ramsey, Andrew James.
Cricket – Anecdotes.
Sportswriters – Australia – Biography.
Australian Broadcasting Corporation.
796.3580924

Cover design by Matt Stanton, HarperCollins Design Studio
Cover images: Caricature sculptures of Shane Warne and Steve Waugh by Anthony Chandler
Internal photographs © Andrew Ramsey
Typeset in 11.5/17pt Adobe Garamond Pro by Kirby Jones
Printed and bound in Australia by Griffin Press
The papers used by HarperCollins in the manufacture of this book
are a natural, recyclable product made from wood grown in sustainable
plantation forests. The fibre source and manufacturing processes meet
recognised international environmental standards, and carry certification.

5 4 3 2 1   12 13 14 15

To Michael
for kindling the flame
Ashes to ashes

Contents

Foreword

L ife on the road as an international sportsman is tough.

'Yeah, sure!' I hear the response, as you read the above line. 'Fame, fortune, business-class flights, five-star hotels … real tough!'

But I ask you to read those first four words again. Life on the road … it is tough.

Tough in any profession, at any level. If you travel enough – on the international cricket calendar that can be up to ten months of the year – you doubtless understand what I'm saying here.

Not whingeing, not complaining, simply stating that it's a gruelling schedule that presents a tremendous challenge to any athlete who embarks on such a journey.

But then again, let's be honest … there are undoubted benefits to be enjoyed. Huge contracts, lucrative commercial endorsements and, for some, a public profile that ensures they will never be left standing for too long in a queue whilst attempting to get a seat in the best restaurant in town.

However tough we players may think that travel and time away from loved ones is, we need only cast our minds to a group of committed men and women who share the same demanding schedules while deriving nowhere near the same pay or recognition as the players.

That group is the cricket journalists who report on matches the world over.

It's a diminishing group in this age of changing technology and budget cuts, as fewer and fewer news organisations send correspondents to anything other than tournaments that have the word 'Cup' in their title.

For as long as the game of cricket has been played internationally, there have been journos 'on the tour'.

Fortunately for me, and greatly beneficial to my being able to increase the number of people I call friends, I played in possibly the last era of professional cricket to have a full-blown media pack that regularly travelled for the entire duration of tours.

Always an intelligent collection of personalities, this group of odd bods and sometimes misfits would devour every ball of every match, analyse it, write or talk about it, and share their thoughts with the world in print, through the airwaves or on camera.

In times gone by, that discussion would often continue later into the evening, after play, over a drink or two with the players themselves. Not so much anymore.

I liked to get to know these guys when the chance arose, and I am better for the experience. I didn't always agree with their opinion or how they expressed it, but found my time at the top level a more fulfilling experience for having forged a few of those relationships.

Andrew Ramsey, or 'Rambo', as he was more affectionately known by the player group, recounts many of these shared adventures in this book, and I've no doubt all will enjoy his work.

Rambo was a highly respected member of the media corps that travelled regularly with the Australian team – a bloke you were always happy to talk to, either professionally or socially.

The journalist's is an extraordinary existence when on the road, and memorable tales have emerged from the many and varied situations they would get themselves into, and usually out of.

Often the press contingent would experience so much more than the players on a tour. As much as we tried to get out and about, the reality was that most of our time was spent training, in meetings at the hotel, playing at the stadium, on a bus to an airport, or travelling at 30,000 feet to the next destination.

For the journos it was often all that, plus more. Taking every chance to get off the beaten track and experience, taste, and live a different culture. Most times that was done out of interest, though sometimes it became a matter of survival!

For these guys, life on the road is truly tough. They don't do the job for the huge pay cheques, because for them they don't exist. Nor for the fame and public profile, for these rarely accompany the job either. And they certainly don't do it in an attempt to skip the restaurant line.

They do it because they love the game. The same reason, at the end of the day, that we did it as players.

Life on the road is tough. But as you are about to experience, it's bloody entertaining as well.

Adam Gilchrist
August, 2012

1

Hong Kong Sixes, October 1993

Always remember you're not a player. You can bask in their reflected limelight. Share their lifestyle, their company and their secrets. Even meet their wives and girlfriends and be entrusted not to mention one in the presence of the other. But critics must never confuse themselves for cricketers.

This first rule of cricket journalism also happened to be the first one I broke. Having it bluntly pointed out less than a day into my inaugural overseas assignment was mildly embarrassing. Being set straight by Mark Waugh, while we shared an immigration queue at Hong Kong's Kai Tak Airport one Wednesday night in October 1993, was downright humiliating. Though not a total surprise.

The cursory research I'd undertaken prior to my maiden international tour revealed the younger Waugh twin did not suffer fools. And that he considered folly the unifying trait of the world's cricket media. He viewed press relations in the same way he handled mediocre spin bowling. With bored detachment ranging to blatant contempt. According to intelligence gleaned from more seasoned reporters, when it came to relations with journalists he was one of those who could put the 'prick' in prickly.

Up until that airport exchange, I felt I'd made a fairly seamless transition from suburban news reporter to globe-hopping cricket correspondent, even if my selection of in-flight reading material had screamed 'rookie error'. In an ill-considered attempt to understand what I was getting myself into, I had tracked down a copy of an unsanctioned, tell-all account of the Australian cricket team's 1991 tour of the West Indies. In the years since its publication, the book had partially lifted the veil on the life of touring cricketers, and exponentially raised the ire of the nation's cricket elite. It also caused an irreparable fracture in the relationship between the players and the journalists who shadowed them.

So by the time I stumbled on to the scene, the golden era of shared confidences and front-bar camaraderie had been replaced by suspicion and a 'them-versus-us' climate of mistrust. Consequently, it wasn't the smartest choice of airport reading. Having it in my possession would only confirm the players' misgivings that I was the enemy within. And unveiling it in transit would have the same effect as walking onto an El Al flight brandishing a copy of *Mein Kampf*. In my own defence, I was banking on being seated at the back of the plane while the cricketers enjoyed their customary luxury up front. Among the many divides between players and press, the business-class curtain has long been one of the least subtle. As such, I reasoned I would be able to skim through the offending text in economy-class anonymity, commit any relevant passages to memory, and abandon the evidence in my Row 50 seat pocket.

That ploy failed spectacularly because I was not part of a traditional overseas cricket tour. I had been plucked from professional obscurity to be the sole Australian reporter accompanying half a dozen of the nation's best cricketers, and their veteran coach, on an all-expenses-paid, long weekend to a location where you're more likely to find cricket on a menu than a suburban park.

Hoping to build on the success of their debut tournament a year earlier, organisers of the Hong Kong International Cricket Sixes had decided that greater media coverage would help their ambitious six-a-side tournament gain exposure, if not credibility. To achieve this aim, the tournament's principal sponsor – a large Hong Kong-based airline – offered to fly a small number of cricket scribes from around the globe to experience their event and enjoy their hospitality.

Upon checking in, I learned the sponsor's generosity extended as far as business-class seating for members of the fourth estate. This was the sort of lavish treatment usually reserved for journalists of immense influence, or for travel writers. It also meant spending eight hours seated amid the playing group in territory that, if not outright hostile, was mildly unnerving. Especially for a young reporter already swimming in self-doubt and clutching only an incendiary book for moral support.

With feigned bravado, I took the first available opportunity to introduce myself to the captain – of the cricket team, not the aircraft. Although I doubt the response would have been any more underwhelmed had I burst through the cockpit door and announced to the flight crew that I constituted the Australian cricket press for the next seventy-two hours. Ian Healy, burdened with the national captaincy for the entire weekend, summoned his deep reserves of diplomacy when I told him who I was and why I was there.

'Oh, okay. Great to have you on board,' he smiled, with a sort of pained sincerity.

He then extended his battle-gnarled fingers and firmly shook my hand. Healy's day job was Australia's wicketkeeper, and he was part of a collective that earned its livelihood by stopping rock-hard projectiles, often hurled at high speed. You can spot the ex-'keepers at any past players' reunion. Their fingers resemble root ginger. Due to their unforgiving profession, they are also well versed at passing off a grimace as a grin.

'I didn't expect there'd even be a journo on this tour,' he said, smile firmly in place. 'So, you're with Australian Associated Press. Where exactly will your stories end up?'

I gave my oft-rehearsed spiel about how AAP copy was sent to most of Australia's metropolitan and regional newspapers, and that its broadcast scripts could be used for radio and television news bulletins. By this stage, the skipper's well-toned smile muscles must have been aching with fatigue.

'Okay, well it's good to meet you,' he said, as he edged back to his seat. 'And we'll catch up over the next few days.'

Then, to make sure I understood my role, he added: 'Not that I reckon there'll be too much worth writing about. This weekend's just a bit of fun.'

I withdrew to study my travel companions in closer detail, and the news hound in me was appalled by what I didn't see. The behaviour of these notoriously overpaid, overexposed sports stars was disgracefully impeccable. They could have been any bored, restless commuters, albeit in matching travel outfits. They dozed or flicked half-heartedly through magazines. They engaged in listless conversations or stared blankly at the tiny televisions blinking in their faces. Where were the indulgent acts of rock-star hedonism? Shouldn't they be spinning tales of past heroics to a coterie of enthralled groupies? Or trying to set a new Melbourne–Hong Kong beer-guzzling record?

Even their appearance was remarkably unremarkable. Unlike tennis players, cricketers don't sport one forearm demonstrably larger than the other. Their ears don't ooze like raspberry flummery, nor their necks bulge like baobab trunks as is the case with rugby front-rowers. And very few display the social graces of *Australopithecus*, which immediately distinguishes them from other football codes.

The striking exception to this uniform ordinariness was twenty-one-year-old Matthew Hayden. His shoulders were obviously on loan from an Olympic butterflyer. His chest filled out his white shirt to the point where it could almost accommodate Cinemascope movies. In a sport historically populated by tall, lean bowlers or short, nimble batsmen, Hayden had swaggered on to the international scene with the physique, and occasionally the technique, of a champion axeman.

Born and raised in rural Kingaroy, home to Australia's peanut-growing industry, Hayden's spirit was as lithe as his body was basalt. His love of life outdoors, especially surfing and fishing, was reflected in his approach to cricket. He lived to toil under the baking sun, often batting for days on end. True to character, he had also slipped out of the team travelling kit and into shorts and T-shirt as soon as the seatbelt warning lights dimmed.

Huddled into his seat's confines, he provided my in-flight entertainment when his lunch arrived. He set about transforming his miniature bread roll, paper-thin fillets of smoked salmon and various salad garnish items into a gourmet sandwich. The dexterity with which he sliced a cherry tomato, battling airline cutlery and a wobbly tray table, led me to ruminate he might have a future as a chef once his considerable cricket skills began to wane.

With the lunch items cleared, Hayden asleep, and fear of physical attack preventing me from pulling out my book, I shifted into the vacant window seat next to me and stared dolefully down at the lush, emerald landscape unfolding far below. I was just starting to drift off when a vaguely familiar voice snapped me from my torpor.

'Hard to believe that fifty years ago, our boys were fighting and dying in the jungles down there,' Australia's cricket coach, Bob Simpson, opined.

Given his sudden appearance in a seat that was technically assigned to me, I assumed this was not a rhetorical observation. I also surmised that the dense tropical canopy beneath must be Borneo. At almost thirty years my senior, and as Australia's serving Test captain at the time of my birth, Simpson had a knowledge of wartime geography far superior to mine.

'That puts cricket in a bit of perspective,' he added, as he leaned forward to share the view.

Simpson was widely regarded as one of the most gifted technical coaches in world cricket. He was famous for being able to spot flaws in a batsman's game simply by watching him bunt a few balls in the practice nets. Assessing the inherent weaknesses in a greenhorn reporter apprehensively tackling his first international assignment presented much less of a challenge.

As well as his formidable cricket credentials, Simpson was a shrewd politician. The rule book he employed when dealing with the press was more Machiavelli than Marylebone. He used our first unofficial chat to point out that the coming weekend was little more than a public relations exercise for his team.

'Some of these guys have been on the road pretty much non-stop – at home, in New Zealand, in England – since the start of the last Australian summer,' he said, finishing on an upward inflection for emphasis. 'That's almost a year ago. So while we'll be doing our best this weekend, I wouldn't be expecting us to dominate.'

He then leaned slightly further forward and gave an almost imperceptible nod, which I understood to mean we had just engaged in a briefing, rather than a greeting. In other words, there was to be no screaming 'Aussies Hit for Six at Sixes' headlines in the papers back home if results didn't measure up to expectations. Point made, he returned to his seat alongside Healy, which at least explained how he knew who, and what, I was.

My discomfort level was rising, exacerbated by my restless attempts to work out the reason for my unease. After all, these were mostly men of my age – late twenties or younger. By rights, I should have felt more at ease in their company than in that of the politicians, business leaders and academics I had regularly interviewed over five years as a journalist. But these guys were completely different. They were celebrities. They had capabilities beyond the rest of us. Members of a fraternity so exclusive that, despite being the life's ambition of countless Australian boys for more than a century, only 350 had gained admission. If they weren't aloof and unapproachable then, in my mind, they should have been.

Such was my level of anxiety, I was relieved when word came from the flight deck that we were preparing to land, even though it was well known that, in terms of accessibility, Kai Tak was not so much an airport as a Chinese box. Successfully putting a Boeing 747 down on a reclaimed runway jutting into Victoria Harbour through an approach ringed by hills and high-rise buildings meant pilots had to throw their aircraft around like two-stroke go-karts negotiating a tight chicane. To even attempt landing at Kai Tak, commercial pilots needed to have undertaken specialist training. Or so I had been reassured.

Rugged peaks, some more than 600 metres high, strayed frighteningly close to the tarmac's north. As we skimmed the bobbing lights on the harbour, we weaved among the lofty residential towers of western Kowloon until the sight of red and white warning billboards on the flank of a small hill signalled it was time for the pilot to swing into a fifty-degree starboard lurch. Passengers on the inside of the 'Checkerboard Turn' now found themselves staring directly into the lounge rooms of stoically oblivious families.

The aircraft was then violently righted back to almost horizontal, and those of us on the port side noticed we were barely fifty metres above the earth. I swear I could discern the brand name, not just the picture that was showing, on a television set one young couple impassively watched as we roared past their window. One final deft, upward flick of the port wing, and we met the ground. Engines screaming, we hurtled to a standstill on what appeared to be a bituminised jetty and then parked between a four-masted replica junk and a Panamax freighter.

It wasn't only the landing trauma that convinced me to stay seated while the team readied to disembark. I was in no hurry to join them. Our relationship was but hours old, yet I sensed we could already both benefit from some time apart. Unfortunately, that strategy didn't take into account the human traffic jam at passport control. It also exposed another deficiency in my pre-departure research.

I was unaware of the internal demarcation system that Australia's elite cricketers observed, whereby touring parties were split into two roughly even sub-groups. The cool, good-looking players and officials dubbed themselves 'Julios', in deference to suave Latino crooner and renowned ladies' man, Julio Iglesias. The rest were known as 'Nerds', as in ... well, nerds.

I had unwittingly joined an immigration queue that included card-carrying 'Julios', Damien Martyn and Mark Waugh and, despite my stalling tactics, we were once again neighbours. Hell-bent on avoiding eye contact or small talk, I rummaged through my collection of travel documents, only to look up and find Mark Waugh glaring dismissively at me over his right shoulder. As he turned, he shifted his gaze to the carpet between my feet where the remainder of my self-esteem was about to land. We hadn't officially passed into Hong Kong, but I was made aware that a far more strict border had been illegally crossed.

'I reckon you're in the wrong line, buddy,' he monotoned, before turning back to an approving nod from his teammate.

There was no point in pleading a novice mistake. I had been caught red-handed. Sharing the players' business-class sanctuary could be explained away as an organisational oversight. Continuing the charade in public was plain impertinent. I needed to be reminded of my place, and my place was not on the Australian cricket team. My cheeks glowed crimson. Sweat began to form on my upper lip. This is not the recommended look when you're approaching a foreign nation's passport police, unless you're a devotee of the full body cavity search.

I hurriedly scooped up my belongings and stumbled blindly away from the source of ridicule, only to find the adjacent queue home to designated 'Nerds', Jamie Siddons and Tony Dodemaide. Blind panic set in. Doubled over, clutching a disarray of documents to my stomach, I scuttled across the arrivals hall searching for a line devoid of cricketers.

I looked like a bank bandit fleeing with a heist of loose notes. Or a heroin smuggler nursing a gut full of rupturing condoms. I eventually took up a position, squatting and sweating, as the final member of the 'All Other Passport Holders' clique.

As I tried to rearrange my papers and my demeanour, I offered a silent prayer for my queue to suffer lengthy processing delays. Anything to put me further behind the cricket team as it disappeared into the Hong Kong night. To ensure that outcome, I waited for my suitcase to complete its third lap of the baggage carousel before I hauled it clear. Emerging from the final security scan, I scoured the crowd of reunited families and beckoning taxi drivers to find no trace of the Australian players. They had vanished into the throng. But further humiliation was heading my way.

A stern gentleman approached me, clad in crisply laundered white tunic, dark trousers complete with razor-sharp creases, and shoes that were just as black, but decidedly more lustrous, than my mood. He looked like a young Bruce Lee, from the days when he was busting criminals in the employ of the Green Hornet. Minus the leather mask. Most disturbingly, 'Kato' was armed with what appeared to be an elaborate white table tennis bat from which a couple of small bells dangled and which bore, in angry capital letters scrawled in black felt pen, my name and flight number.

It turned out that the same sponsor who had arranged for me to fly among the team also wanted me to share their hotel transfer. I felt nauseous. I tried to argue my case for independent transport, but Kato didn't care for the inviolable protocol that prevented journalists ever setting foot on the Australian team's bus. Along with the dressing room, it's a universally recognised safe haven. In the cricket universe, anyway. Media representatives are invited on to the bus about as often as women are asked to enter the Catholic priesthood. None of this helped crack Kato's stony countenance. He had a schedule to keep and I was keeping him from it.

He frog-marched me to the idling, twelve-seater minibus, and I dragged myself aboard to be greeted by seven sickeningly familiar faces. None of them tried to disguise their impatience, as they glared at the slowcoach boarding the team coach. My half-hour of deliberate dawdling must have seemed decidedly longer in the confines of the bus. As a result, the late-night air was heavy with resentment as we shared a wordless ride into the heart of Tsim Sha Shui.

By the time we reached the reclaimed swamp that had grown into the soaring commercial centre of the Kowloon Peninsula, the overworked air conditioners and ad-hoc wiring that dangled precariously from grimy apartment blocks lining the road from the airport had given way to a Manhattan-like skyline. The choked streets were bathed in neon and bordered by designer boutiques. With the bus becalmed in a gridlock of imported luxury cars, it was easy to forget we had arrived on the doorstep of the developing world.

That was until I noticed an ancient woman carrying a large swaddling of bulky possessions on her back, stop and gently lay her burden on the footpath. She then stepped down from the kerb, and positioned her bare feet on a metal grate that covered an entrance to a stormwater drain. In full view of the motionless traffic, she yanked down the pants of her coarse blue 'Mao suit' and, inconvenienced neither by her age nor by stage fright, dropped into a textbook Asian squat. Without so much as a glance around her, she unleashed a torrent of excrement that would have done a disgorging cement truck proud. Until that moment, I had no idea a forty-five-kilogram woman could pack a hundredweight of shit. When the flow finally stemmed, she simply hitched up her strides, repositioned her pack, and resumed her journey. The whole episode had taken less than two minutes. In that time, I was cured of any jet-lagged delusion we were stuck on Fifth Avenue. Or thoughts of an ocean swim.

Relief arrived for me soon after, when we finally reached the hotel. Mercifully, the tournament organisers had seen fit to house journalists and players in separate, if adjacent, accommodation. As the bus doors swung open, I hurtled down the stairs with all the intent of a liberated hostage. I was in a savage hurry to draw the curtain on day one of my career as a travelling cricket writer and to steel myself for the reception that awaited on day two. I knew from experience how quickly the professional relationship with top-flight sportspeople could turn from suspicion to odium.

Months earlier, I'd sought comment from the former Australian Test cricket great Rod Marsh, in his guise as head coach of the Australian

Institute of Sport cricket academy in Adelaide. I phoned him at his home one June morning, in the wake of Australia's thumping Test win over England at Lord's, a victory orchestrated by opening batsman, and recent academy graduate, Michael Slater. The call's purpose was to establish how Marsh felt about his young academy alumni – Slater and Shane Warne – playing such pivotal roles in Australia's unfolding Ashes success. Initially, the former Test vice-captain was cautious about singing the praises of the young stars too loudly. He also wanted to paint their achievements against the backdrop of an English opposition that was modest at best, and plain inept more often. As the interview progressed, Marsh warmed to the latter theme.

'Take Michael Slater's innings,' he railed. 'Sure it was a good knock, but there's a lot of blokes in this country who would've given their right arms to bat against that England attack. Michael will probably admit he's made better thirties or forties in Sheffield Shield cricket than that 150 he made at Lord's.'

It was when he issued a pointed warning to aspiring Australian players against travelling to England to play county cricket in the misguided belief it would improve their skills that he outdid himself. Or undid himself.

'They go over there and face bowlers who are really just pie throwers, and they're not going to learn anything about the game.'

At that point, I placed a small asterisk in the margin of my notebook. Even a trainee cricket writer knows a headline when it happens along. The priceless quote became the hook for a story that created a stir on either side of cricket's oldest rivalry. Sent out to the world on the AAP sports wire, it was seized upon by the British press. Some supplemented the yarn with an equally spirited rebuttal from England's Test bowling coach, Geoff Arnold. Others took it upon themselves to phone Marsh directly and challenge his assertion. These calls were invariably placed in the small hours of the Australian morning, and were not especially well received.

Marsh then angrily claimed his words had been twisted out of context. In fact, he reckoned there had never been a context. He flatly denied ever using the term 'pie throwers'. Of course, journalists' propensity to engage in a bit of literary licence is as widely recognised as their dubious fashion sense. The craft is built on an ignoble tradition of tweaking the occasional quote to justify a headline, or simply to generate one in the first place. But at that stage of my fledgling career, I was neither creative nor canny enough to fabricate such a cracking description of England's hopeless seamers. Thus, a scar was born.

I had burned my first cricket contact even before I had become a proper cricket writer. For what it's worth, I stand by the authenticity and accuracy of that quote. Marsh similarly swears it's a concoction. As a consequence, he has since refused to speak to me, or acknowledge my presence. Except for the time, years later in England, when we crossed paths in the lobby of a Manchester hotel. He indicated our dispute might be best sorted out in the car park, an offer I politely declined.

It's safe to assume that the Kowloon Cricket Club has seen its fair share of, if not pie chuckers, then certainly dumpling dispensers. It was the quintessence of village cricket, albeit in a village under siege from a forest of concrete towers, the constant howl of lorries, buses and low-flying passenger jets, and air that carried the colour, odour and taste of diesel. In the countdown to the Dependent Territory's impending handover to the People's Republic of China, the KCC stood as an enduring symbol of the irreconcilable contrast between Hong Kong's genteel, imperial past, and its chaotic, dynamic future.

Vaguely heptagonal in shape, the club's playing field was immaculately maintained. One of its sides was dominated by a lavish art-deco-influenced clubhouse that would not have looked out of place adjoining the eighteenth green at a New England country club. The Members lounge walls bore photographic tributes to the decidedly Anglo, and occasional Indian, heroes of glories past. They stared agelessly at the club's parade of daily regulars, who sipped European lager from dimpled pint mugs, or ice-laden cocktails, the condensation from which streamed down the sides of highballs in the clawing humidity and formed deep pools on the dark wooden bar. This tribute to the most English of games also incorporated a broad players' balcony that provided a sweeping view of the cricket ground, and the encroaching squalor.

The venue's intimate feel was enhanced by an array of corporate hospitality tents erected along its numerous edges for the six-a-side frolic. They helped ensure the cricket carried the air of a food and wine festival. The specially invited local and international guests occasionally looked up from the free fizz and tasting plates to try and make sense of what was happening out on the lawn. I sat perched on a plastic chair, wedged between the knee-high boundary fence and the brick wall of the curators' shed, earnestly trying to answer that same question. Even though the Hong Kong Sixes had secured the talents of superstars such as Sachin Tendulkar, Viv Richards, Javed Miandad and Aravinda de Silva, the matches carried only a passing resemblance to cricket as I knew it.

For a start, once the roles of bowler and wicketkeeper were assigned, the non-batting team was left with just four fielders. Consequently, boundaries were scored pretty much every time bat made contact with ball. It reminded me of the backyard games played with childhood friends, albeit with vastly superior skills and no hibiscus bush at short extra-cover. Even the synthetic pitch and iridescent orange stumps suggested 'Mudamuckla Thirds' rather than prestigious international cricket event.

Players mixed freely with all elements of the crowd between, and even during, the two-day roster that was stocked with forty-five-minute matches. Well, not quite all elements. As I skirted the field, seeking out feature interviews to try and justify, as well as announce, my presence, I noticed the Australians were strangely elusive. When they saw me approaching, wielding my dictaphone and a look of grim intent, they would smile apologetically before melting into the crowd.

Sadly, Australia's major media outlets showed a similar lack of appetite for my hourly radio scripts and detailed newspaper reports. Worse, my hope that a story of major global significance would erupt in front of me was proving disappointingly delusional. The only potentially newsworthy incident emerged when Pakistan's Inzamam-ul-Haq was prevented from fulfilling the tournament requirement that each member of the fielding team bowl an over apiece.

In the early stages of the weekend, Inzamam's bowling had shown the same economy of effort that was to distinguish the bulk of his career. To the extent that, in 2006, he famously couldn't be bothered leading his team back on to the field when captaining in a Test match against

England. In Kowloon, he simply stood at the non-striker's end and tossed the ball, like a heavily sedated baseball pitcher, towards bemused batsmen. I noticed it was the same sort of nonchalant indifference he showed when throwing down vegetable pakoras between games. His unique bowling action provoked tittering on and off the field, but nobody seemed too concerned given the event's picnic nature.

However, as the tournament progressed towards the prize-money matches, rumblings surfaced that such a flagrant bending of the game's laws did little to enhance Hong Kong's hopes of securing a permanent berth on the world cricket calendar. It was therefore agreed that Inzamam would, in the final matches, play solely as a batsman and a fielder. Which meant he played only as a batsman, since he was as reluctant to chase and retrieve as he was to adopt a legal bowling action. My one hope of a story with international implications was accordingly snuffed out. My problem, I learned years later, was that I had been watching the cricket. Subsequent reports eventually surfaced of illegal bookmakers using the relaxed atmosphere at Kowloon to take their corrupt business proposals to some of cricket's biggest names.

By the time Sunday's grand final came around, my enthusiasm for the cause had dipped about as low as Inzamam's bowling arm. With England and Sri Lanka slugging it out for the title, any story I wrote about the climax would be little more than typing practice. Even the novelty of England eventually winning an international cricket trophy failed to generate interest back home. I also accepted I was not about to gain friendship, trust or even eye contact from the Australian team, and was therefore firmly of the view that my first international tour would also act as my cricket-writing swansong.

England's win did, however, provide cause for celebration among the pair of genuine Fleet Street cricket scribes who had also been shouted a weekend in the Orient. They generously included me in their knees-up, apparently mistaking the exclusivity of my role for seniority. That's how I learned the gulf that ran deep between players and the press did not likewise extend to professional rivalries within the cricket-writing fraternity.

In the spirit of journalistic camaraderie, we toasted England's resurgence as a global cricketing powerhouse at Hong Kong's famous

Foreign Correspondents' Club. Throughout conflicts in Korea and Vietnam, it had heard a litany of war stories, and several more were recounted that evening. The sense of isolation and ostracism I had nursed over the preceding seventy-two hours gave way to warm encouragement, not solely because of the beer buzz, as my new friends regaled me with tales of press box intrigue, dressing room gossip, and glamorous globetrotting. My interest in cricket writing was being rekindled, pint by pint.

In a shameless attempt to bolster my own stocks, I told my one and only worthwhile cricket anecdote. Not the one where an opening batsman filleted a cocktail tomato. Rather, how my recent interview with Rod Marsh had given rise to a headline, and a hatred. As the story unwound, I noticed a grin growing across the face of the audience member who hadn't left the table to fetch more beer. Then, when I delivered the punchline, he swivelled in his chair and cackled to his mate at the bar: 'Hey Charlie, you won't believe it. He's the pie-chuckin' geezer.'

It was the moment I became a cricket journalist.

2

From Nuriootpa to Newsroom
to New Zealand, February 1998

I t's tempting to assert I'd been embedded with the Australian team
to Hong Kong in recognition of my shimmering journalistic talent.
But that would also be a gross falsehood. The bald truth remains I was
the spare body in the office with a free weekend when the sponsor's
invitation arrived.

At the time, I was working as a general news reporter in a five-person
AAP bureau in Adelaide. Given the paucity of staff proportionate to
the demands of a round-the-clock news wire service, diversity was our
office's stock in trade. Court reporting, state politics, business stories,
police rounds and sports events were among the variety that ensured days
were anything but routine. It also meant I possessed subject knowledge
roughly as broad as Lake Eyre. And almost as deep, keeping in mind
that the giant saltpan filled just four times in the twentieth century.

So while I could boast versatility, I was under no illusions as to my
journalistic influence. The generalists in any newsroom might account
for most of the legwork, but it's those who report specialist rounds that
carry a public profile, earn the marginally bigger bucks, and get the
overseas trips. It just happened that one of those specialists – AAP's
national cricket correspondent – was nominally based in Adelaide when

not trailing the Australian team around the globe. It was his name on the invitation when it lobbed but, having just returned from a four-month tour of England, he needed a weekend in south Asia watching a six-a-side carnival in the same way an insomniac requires a triple-shot espresso as a nightcap. In fact, management withheld news of the prospective Kowloon commitment from him for fear he might consider self-harm.

Instead, our bureau chief ran a brief audit of potential substitutes, and I ticked all the necessary boxes. I held a valid passport, had no conflicting obligations, and maintained a passable knowledge of cricket. No sooner were the organisers notified of the switch than my first pangs of unease began to stir.

That was because, while my credentials as a cricket writer were decidedly shaky, they were considerably more robust than my expertise as a cricketer. Indeed, my playing skills were so limited that I pioneered a new category of 'all-rounder' during my time with the Nuriootpa Cricket Club in the Barossa Valley. My dual specialty was batting at number eleven, an honour bestowed only because cricket teams don't stretch to a number twelve, and fielding as far from the action as possible while remaining within the field of play. So adept was I at patrolling cricket's equivalent of the Mongolian steppes – deep fine leg – I was entrusted with that duty for the duration of every day we spent in the field. At both ends of the ground. Consequently, most of the runs I contributed over five years of senior cricket were my glacial gallops from one extremity of a parched oval to the other.

In spite of my glaring shortcomings, my place in the first XI was guaranteed by two unrelated but equally relevant factors. A small country town's lack of selection alternatives. And my quasi-official role as author of the cricket club's diary notes in the local weekly newspapers. I learned quickly that the pen was mightier than the slow-turning off-break. Writing granted me a status that my cricket would never deliver. So, despite only being able to converse with my teammates on the rare occasions we gathered to celebrate the fall of an opposition wicket, I stuck at the game that had been my passion from a very young age.

My earliest cricket memories remain the most vivid of a sport-obsessed, self-contained childhood. They took shape during the 1971–72 Australian season, when an all-stars World XI toured in place of a South African team for political reasons that I tried, but failed, to comprehend. During that sweltering summer, respite was provided by a small metallic electric fan that resembled the propeller housing from a miniature Messerschmitt, and stood alongside our equally antiquated television. The cooling breeze allowed me to focus my attention on the fuzzy images of white-clad cricketers against a grainy grey background.

The sight that both mesmerised and terrorised me was Dennis Lillee, loping in on his twenty-pace run-up, launching himself into a spring-loaded delivery stride, and directing his menace at hapless batsmen. The grace and controlled power of his bowling contrasted with his wildly exuberant celebrations whenever another one fell. His ferocious spell in Perth, which yielded eight of the world's best at a cost of just twenty-nine runs, screamed from the front page of the next day's newspaper, accompanied by a close-up photograph of Lillee, frozen as he prepared to unleash, with eyes narrowed at his prey and his right wrist cocked like a cobra alongside his chunky sideburns.

'This is how Lillee appears from 22 yards away, just before another thunderbolt arrives', the caption trilled.

When the day's heat dimmed, I would become Dennis Lillee. I charged up and down the backyard trying to replicate his idiosyncratic bowling style. So dedicated was I to this task, I wore a track of tiny, browning footmarks that spelled out its own Morse tale of delusion along the length of my father's cherished lawn. Over after over, I would charge in, right arm flapping at my side like a one-armed surfer paddling out beyond the break. Carefully synchronising the finale to avoid becoming ensnared in the drooping wire cables of the clothes line, I then launched myself skyward with the grace and athleticism of an emperor penguin heaving itself onto an Antarctic ice shelf. Finally, in an uncoordinated whirr of arms and legs, I would let loose a tennis ball that smacked into the whitewashed back wall of our house with all the force of a drop volley. I would then scowl at the brickwork, flick beads of imagined sweat from my forehead, and retrieve the ball in order to start the long trudge back to my bowling mark, beneath the low branches of the walnut tree. I would repeat this charade until nightfall. Or until my exasperated father switched on the sprinkler.

When it was too dark, too wet, or too obviously football season to indulge my backyard cricket fantasies, I immersed myself in the array of monthly Australian and English cricket magazines that my father on-passed. This was not great news for my schooling, as I devoted more time to studying England's Sunday League than I did to my grade three English homework. Each night, I would clamber into bed and await Dad's appearance to turn out the light. That was when I would badger him for stories about the great cricketers he had watched as a boy, for details of upcoming games we might attend, and for answers to troubling conundrums of the time, such as how a towelling hat with no brim could offer any protection from the sun. He never visibly tired of these inquisitions that were the high points of a young boy's day, and only partly a ruse to delay the onset of sleep.

During the winter of 1972, with Ian Chappell's team battling for the Ashes in the Old Dart, I bounded out of bed on many a frosty Barossa morning to excitedly pore over the details of the previous night's action. These had been fastidiously documented by my father in a miniature scorebook while I slept. I was fascinated by the notion of cricket being played through the dead of night, on the other side of the world, and equally impressed by Dad's dedication to staying awake into the wee hours, tuned to the BBC commentary and recording the details for my benefit.

One morning over breakfast, as I scoured obsessively through the previous night's happenings, I boldly announced to him that one day I too would travel to England as part of an Australian touring team. Displaying all the patient diplomacy of parenthood, he simply smiled and nodded. And doubtless offered up a silent prayer for the future of Australian cricket lest its playing stocks dwindle that low.

'What would be so good about that?' he inquired, ignoring the selection opportunities likely to beckon for an athletically challenged trundler who specialised in bowling at three-bedroom rental properties.

'I could go to the cricket every day,' I replied, after considered thought. 'And I'd get to see a lot of different places.'

Pausing only to light one of the succession of Wild Woodbines that – along with several 'steaming mugs of java', his romanticised description of cheap instant coffee – comprised his breakfast, he decided this conversation had run its useful course.

'You'd certainly see a lot of cricket grounds,' he said, before resuming his hiding place behind the thick, heavy type of the morning broadsheet.

As my junior cricket career developed, there was not the slightest suggestion this aspiration would be fulfilled. In fact, my playing prowess threatened to take me nowhere other than the outfield. Cutting my run-up by around ninety-eight per cent, a move that delivered no discernible loss of bowling speed, and bolstering my batting repertoire to include a leg glance as well as a forward defensive prod, somehow landed me the captaincy of the town's under-fourteen team. But from there, the career path led unfailingly downhill.

Elevation to senior ranks at age fifteen meant I was forced to face grown men who bowled at speeds that seemed not far short of Dennis Lillee, and who also shared the Australian team's propensity for sledging. In one of my first A-grade outings, our team was copping another of our painfully regular whippings. Set around 800 runs to win off our allocated sixty-five overs, our top-order batsmen dug deep in the face of overwhelming adversity to lift our score creditably close to triple figures. But by the time I made my nervous appearance at the very tip of an extended tail, the opposition bowlers and fielders justifiably felt they were only one on-target delivery from victory. I strode to the middle with all the conviction of a vertiginous tightrope walker, where I was met by teammate 'Ted' Lange who, being a year ahead of me at school, took on the role of senior partner. Ted's assessment of our predicament was blunt yet bright.

'I guess we just hang around for as long as we can,' he suggested with a shrug of his shoulders.

The sight of two barely pubescent tailenders placing a pointless value on their wickets became a red rag to a bully. During the first fifteen minutes of our obstinacy, we were the targets of constant, if benign, chirping from surrounding fielders.

'If ya get out now, I'll give you both a lift to the pub and shout yuz ... a Coke,' one heavily moustachioed opponent grinned.

But as our defiance yielded a couple of tentative boundaries, the other mob's humour dissipated.

'It's getting late, so why don't you little cunts fuck off home to bed,' a paunchy fielder wheezed as he stalked past.

The other mob's star player, a former South Australian Sheffield Shield all-rounder and notoriously combative grade cricket curmudgeon, then took it upon himself to end our upstart resistance. He resorted to bowling over after over of 'donkey drops', cloud-seeding full tosses that lobbed in a steepling arc so as to fall almost vertically on the batsman from a huge height. Difficult to bowl, they were even harder to hit. The only foolproof way to negate them was to crouch over the stumps, as if vomiting out of a window. You then braced yourself for the inevitable thump between the shoulderblades, as a 160-gram leather-encased missile hurtled from the troposphere.

Ted and I decided against this tactic, partly because of its lack of aesthetic appeal, and partly because it seemed as far removed from the essence of cricket as bowling the bloody things in the first place. Instead, we swatted and swung, as if trying to sweep away raindrops before they reached the ground, until Ted eventually toppled his stumps in the process. Mission accomplished, our tormentor turned on his heel, snatched his cap from the umpire, and made a bee-line for his car.

Entire books have been penned about the rapier-like on-field repartee that's passed between cricketers down the years. Nobody I played against seemed to have read them. In the heat of battle, you copped plenty of abrasive character slurs, but rarely any Wildean wit. And the notion of cricket at any level being a bastion of fair play and gentlemanly fellowship has long been as much a quaint relic of the past as Dennis Lillee's facial hair. The Australian way has long been that winning takes precedence over all else.

That's why, when regularly criticised for their ugly on-field demeanour, indignant Australian teams point to the cricket culture in which they were raised. Their 'gamesmanship', or 'mental disintegration' as it became euphemistically known, was explained away as a product of the playing apprenticeship that all budding Australian cricketers served. The mantra was: 'Be as unpleasant as you want during playing hours, then slap the target of your invective on the back at day's end and remind them all's fair on the field of combat.' Unfortunately, over the decades, Australian teams have struggled to grasp that this philosophy isn't universally shared. And as the game outgrew rubber-spiked batting gloves and buckle-up pads, so too did rivals' preparedness to silently endure sustained, sometimes personal abuse that the perpetrators often dismissively scoffed should simply be washed away at day's end by a cold beer. Or a glass of Coke.

By the time I turned twenty-one, I was in possession of dual careers that offered equal futility. On summer weekends, it was fielding. On the days between, it was in the teller's box at a local savings bank, a job that saw about as much diurnal variation as a Beijing barber. Even though it provided enough money to regularly re-sole my cricket shoes, there was no hiding the fact that my interest leaned more towards words than numbers. And that my sporting talents were better suited to watching than playing. So in a reversal of accepted employment protocols – causing my long-suffering mother further angst – I quit my job and my cricket and set about applying to study journalism at university.

Two-thirds through my three-year Bachelor's degree, I was offered a cadetship with *The Advertiser*, Adelaide's metropolitan morning newspaper. Among my first chores on the cadet roster was a three-month stint in the sports department, collating pigeon-racing results and negotiating the vipers' nest that is mid-week ladies' bowls. But in observing my senior colleagues, I also realised that sports writing provided a guaranteed leave-pass from the office. In the days preceding blanket live television coverage of even the most trite sporting events, writing about sport could only be meaningfully carried out by attending sports venues.

This became a powerful drawcard, given that I had not entered journalism with a burning need to change the world. I just wanted to see it. And in the increasingly desk-bound culture of modern newspapers, sports writing offered a rare professional licence to work and live remotely. Very remotely, as it turned out. This enticement, married with my undimmed interest in cricket, became the thin thread that linked subsequent career moves to the wire service, and then to *The Australian*, the national daily broadsheet.

That's where my first genuine opportunity arose. And as with the brief Hong Kong excursion, it came through attrition, rather than acumen. Early in 1998, Australia's cricketers were in the midst of another sixteen-month, non-stop touring stint that had begun in India, then taken them around Australia, to South Africa, an Ashes campaign in England, followed by another Australian summer. A return bout in India loomed, but before then a four-match limited-overs series in New Zealand had been thoughtfully shoe-horned into the schedule.

Even though Australia's selectors had acknowledged the issue of excessive player workload by introducing distinct teams for the Test and limited-overs formats, they had been unable to prevent a raft of battle-weary cricketers falling by the wayside throughout the course of a gruelling home season. Consequently, the squad that freshly installed limited-overs captain Stephen Waugh led to New Zealand contained the bare minimum of twelve players, and included off-spinner Gavin Robertson, who had been virtually hauled from Sydney grade cricket to make up the numbers. I was similarly plucked from obscurity to fill in for *The Australian*'s chief cricket writer, Malcolm 'Big Mal' Conn, whose travel fatigue helped him form the sensible view that our newspaper should mirror the game's evolution by nurturing separate Test match and limited-overs correspondents. I happily volunteered my services as the one to follow the coloured-clothes version.

While the New Zealand assignment featured proper matches with eleven players per side competing on turf pitches, and covered by a press corps of greater than one, it was also distinguished by the calibre of players not taking part. Remaining in Australia to nurse ailments from the summer just gone, or nurse their pain at exclusion from the one-day squad just named, were Shane Warne, Glenn McGrath, Jason Gillespie, Mark Taylor and Ian Healy. The recast touring party did include Mark Waugh, who I studiously avoided as we made our way through an almost deserted Christchurch Airport on arrival. It proved a shrewd move, not because the 'Julios' once again had me in their cross-hairs. Rather, it enabled me to bypass a lengthy delay as the Australian batsman was instructed by New Zealand customs officials to remove grass and dirt residue from his cricket shoes lest they be a repository for caltrop. It wasn't the only additional baggage he was carrying. With

Warne's late scratching, Mark Waugh had been installed as Australia's vice-captain.

On day one, to help acclimatise to the crisp, clear South Island climate, the entire touring party was invited by local cricket officials to a barbecue lunch and a round of golf at Christchurch's famous Shirley Links. As exclusive as it was impeccable, the Christchurch Golf Club offered the cricketers, as VIP guests, *gratis* use of its heavily tree-lined fairways and lovingly clipped greens. Journalists could also play, provided we each stumped up the $100 green fee. And waited half an hour after the players teed off, so as to eliminate any risk of the rival parties' paths crossing. We collectively agreed to forego the golf.

The reason the media was allowed to intrude in the first place was the staging of a low-key press conference under the eaves of the mock-Tudor clubhouse's pitched roof. Stephen Waugh immediately seized the opportunity to quash any speculative leadership aspirations his new deputy might be harbouring.

'I waited a long time to become captain of Australia,' he said, with the barest hint of a smile when asked if he might consider sitting out one of the upcoming matches to give his brother a go at the helm.

Undaunted, Mark ventured that he was ready for the challenge in the event that one of his twin's notoriously brittle hamstrings was to snap during the tournament. Quizzed further on the extent of his captaincy experience, Mark conceded it did not extend past junior ranks at the family's Sydney grade club, Bankstown.

'That was under-twelves, mate,' Stephen riposted. 'That should hold you in real good stead.'

As fate would have it, one of Stephen's hamstrings did give way as the result of a mid-pitch collision with an opponent. But it happened in the final match of the tour, which meant he remained true to his word. His brother's Australian captaincy aspirations were never realised.

Conscious not to cramp the players on or off the golf course, the four-man Australian press corps opted to take our complimentary lunch at an outdoor table bathed in gentle late-summer Cantabrian sunshine. Out of the blue, we were joined by the Australian captain, who approached bearing a plate groaning with sausages and salad. Under Stephen Waugh's stewardship, Australian cricket was embracing a new era. For starters, the players' partners had been invited to join the New Zealand sojourn, which represented a seismic shift away from more than a century of cricket tradition. It was a revolution that had been canvassed under Mark Taylor, but it seemed family-friendly tours were being formalised by his successor. There had been no prior warning, however, that the brave new world extended as far as voluntarily sharing a meal with the press.

Stephen explained that, from the outset of his captaincy, he wanted to cultivate a convivial working relationship with the cricket media. He lamented as unfair and inaccurate the press's stereotyping of him as taciturn and aloof. Over lunch, he also addressed his distaste for golf, his passion for photography, and a genuine curiosity about the discipline and demands of writing for daily newspapers. He considered himself something of a kindred spirit, due to the success of his recent series of published tour diaries. In turn, we were surprised to find the manuscripts for those books were churned out in long-hand. Australian cricket may have chosen him to lead it into the twenty-first century, but Stephen Waugh was a staunch traditionalist, and not about to embrace such trappings of modernity as the laptop computer.

Had our get-together taken place at tour's end rather than at its beginning, the chat would doubtless have centred on the issue that came to dog him across New Zealand, and then confound him throughout his six-year captaincy. That being idiot spectators who found entertainment in using cricketers as target practice. His views on player safety were well known prior to arriving in Christchurch, but events during the second match in Wellington set Stephen Waugh on a campaign that led him to challenge cricket's custodians, as well as law and order officials, to address a blight that was also to cause him heartburn in Australia, in England, and, most dramatically, in the West Indies.

Wellington's premier cricket venue, the Basin Reserve, is a grass-banked, English-style ground ringed by white pickets and plonked smack in the centre of one of the world's largest traffic islands. While the Windy City's commuters skirt the ground's perimeter, the icy breeze that howls off Wellington Harbour slices a path straight through the middle. Perhaps it was the biting wind that sent the local fans skittish as their team faced defeat for the second consecutive match of the mini-series. It was more likely the standard cocktail of beer and boorishness that accounted for the stupidity that began early on game day, and became more stupid as the afternoon progressed.

While batting, Mark Waugh was grabbed from behind by a pitch invader who vaulted onto the field and charged towards the middle in full view of 12,000 spectators, but who was apparently invisible to a dozen or more motionless security personnel. Worse followed when the Australians took to the field. Those lucky enough to be stationed close to the centre only copped abuse, although four golf balls did find their way to the pitch's edge. Mark Waugh, a far keener golfer than his brother, contemplated slipping them into his pocket, until closer inspection revealed the missiles were as damaged and useless as the folk who launched them. It was those Australians occupying the fielding outposts who bore the brunt. Food scraps, pieces of fruit, and any other available detritus was flung until the Basin Reserve surface resembled the aftermath of a trailer park tornado. Stuart Law heard a glass sauce bottle whistle past his head, about the same time as his career flashed before his eyes.

At the post-match media conference, Stephen Waugh unloaded on cricket officialdom for its unwillingness to acknowledge, let alone tackle, this straightforward workplace safety issue. In challenging authorities to make a stand before someone was badly hurt, he stressed the problem was more endemic to one-day cricket than to New Zealand. That's despite its South Island university city of Dunedin gaining infamy for an incident years earlier when Australian bowler Greg Matthews dodged a toilet seat flung from the bleachers. And while fielding in front of the notoriously raucous western stand at Auckland's Eden Park, Michael Bevan once felt a hefty thud on the ground nearby, and turned to find an intact, frozen flounder staring up at him.

By the eve of the final match in Auckland, the Wellington uprising remained the only story of significance to have emerged from the tour. Even that excited about as much interest from sports editors, preparing to welcome a new football season, as it did among cricket's ruling bodies. As was the case in Hong Kong, I had failed to announce my arrival as a serious cricket writer to the newspaper's decision-makers back in

Sydney. There was little danger of my byline becoming a household name, even in my own home. Then, on the penultimate day, I received an early-morning phone call from my boss, a Northern Irishman whose deeply held, old-school newspaper ethics included a fierce loyalty to his staff working on the road. He was on the hunt for a back-page 'splash' for the weekend paper, that section's lead story regarded as pole position within the fraternity. Sports writers rate coverage on the back page as far more prestigious than the front.

'Mayut,' he began in his lilting Belfast brogue, 'I've harrd a whusper that Steve Waugh might be lookin' at playin' cricket in Oirland next yearr. Might be worth checkin' out.'

In light of the already absurdly overcrowded international playing schedule, I suspected it was not much more than gossip. But I respected the boss's judgement. Plus, it carried the prospect of a back page byline and that position's accompanying credit points. So I phoned the skipper in his room. These were, after all, the last days of cricket teams travelling without a dedicated media officer to act as the first and final point of obstruction for journalists chasing access to players.

Stephen Waugh's phone was diverted to the hotel switchboard operator, who helpfully, if indiscreetly, told me the Australian captain had blocked all incoming inquiries after a local breakfast radio host had woken him with a prank call some time prior to dawn. I hadn't even had a chance to run my rumour past him and already I had inadvertently stumbled across a possible yarn. I could already see the headline: 'Kiwis Declare Waugh as DJ Puts Aussies in Spin'.

Sensing my luck might finally be in, I bolted to the hotel lobby to see if any other similarly loose-lipped staff might know of the captain's whereabouts. As I jumped out of the lift, Stephen Waugh and his wife, Lynette, slipped quietly in. I furiously waved my left arm between the rapidly closing doors to impede their escape, and by the time I joined them and spent six floors scouring my pockets for a notebook and pen, Stephen was in no doubt that I was chasing an interview. His wife simply thought I was deranged.

Standing in the corridor outside his hotel room, he confirmed that the Irish Cricket Union had indeed approached him, and that he was seriously mulling over the offer.

'There are still a few things to consider, but I'll probably make a final decision next week,' he said.

That was all I needed to get me in the paper. I returned to my room, chuffed at unearthing a couple of passable stories in the space of fifteen minutes, while exerting little more effort than pressing the phone keypad and the lift call button.

My sports editor must have been equally impressed by my diligence at writing his story, which duly filled a hole on the back page. That's because, upon my return to Adelaide, he offered me a transfer to the paper's Melbourne office. Australia's self-proclaimed sporting capital, Melbourne is to the nation's sports hacks what Washington is to political junkies, and what London is to the sunlight averse. In addition, there was the possibility that I might be installed as the paper's auxiliary cricket correspondent. To oversee coverage of the Australian team when and where they donned the yellow pants. On sharing this news with a friend I was told, for the first of countless times over coming years, I had just scored the world's best job.

3

Australian Summer 1998–99

'You're the Michael Bevan of journalism,' chortled one of my new colleagues, upon learning my specialty was to be fifty-over cricket.

'You'll probably never meet Mark Taylor … but you might get invited to Brendon Julian's wedding,' another chirped, highlighting the new selection policy that meant Australia's Test and one-day teams featured markedly different personnel.

Gone was the previously accepted wisdom that the nation's foremost eleven cricketers were the best choice for both long and short versions of the game. Come the end of the twentieth century, Australia fielded two distinct teams. Those deemed to be lacking flamboyance – Taylor, Healy, and Justin Langer – were deemed TMOs (Test Matches Only). Those whose talents resembled the local pub buffet – a little bit of everything, but nothing too elaborate, such as Julian, Shane Lee and Ian Harvey – were pigeon-holed as one-day specialists. And for their sins, were forced to appear in public clad head to toe in hectic yellow.

Those demarcation lines weren't so strictly enforced in my new office, so I was free to turn my hand to 'real cricket' issues, as required. And in the summer of 1998–99, there was no shortage of real stories. Players taking money from bookmakers. Players taking industrial and legal action. Players taking a tumble, on the field and in seedy nightclubs. There even emerged a most undignified class president-style national popularity contest between Stephen Waugh and Shane Warne to try and sway opinions on who should take over from Taylor as Australia's fortieth Test captain.

As a result, cricket became a favoured discussion topic at daily editorial conferences, even among those senior editors who knew little of the sport other than its strong following among readers, and therefore advertisers. 'National sport, national paper' was how one of the more intuitive executives once described the nexus between our paper and cricket. With the Australian Test team touring Pakistan, where many suspected the match-fixing scandal that was sullying cricket's reputation was rooted, the combination of international sport, celebrities, corruption and sex – the latter, in this case, referring to gender – were ingredients thought too spicy to be restricted to the sports pages. So no sooner had I arrived at work one Tuesday morning than I received a call from a features boss delivering an edict from the paper's editor, who had earlier pronounced that any journalist who could not research, draft and produce a decent full-page feature article in less than a day belonged, like hot-metal type and understatement, to a bygone newspaper era. And it was a full-page, 1,000-word feature for the next day's paper that was needed.

In true modern newspaper style, whereby the demand for immediate content took precedence over detailed research and quality writing, it was an idea constructed from reverse logic. The editor had burst into the morning conference having learned, to his undisguised amazement, that one of the most fearless inquisitors delving into the subcontinental bookmakers' affair was not only a highly respected Pakistani journalist, but also a woman. The article, therefore, became an adjunct to the image the boss had already decided would illustrate it.

'This is a great yarn,' he ranted, as the acolytes around the conference table nodded in sage agreement. 'A woman is showing the guts to take on the elitist, male world of cricket and expose the sport for what it is. So we need to get a photo of her. With her face covered by a veil. Only her smouldering, dark eyes showing. Steely with resolve. It'll be a great image.'

One of the more worldly among the coterie, aware that not all Pakistani women conformed to ultra-conservative traditional dress standards, summoned the courage to pipe up: 'but there's a good chance she might not even be in *purdah*.'

'I don't care where she is,' the boss exploded. 'I just want someone to track her down and get a photo.'

That someone was me and, over the ensuing hours, I exhausted my limited pool of cricket contacts to find the woman in question – Fareshteh Gati-Aslam, coordinating editor of Karachi's biggest-selling English-language newspaper, *News on Sunday*. As hard as I tried, I just could not make the truth fit the prefabricated premise of an oppressed Muslim woman engaged in a life-and-death struggle to expose the dark forces corrupting cricket, while at the same time battling the inequalities foisted upon women climbing the corporate ladder in an Islamic republic.

Given I was yet to set foot on the subcontinent, Fareshteh helpfully pointed out that female sports reporters in that part of the world largely enjoyed far greater acceptance and equality than many of their Australian women counterparts. She even agreed to pose for the freelance photographer we had commissioned for the much-awaited picture – in her sleeveless, saffron-coloured *salwar kameez* and matching *dupatta*, revealing more flesh than most of her Australian newsroom contemporaries would, and without a trace of headwear, Islamic or otherwise. I attributed the lack of recriminations when the story appeared next morning to a managerial attention span that rarely outlived the twenty-four-hour news cycle.

There are other occasions, however, when prescriptive is the only option. Like Boxing Day's traditional, mawkish front-page picture story extracted from the Australian team's annual players' Christmas luncheon. There was a time, I was assured, when this event crackled with the spirit of the season. A revealing snapshot of a cricketer's life outside the game. Confirmation they owned clothes other than creams and tracksuits. Family album glimpses of wives and girlfriends, in the days before they became a sideshow in their own right.

By the time I happened upon this ritual on Christmas morning, 1998, it had already begun its degeneration into just another contrived media opportunity. A handful of journalists mingled awkwardly as unimpressed waiters skulked around the edges of the inner-Melbourne hotel meeting room set aside for the charade. Even the free drinks added to my sense of unease. What was the etiquette for attending someone else's party at 11 a.m. on a Friday? Champagne would appear too celebratory. Beer a touch desperate. Mineral water a tad puritanical. I opted for adult, yet professional, and asked for a dry ginger ale. The young waiter scanned the selection of already opened bottles, snorted his contempt, and then dragged himself indignantly towards the kitchen, never to re-emerge.

The players with young children filed slowly into the room and self-consciously unwrapped specially provided gifts for the benefit of television crews that lurched from scene to scene in a tangle of cables and confected urgency in search of the cheesiest pictures to sit alongside vision of local church services, foreign backpackers at Bondi Beach, and grabs from the Queen's Message that perennially fill Christmas night TV news bulletins.

Several of the younger, childless players attempted to melt into the background with their ill-at-ease partners. Some declined to front at all. Michael Slater and his wife, Stephanie, wore matching headbands from which miniature pairs of felt-covered reindeer antlers waved, and were the only ones to actively court the cameras. The remainder of the gathering carried looks most often seen at an office farewell. The ones where people cling to the walls, push a slice of too-much-mock-cream sponge cake around a saucer, and anxiously await handover of the gift and plus-sized card so they can return to the refuge of their desks. We were all there for no reason other than we had to be and, accordingly, struggled with the pretence that we were partaking of a spontaneous outbreak of Yuletide celebration.

'It's just what you get used to, and for the past ten years this has been the reality of Christmas for our family,' Judi Taylor, wife of the incumbent Test captain, observed as she sipped orange juice, her eyes fixed on sons William and Jack, who were insistently whispering to their father. Doubtless unnerved by the intrusion of three camera crews jostling to get in their faces. 'People ask me if it's a nuisance to pack up the boys every year and have Christmas away from home in Sydney. But it's all they've known. They're just getting to that age where they're asking the question themselves. I tell them, "If Daddy's not working in Melbourne, it means he hasn't got a job. And that means he isn't earning any money for Christmas."'

She respectfully declined to speculate on whether that scenario might change next year. Taylor was expected to announce his retirement at the end of that summer's Ashes series, but his wife was far too media savvy to let any hint of his intentions slip to a journalist who kept peering over her shoulder towards the kitchen in the vain hope his soft drink might emerge.

Even when Taylor did stand down two weeks later, it only served to stoke greater conjecture as to who would fill his shoes. As the one-day team's leader, Stephen Waugh carried the favour of legitimate bookmakers. But when injury once again forced him to the sidelines during the limited-overs series that followed the Ashes, Warne seized the chance to push his case.

In keeping with his mesmeric bowling talents, there were times when Warne's life was utterly unfathomable. He had begun the summer of 1998–99 in a fog of self-doubt, publicly wondering whether his recovery from recent shoulder surgery would allow him to return to international cricket. While still completing his rehabilitation, it was revealed he had accepted $US5,000 from an illegal bookmaker in Sri Lanka four years earlier. Then, a month later, he was at his brilliant best, leading Australia to a one-day tournament victory and whipping his players into a frenzy of self-belief with his football-style captaincy built on inspirational on-field deeds. At one point, he even played the unlikely diplomat, emerging from the MCG change rooms like a pantomime hero clad in tracksuit pants, polo shirt, sandals and protective helmet to call for an end to another bout of missile throwing from drunken fans, which threatened to curtail a match against England. It was a symbolic moment. Warne revelled in the role of people's champion. The populist underdog.

However, Australia's cricket administrators did not share his love of a punt. And it would have taken a huge leap of faith to install him as their next Test captain, a position that stands alone on the Australian sporting landscape for its hybrid of statesman and sportsman. With the game already lurching from one crisis to the next, Warne was seen as simply too high risk. His ability to court off-field controversy countered his unquestioned talents with a cricket ball. Regular appearances in the tabloid gossip pages were not the look Australians wanted in their loftiest sporting office. Unless you could successfully show you had resolutely changed your ways, as Ricky Ponting later proved able to do.

Raw talent had seen Ponting hailed as the Australian game's future, even before he made his first Test appearance as a twenty-year-old. But the assumption that he would inevitably rise to the top job came into question at the height of that summer's captaincy debate when he was struck by a bouncer in Sydney. Not in the heat of battle, but in the swill of a Kings Cross nightclub. Ponting met the enforcer, a one-time rugby league professional, when he angrily objected to being refused another drink in the pre-dawn hours following a day-night match at the SCG. That's all Ponting can remember, with the bouncer's intervention and unconsciousness following one another in rapid succession.

Not even journalists frequent sordid nightspots at that hour of the morning, so the misdemeanour remained a carefully concealed secret for two days. But Australian cricket officials have no idea how close that story came to being splashed across the national broadsheet long before they chose to go public. Sadly, but not altogether surprisingly, the journalist into whose lap the yarn almost landed was similarly clueless. I was at the reception desk of our Sydney hotel at the same time the cricketers' bus was preparing to depart for the airport. Alongside me stood the Australian team manager on the house phone to a nameless member of the squad, who was still obviously holed up in his room.

'Well, quick as you can, mate, everyone's in the bus. And we're already supposed to be on the road,' the exasperated official muttered, eyes squeezed shut, his left elbow resting on the counter as he slowly massaged his temples with thumb and middle finger.

With just a waft of perspicacity, a tincture of curiosity, I could have established that something was seriously amiss. All it needed was for me to plant myself in a lobby chair opposite the bank of lifts and wait for the errant cricketer to appear. Even if the shabby demeanour of the youngest member of the Australian team didn't appear suspiciously out of place, the crescent-shaped purple bruise that was blossoming beneath his left eye would have provided at least one vital clue.

Instead, my finely honed journalistic instincts, coupled with my own urgent need to catch a morning flight, led me to conclude the manager was simply on the case of another tardy cricketer who had dallied too long over his morning toast and coffee. At no stage did it cross my inquiring mind that he was, instead, already piecing together a strategy to deal with a concussed, hungover, sleep-deprived batting prodigy whose immediate playing future was suddenly as clouded as his judgement. Well, it did occur to me. Two days later, when a chastened and battered Ponting was paraded before a media conference in Hobart to admit he suffered from an alcohol problem.

My need to nurture some meaningful contacts within the cricket team, and across the wider cricket world, thus became as painfully obvious as Ponting's shiner. Those who knew such things told me the only way to successfully and regularly break stories was to have at least one reliable source willing to pass on information from within the playing group, one at the selection table, and one inside the Australian Cricket Board Room. As things stood, I was hard pressed getting a nod of recognition from the team scorer.

The job was much simpler when political upheaval, personal spats and outbreaks of violence unfolded on the field of play in full view of everyone. For all of those to surface in the course of a single afternoon would have been unheard of until that fractious summer finally blew its lid on a typically stifling January day in Adelaide. Ross Emerson, an investigator with Western Australia's Ministry for Fair Trading who, in his spare time, also served as an international cricket umpire, sparked the mayhem when he publicly outed Sri Lanka's record-breaking off-spinner Muttiah Muralitharan as a chucker. For the next seventy-two hours, international cricket wobbled violently, and almost fell clean off its axis. It wasn't quite match-fixing, but it was a fairly serious case of muscle-flexing.

In judging that Muralitharan bent the rules by straightening his arm, Emerson triggered an unprecedented risk to cricket's governance. Sri Lankan captain Arjuna Ranatunga responded by threatening to take his team not just off the field that afternoon, but out of the country. Their match against England then stalled for a quarter of an hour while urgent peace talks took place boundary-side. Upon resumption, the match degenerated into an unedifying display of finger-pointing, name-calling and shoulder-charging. There was even an attempted head butt. Central to much of this unpleasantness was Ranatunga, which prompted his rival skipper, Alec Stewart, to famously scold from behind the stumps, 'Your conduct today has been appalling for a country's captain.'

Ranatunga duly faced five charges under the International Cricket Council's code of behaviour. They were to be heard at Adelaide Oval's administration offices two days after the match, which had already entered cricket folklore as the most bad-tempered and distasteful since England's Bodyline tactics had threatened to incite mob violence at the same venue sixty-five years earlier.

The passage of thirty-six hours had failed to quell inflamed nationalistic passions when the hearing convened. Several Sri Lankan supporters positioned themselves outside the Oval's entrance gates, and posed for photographers and camera crews as they shouted, sang and waved a large cardboard placard daubed with the words 'Free Arjuna, Hang Emerson'. As far as protests go, it would not have looked out of place at The Hague's International Criminal Court, rather than a response to a cricket umpire's call of 'no-ball'. But as events over ensuing days confirmed, this matter had evolved into far more than a regulation code of conduct hearing.

Adding to the melodrama was the mysterious decision to adjourn the Adelaide inquisition and have it reconvened the following evening in Perth, the site of Sri Lanka's next match. When that in-camera four-hour session subsequently wound up on a hot, still Thursday night, the story only became stranger. Instead of copping the six-match ban that most believed was the minimum penalty he deserved, Ranatunga emerged with a suspended sentence and a fine of seventy-five per cent of his match fee. Around $160. The verdict was delivered by ashen-faced match referee, South African Peter van der Merwe, who read a brief statement and took no questions, due to legal constraints.

The players and officials who had sat around for hours at the hearing before being dismissed without a word of evidence being heard made little attempt to hide their fury. I was similarly unimpressed. Not because of the verdict, but due to the conspicuous lack of detail as to how it was reached. Editors are notoriously intolerant of reporters telling them 'but that's all I could find out'. So on my return to our hotel, I was thrilled to be singled out by an Australian Cricket Board official who motioned frantically from a table in the foyer bar.

'What did you write about the hearing for tomorrow's paper?' he asked, as if shooting the evening Fremantle breeze. He showed no surprise when I told him my commentary was minimal, and I was not looking forward to the imminent call demanding a more substantial follow-up for the next day.

'There's a lot of people in world cricket who are seriously pissed off by the way this has played out,' he whispered, glancing furtively around. 'Nobody can comment about it publicly. But if you were to receive a full off-the-record briefing on what took place in that hearing room, there would be nothing to stop you from writing it. Someone who was present for the whole thing will be having a drink in the bar in a few minutes. Might be worth joining him.'

I tried to exude a George Smiley-esque air of insouciance as I sauntered to the bar and ordered a gin and tonic. But the sudden appearance of my informant set off a fit of anxiety that saw me snatch a glass of neat spirit and a bowl of rice crackers from the startled barman, and attract the attention of most patrons as I hustled to our rendezvous juggling a drink, notebook and dictaphone, leaving a trail of bar snacks in my wake.

Still angry from the night's events, the official overlooked my state of unpreparedness. He focused, instead, on the details of how the Sri Lankans had used the hearing's adjournment in Adelaide to engage a couple of well-heeled Melbourne lawyers, even though legal representatives had in the past been excluded from hearings that dealt with on-field indiscretions. That's because the guidelines that govern cricket are laws in name alone. If the wigged ones got involved, a restraint of trade would be lodged each time a batsman was incorrectly given out, and bowlers' appeals would echo all the way to the High Court.

The legal eagles zeroed in on van der Merwe's hopelessly compromised dual role as the case's prosecutor and adjudicator. They challenged, on a legal technicality, the legitimacy of damning umpires' reports that cited Ranatunga for intimidation, among other charges. And van der Merwe himself was accused of bias because of public comments he made earlier in the tournament when he had conceded Muralitharan possessed 'an unusual' bowling action. They argued the charges should be thrown out and threatened that, if they were pursued and Ranatunga was banned, the tour would be immediately abandoned.

But their trump card was the assertion that the ICC code of conduct, the manifesto to which every playing member of the Council – Sri Lanka included – had willingly subscribed, was legally flawed and would not survive a court challenge. In short, if Ranatunga was suspended, the matter would be before Australia's Federal Court within hours, and an injunction gained to ensure he could continue playing. Van der Merwe knew there was no point imposing a suspension because the code of conduct that Ranatunga was accused of breaching had been written by cricketers, for cricketers. It was a gentleman's agreement, not an enforceable contract and, as such, would collapse under court scrutiny. And once this cornerstone of the game's on-field disciplinary framework was demolished, other pillars that it unsteadily supported would also begin to crumble.

In the end, all the referee could do was make his muted point by imposing the maximum six-match ban but, like a condemned man shouting from the gallows 'justice will be done', he had no choice but to make a mockery of the process by suspending that sentence. Ranatunga had beaten the charges and, in doing so, exposed the archaic spirit of cricket for being as real and as contemporary as Jacob Marley.

With the mystery of the disappearing punishment neatly solved, I returned to my room around midnight and fired off a note to my sports editor in Sydney, to make sure he was aware that I had worked doggedly through the night chasing down every available detail. And that, thanks to investigative journalistic skills hitherto unknown to both of us, I would be filing, when I arose, a forensically assembled account of how Sri Lanka's captain had slipped the noose. I selectively omitted that all I had done to piece together this information was make sure the rattling of ice cubes didn't impinge on the audio quality of the interview.

* * *

Stephen Waugh was sitting at home, tuned into an episode of *Sesame Street*, when he received a phone call confirming he had been appointed as Australia's next Test captain. Around the same time, I was hunched over an ironing board in my Melbourne flat, trying to eradicate the creases embedded in much of my wardrobe following a summer of suitcase living, when I received similarly joyful news. Obviously impressed by my unravelling of the Ranatunga case, the boss wanted me to head to the West Indies at the end of Australia's four-Test series there, and assume the paper's coverage for the ensuing seven-match one-day tournament. And then follow the team through to England for its 1999 World Cup campaign. All up, three months on the road.

Waugh's promotion represented the hard-won achievement of a life-long ambition. For me, being part of a cricket tour to the Caribbean and Great Britain was the realisation of a similarly cherished childhood dream. I danced an ungainly jig, punched the air in silent exultation, and snapped back to reality too late to prevent a dark scorch mark being seared into the sleeve of a white T-shirt. Images and words from formative years spent studying every available cricket publication came swirling back in such a violent cascade that I had to take a seat lest they knock me down.

The glossy black-and-white plates incorporated in hard-backed, serious cricket texts hidden away in cardboard cartons in my grandfather's woodworking shed. The smell of damp sawdust, and the delicate curls of wood shavings that crunched underfoot as I carefully lifted each musty volume from its resting place, and scanned the images, scattered like treasure amid the yellowing pages of unfathomable text. Of Lindwall and Harvey, Trueman and Cowdrey, with their heavy high-cut boots, long-sleeved cable-knit jumpers and quaintly captioned deeds ('Benaud turns to leg as England's slips cordon looks on'). All played out in front of ordered terraces of attentive spectators, clad in gabardine overcoats and smart fedoras at venues with mysteriously reverential names – Old Trafford, Trent Bridge, The Oval – that could not be found in any atlas.

The parade of monthly magazines that filled so many secluded schoolboy hours through the height of summer and the depths of winter. Their tales of rum-soaked spectators jammed into the heaving grandstands at Sabina Park and Bourda, with even larger crowds clustered around the adjoining market street stalls, and clinging to precarious vantage points beyond the perimeter fences. The giddy combination of romanticism and athleticism conveyed by action photographs of lissom cricketers bearing grandly baroque names – Vanburn Holder, Uton Dowe, Raphick Jumadeen.

Amid the tumble of dislodged memories, and the early pangs of doubt as to my ability to carry off such a mission, was a nagging need to share my news with someone. Not just someone, but with my dad. Surely making good my pre-pubescent threat to be part of an Australian cricket tour to the Old Dart would excite in him the same thrill and pride that coursed through me. But he had long stopped taking calls. Hounded by the dual demons of addiction and self-loathing, he had opted out of our shared future just weeks after I'd turned twenty-one. A lifetime of moments not yet shared atomised in a cloud of exhaust smoke and unanswered questions. The remnants folded neatly into a brown paper bag that I collected, along with a putrid Datsun sedan and a precisely measured length of garden hose, from the local police station one mid-winter Sunday morning. The light had been forever extinguished.

4

West Indies, April 1999

In the Jet Age, it's not unreasonable to assume that if you travel virtually non-stop for forty-eight hours in vaguely one direction, you'll likely end up fairly close to where you started. Either that, or in the Caribbean. It's hard to imagine anywhere being as remote from somewhere else as the West Indies. But the benefit of long-hauling from Melbourne to Bangkok, to London Heathrow, to London Gatwick, to Barbados, and finally to Antigua was the opportunity to consider, at length, how I might best tackle the upcoming eighty-four-day assignment. And how to better survive the homeward leg.

Mild tranquillisers were the obvious answer to the latter. The puzzle of the former was not so simply solved. That was largely due to the conspicuous lack of pre-departure briefings, warnings or handy hints from my employer. Apart from repeatedly stressing the newspaper's significant financial outlay to have me cover two limited-overs cricket tournaments in opposite corners of the North Atlantic, the only direct input from my superiors was 'make sure you send an overnight news list outlining what you'll be writing for the next day, so we can take it into morning editorial conference'. In other words, this is how you can make life easier for us. In terms of information flow, it was a strictly one-way street.

Through contacts at the Australian Cricket Board, I had secured a list of the team's hotels and as much detail of the itinerary as could be planned, and passed them on to the newspaper's travel consultants. In return, head office sent me a reconditioned laptop days before departure, with assurances that it had been configured so I could file copy directly to the sports desk from anywhere in the world. Apart from that, not a single discussion on how to maximise returns from this exorbitant investment. No meetings to go through their expectations and demands. Even less dialogue about how best to overcome unexpected technology glitches, communications breakdowns, travel disruptions, or possible internment.

'Hope it all goes well. And don't forget to write,' was the knee-slapping advice from the newly appointed sports editor as I scurried about collecting vaccinations, visas and every configuration of electrical and phone plug adaptors known to humankind. The most useful intelligence, as ever, came from fellow cricket writers, many of them competitors who had undertaken tours for rival publications.

'Don't bother about the calendar because there's only two sorts of days on tour – playing days and non-playing days,' one advised.

'Make sure you don't become separated from the team, even if they change their travel plans at the last minute,' forewarned another. 'If you do and a big story breaks when you're not with them, just save yourself the grief that will follow by resigning on the spot.'

And most pragmatically, for filing 'live' stories documenting events that continue to unfold through the Australian night after the next morning's paper has gone to print, 'only write what you've seen, because historical facts can't change'. Even if it meant the copy people read next day was hours out of date, it was better than boldly predicting the future and rendering your publication an instant collectors' item. History best knows Boston's *Christian Science Monitor* for its plucky but unlucky 1912 headline 'Passengers Safely Moved and Steamer Titanic Taken in Tow' that appeared after the mighty liner had settled on the Atlantic floor.

In case we were unclear as to why so many made the epic trip to the Caribbean, it was spelled out in bold letters above V.C. Bird

International Airport as we filed, zombie-like, across the tarmac. 'Welcome to Antigua, Home of 365 beaches – One for Every Day of the Year.' The marketing pitch even extended to the stamp banged into my passport by a bored immigration officer that cheerily proclaimed 'Antigua – The Beach is Just the Beginning'. This was not especially comforting news for those of us stricken with travel weariness who, after two sanity-sapping days of aircraft and airports, were praying to our respective gods that we had, in fact, reached the end.

Squinting into the harsh light of a cloudless afternoon, and sweating sourly into clothes that seemed so appropriate for the onset of a Melbourne autumn earlier in the week, I almost wept with relief when my battle-scarred brown suitcase made a belated appearance on the baggage trailer. It was a triumph not shared by my travelling companion and journalistic competitor for the coming three months, Robert 'Crash' Craddock. Although employed by the same media megapoly, Crash would be filing for rival daily metropolitan papers throughout Australia. In addition to being one of the world's foremost cricket writers, Crash was also one of nature's true gentlemen. Unfailingly good-natured and generous to a fault, he met the news of his misplaced luggage with admirable calm. Even allowing for his perpetually sunny Queensland disposition, I suspected this was more likely exhaustion than equanimity.

After an hour of waiting in vain hope for a sighting of the suitcase, we engaged the services of Marlon, a sinewy taxi driver whose appearance was as far removed from my preconception of a Caribbean cabbie as Crash's luggage was from BA Flight 2157. Instead of cut-off denim shorts, dreadlocks and tri-colour Rasta hat, he wore a crisply pressed sports shirt, fawn slacks and brown leather loafers. His huge grin revealed teeth that were emblematic of the West Indies itself. A disparate set of sovereign entities, loosely fitted together and, as became obvious when he worked over a wad of cinnamon-scented chewing gum, committed to pursuing their individual cause rather than the collective good. He could easily have eaten an apple through a tennis racquet.

My initial view of the West Indies from the back of Marlon's taxi became burned into my memory. Not because of any exotic beauty, but because I feared succumbing to sleep at that point might render me unconscious until the following Thursday. I studied, with eyes willed apart, through a window also fully opened to try and catch the recuperative nor'-easterly zipping in off Winthorpes Bay, the intermittent villages, scrubby, treeless hills and low-lying vegetation that gave the impression the biggest of the Leeward Islands was both unloved and uninspiring. But the signs pointing to its network of rugged coasts and protected coves, which once hosted slave traders and pirates, could have been lifted from Robert Louis Stevenson. Jolly Harbour. Runaway Bay. Betty's Hope. All that was missing was a hint of treasure, buried or otherwise.

I asked Marlon if the small, brightly coloured houses that flashed by, clustered in hamlets, were the retreats of Antigua's celebrity property owners, who supposedly included Giorgio Armani, Silvio Berlusconi and Oprah Winfrey. He laughed uproariously and told us we were unlikely to catch sight of any of the cashed-up, sun-seeking tourists – famous or not – while exploring the island's unremarkable interior. They stuck fast to their resorts and shoreside villas, and kept their gaze firmly fixed on the sea. Should the local tourist board wish to turn visitors' attention to what's on offer inland, they might consider a new slogan. Perhaps: 'Antigua – It's Behind You'.

As Marlon pulled into the driveway of our hilltop hotel, I was suddenly panicked into thinking I had somehow passed out long enough during the ride for him to have missed a turn-off and ferried us, instead, to the Greek islands. Whitewashed walls and a stone staircase that led to a line of bougainvillea-fringed rooms, the courtyard balconies of which looked out over an aquamarine sea which lapped half-heartedly at a stretch of bleached sand. A solitary thought consumed me as I stared, mesmerised, across Dickenson Bay. Sleep. But no amount of throat-clearing, impatient huffing or high-pitched wailing could summon a body to the reception desk. I had been forewarned about Caribbean efficiency.

'Most of their hotels offer twenty-four-hour room service,' Big Mal had once lamented. 'But sometimes it can take even longer.'

We eventually unearthed the staff, crowded into an otherwise empty dining room and gazing in mortal dread at a vintage television set. The squeals that accompanied our entrance were, thankfully, in response to the live telecast of the third Test in nearby Barbados, which had reached its critical juncture. These were the days when West Indians still expected their team to win cricket matches, largely because they could still call on the talents of match-winning cricketers. Two of those – Brian Lara and Courtney Walsh – were responsible for the break in service at the Trade Winds Hotel. The pair needed to find six runs to secure a West Indian victory. The Australians needed a wicket to achieve theirs. As Walsh was the least-credentialled batsman Test cricket had seen, the odds were with the tourists. But given the veneration afforded Lara's rare talents, providence sided with the locals.

Even for the terminally sleep-deprived, it was impossible not to get swept up in the emotion. A grey-haired gentleman in bib-and-brace denim overalls squeezed the hands of a member of the housekeeping staff as they nervously edged closer and closer to the screen. A young man with a clip-on bow tie covered his face with his hands as Jason Gillespie ran in to bowl, but then peeped through spread fingers at the moment of delivery. Each successful defensive push or studied leave was met with shrieks, flashing white grins, and heart-wrenching anxiety. I had not yet met any of these people, but I so wanted their team to triumph because it clearly meant everything to them. When Lara ended the suspense with a typically expansive boundary, the staff hugged, danced and cried. I would have joined in, but feared passing out amid the jubilation.

When I surfaced from my fifteen-hour nap, the hotel staff had resumed their duties and an influx of Australians, including the touring Test match press corps, were keeping them busy. Even though my tenure did not officially start until the final Test had ended, my colleague Malcolm Conn, whom I was relieving, suggested if I was in Antigua, I might as well be involved in the series decider. It was simply a matter of ensuring my freshly prepared laptop was match-ready. I may as well have been asked to find Crash's luggage.

The newspaper's computer experts, so intent on ensuring the machine was used only for work purposes that they had gone to the trouble of dismantling its Solitaire program, had also somehow missed the fact it was unable to transmit written material to Sydney from anywhere further afield than Perth. Its internal modem was incapable of holding an international telephone signal, and I could not dial into a local internet server because it had not been fitted with appropriate browser software – no doubt to prevent me trawling the worldwide web in search of online card games. I was essentially travelling with a five-kilogram electronic calculator. When I explained my predicament to Big Mal, he reassured me his machine had worked without a hitch during the first three Tests, and suggested I simply commandeer it at series end. Then he could escort my useless contraption back to where it had been built. A solution so seamless, it was bound to meet head office disapproval.

There was certainly no shortage of material to keep Big Mal, my paper's celebrated cricket columnist and press corps doyen Mike Coward, and me busy leading into the Antigua Test. And most of that fodder was provided by Shane Warne. Not only had he been overlooked for the captaincy, his effectiveness in Test cricket since returning from shoulder surgery was so blunted that his place in the starting XI was also uncertain. Rumours of a rift between Stephen Waugh and his deputy had surfaced so, in the absence of any verifiable evidence, the touring press decided to pool its expenses money and issue a dinner invitation to the Australian coach, Geoff Marsh, as well as the skipper and his lieutenant. The hope was that any existing tensions might spill into the public domain over a bite to eat and a couple of rum and colas.

Warne kept a conspicuous distance from his teammates as we assembled for pre-prandial drinks on the hotel's poolside terrace. For perhaps the only time in his career, he opted to mingle with journalists rather than his fellow celebrities. When it came time to be seated, Marsh and Waugh chose one end of the table for twenty that spanned the length of the portico, ceiling fan whirring ineffectively above them. Warne chose the opposite end, where the recent media arrivals and a couple of heavily sun-kissed photographers were seated. His unspoken hope was that talk at the shallow end would not extend to selection dilemmas for the upcoming Test.

Although facing the greatest on-field shake-up of his headline-studded Test career – he was dropped for the one and only time in Antigua – Warne was nothing if not pleasant, though clearly subdued, company that evening. The only time he spat it was when he bit into a dinner roll sprinkled with caraway. A mouthful of aniseed-infused bread was not what his notoriously unadventurous palate had anticipated. His green eyes bulged wide in horror, and his face contorted like a test pilot subjected to fifteen-plus g-forces. Opting not to discreetly swallow the morsel already in his mouth and avoid the remainder, he instead rasped up the barely chewed lump into a napkin. He then wrapped it hurriedly and frantically summoned a waiter.

'Dunno what they've put in that, pal,' he spluttered, handing over the parcel as if it contained an inexpertly wired bomb.

That was the end of Warne's dalliance with fine dining. He dismissed, out of hand, the menu's seafood delicacies, and instead suggested the chef might like to whip him up a bowl of spaghetti bolognaise. With a side of plain white bread. By contrast, Stephen Waugh's only concern was whether the press corps was indeed footing the entire bill. Upon learning that was the deal, he delighted in ordering a lobster entrée followed by a lobster main course. The Australian captain enjoyed getting one up on the media almost as much as he craved winning games of cricket.

The tiny Antigua Recreation Ground served as the spiritual home of Calypso cricket in the days when the West Indies were a world force. Its very location affirmed its non-denominational appeal – a short stroll from the sleepy commercial heart of St John's, past the imposing grey stone edifice of the nineteenth-century Anglican cathedral, skirting the official home and office of the Governor-General, and the last stop heading east before Her Majesty's Prison. Its amalgam of whitewashed concrete walls and bare steel and timber grandstands only highlighted the fact that the soul of a cricket ground can transcend the sum of its graceless parts. It held scarcely 10,000 people, but when fully packed it pulsed with a passion that left the world's mega-stadia looking decidedly soulless. It was like no other cricket venue on the planet – part open-air nightclub, part house of worship.

The prospect of the home team wresting back the Frank Worrell Trophy after being brutalised in the opening Test of the 1999 series meant the ground was beyond bursting for the decider. Even though it was Easter weekend in a traditionally God-fearing community, the party was in full swing along the narrow walkways separating the terraces from the perimeter walls before a ball was bowled. Heavy-set women sat on upturned milk crates, crouched over huge pots that bubbled with goat curry. Hotplates billowed aromatic smoke as the early morning jerk chicken or shark and bake customers queued. And the pick-up trucks that made the slow crawl to the heavy steel entrance gates on Factory Road unloaded groups of fans who lugged in enormous cooler boxes stacked with bottled beer, rum punch, and all manner of other grog that screamed 'late afternoon security problem'.

Reggae music blasted – at a volume that demanded its own health warning – from the soaring speaker stacks of 'Chickie's Disco', as much a landmark in the Double Decker Stand as Old Father Time perched above Lord's. In the sweaty catacombs under the elevated western concourses, staff dispensed cold drinks and lukewarm rotis, stopping only to strain for a glimpse of the players through the louvred windows above them that opened out at ground level. Almost to a person – hard-partying Australian tour groups and objective journalists included – the crowd buzzed with the expectation of another virtuoso performance from Lara, who had peeled off match-winning centuries in each of the previous two Tests. And none of us was left short-changed. The raw statistics of Lara's sublime second-day hundred, reached off just eighty-two balls, tell a suitably compelling tale. But the drama compacted into that 101-minute innings sustains the memory of all who lived it.

As Lara ambled on to the ground midway through Easter Sunday afternoon, his slightly knock-kneed gait giving him the misleading appearance of a small boy kitted out in too-big protective equipment, customers vacated the bars and food stalls to take up any spare vantage points. Many of the venue staff followed them. Despite being in the form of his life, Lara took a dozen deliveries to score his first runs. He should have been dismissed twice in the space of a single over having reached fourteen, but was spared by the ineptitude of Australia's fielders. Or perhaps they secretly also wanted to see him flaunt his genius one more time. Whatever the truth, they deserved thanks rather than ridicule. Because, for the next hour, Lara conducted a master class as ruthless as it was flawless. No matter how Australia's hapless bowlers attacked him, or where Stephen Waugh deployed his fielders, Lara simply hit the ball wherever he wanted, often times even further. In doing so, he lifted the congregation to the cusp of exalted delirium.

Lara's extravagant back-lift always gave the erroneous impression that he premeditated his strokes, or that he aimed a glory shot at every ball that came along. But like a matador's *estoque* beneath a billowing cape, the flourish helped to mask the menace. He would dip into a slight crouch as the bowler delivered, as if drawing reserves of power from the very pit of his being, then channel that power into the moment bat met ball. It was at that point of contact that he seemed to have at least three shots in his repertoire to achieve the optimum outcome. His ability to subtly transfer his body weight, flex his wrists and angle his blade at the last conceivable instant meant a delivery of full length around off stump could be stroked either through extra cover, squeezed through point, or deflected to third man depending on where the fielders weren't. On this day, once he got into his stride, every choice was unerring. It didn't define the outcome of the Test or the series, but it meant that, in a matter of a few days, my long-held expectations about the joys cricket journalism could deliver had been stunningly exceeded. It also provided something well worth writing home about. When it was my turn to use the laptop.

The Test series completed, those of us travelling with the one-day squad then made the short flight to the island nation of St Vincent, stopping-off point for the sailing haven of the Tobago Cays and site of the first of seven limited-overs internationals. At least it would have been a short hop, had it not been for the obligatory Caribbean airport hiccup that meant an eighty-minute flight was delayed by four hours, thereby ensuring our media contingent eventually landed in Kingstown around midnight. The thrill of working in enchanting locations was already being counter-balanced by the inescapable tedium involved in travelling to and from them.

St Vincent didn't occupy a place on the established Caribbean tourist trail for a number of reasons, one of those being because its hotel staff didn't keep the same flexible hours as local airlines. We were deposited at our final destination in bright moonlight, outside a securely locked front office, by an unhelpful taxi driver. Our frantic rattling of the glass doors finally roused a rifle-toting security guard, who hesitantly unshackled the door. We explained to him about our bookings, our delayed flight, and our need to get to our rooms so we could begin work. It may have been deep into snooze time in the Grenadines, but in Australia it was mid-afternoon and deadline loomed. Displaying the region's legendary commitment to customer service, he told us we'd have to wait until the hotel staff clocked on later in the morning before our rooms could be assigned. He had obviously been trained to guard against tourists trying to break in to steal half a night's sleep, and it was only a barrage of sustained and deliberate falsehoods about us being influential foreign travel writers happy to sabotage the hotel's global reputation that led to lights being turned on, a booking register produced, and room keys dispensed. We snatched them like gulls seizing discarded sandwich crusts, and bolted for the stairwell before he could cock the gun.

My heart sank when I flicked on the room light and noticed the ancient Bakelite telephone handset that dominated the corner desk, with its thick, pre-war cabling snugly tucked into the wall cavity behind a firmly fixed square of tin plate, whitewashed to match the plaster. It made my rudimentary technology appear positively futuristic. Figuring the guy with the gun was as likely to be an IT wizard as he was a tourism ambassador, I abandoned the urge to pick up the museum piece and summon help to access an alternative phone with a detachable line. Instead, I unpacked my Swiss Army knife and set to work, with the tenacity of a prison escapee, chipping into a wall that crumbled like desiccated feta. I finally unearthed a dust-encrusted phone plug that I cradled as if it were an artefact of archaeological significance, and then gently prised it apart to work out a means of making contact between my computer and the outside world.

Then, having thrashed out a hasty preview of the upcoming series opener, I sat in simmering fury as the machine stubbornly refused to connect to the Sydney mother ship. By this time it was past 2 a.m. Caribbean time, and I thought it would be therapeutic to share my rage with the newspaper's oxymoronic IT help desk. My reasoning that they couldn't make a dire situation any worse turned out to be badly skewed.

'What's the asset ID number on that laptop?' the technocrat asked, before my response led to an ominous silence.

'Where did you get this machine from?' he eventually hissed.

I explained in excruciating detail the uselessness of my original hardware, the generosity of my colleague, how he was returning the dud device back to its makers, and how grateful I was that somebody in the organisation was prepared to offer useful assistance so that I could perform my job. None of which made any impression.

'Well you're not authorised to have that machine,' the geek said, fairly bursting with that glee the professionally powerless gain from nobbling others. 'You'll have to return it to Sydney immediately, and we'll see what we can do about getting you set up with a replacement.'

As gently as I could, given the hour and my demeanour, I explained that our mutual employer was spending tens of thousands of dollars to send me away for three months on the understanding I would file stories for the newspaper every day of that assignment. Given the obvious inability of luggage items to find their way to the Caribbean when notionally travelling with a paying customer, I doubted that an unaccompanied laptop would safely make it from Australia before the current millennium ticked over. And it was an even-money bet it could be achieved within the parameters of the next.

'That's not our concern. We're simply looking after the company's assets. You're not authorised to continue using it and we need to recover it.'

Defeated by exhaustion and the obstinacy, I asked roughly how long it would take to commission, build and issue a replacement machine that fitted the cutting-edge specifications of the device staring at me from the dust-strewn floor. A week, maybe two, came the reply. The chill at the far end of the phone was starting to thaw now that I was playing the game on his terms. I reassured him I would have my laptop in the hands of an international courier later that day. Then I hung up, safe in the knowledge I would attempt no such manoeuvre, and that my laptop impasse was an issue I would now have to sort on my own, thereby adding IT consultant to a skills set that had recently grown to include travel agent, telecommunications repairman and excavator. Consequently, sleep – when it finally arrived – was punctuated by the first of what became a regular series of quasi-erotic dreams. The soundtrack to these visions was the high-pitched meshing of acoustic signals that pulsed through a dial-up modem – technology thankfully lost to the broadband generation – which then climaxed at the glorious moment the cacophony dramatically gave way to an electronic echo that announced a connection had been successfully established. I interpreted them as metaphysical proof that the phone line had become my lifeline.

Upon waking, I peered from my first-floor window to find my surrounds bore no resemblance to the miserable, unwelcoming place we had arrived at hours earlier. By daylight, our restored plantation house hotel offered sweeping views of the cobalt blue Caribbean Sea as it met the yellow-brown sands rimming Indian Bay. A stretch of lawn sloped away towards the tip of an undulating headland, where a swimming pool, surrounded by palm trees, sparkled invitingly. A terracotta patio soaked up the morning sun, flanked by a pristine white balustrade draped in pink and white frangipanis, and beyond them bobbed the masts of pleasure craft moored near the exclusive private retreat of Young Island. On my way to the breakfast room, where the newly painted wooden shutters were thrown open to reveal luxury yachts gliding by under full sail, I noted the reception desk was staffed by a couple of immaculately dressed young women who wielded nothing more sinister than staplers.

Crash was already ensconced, wolfing his way through his traditional morning meal. Keen to avoid dairy products, his daily serving of rice bubbles floated in a pool of pineapple juice. Or, failing that, water. The sight of several errant rice puffs on his chin suggested this morning's accompaniment was sticky nectar. His heavy-lidded appearance also told me he had encountered similar communications problems overnight.

'How did you go with the phone lines?' I asked, selfishly hoping I would not be met with news of unmitigated triumph.

'I got it through eventually,' came the tired reply. 'It's not too easy from here, is it?' he added, waving another spoonful of rice clusters in the vague direction of his mouth.

Despite the serenity of our surrounds, events of the preceding hours meant I soon turned the conversation to the shortcomings of the local travel industry, the technological hurdles I faced, the dubious diligence of the Australian-based company that had made our travel bookings. It then evolved to include my blunt assessment of the global media empire that employed us, and its belief that the more modern hotel that housed the cricket team and rival journalists was too lavish for its staff. Crash, who had experienced all these pitfalls many times over, just nodded sympathetically, while the only other patron in the breakfast room remained politely oblivious to my tired grumblings. When talk eventually turned to the upcoming game at the nearby Arnos Vale ground, and I grimly speculated about the adequacy of facilities at a venue that had hosted just eight international cricket matches over the past twenty years, our fellow guest hesitantly approached. His slim physique, deep suntan and outfit of dress shorts, freshly laundered polo shirt and boat shoes led me to surmise he was a successful American businessman who had taken early retirement to sail his days around the Cays. Once again, my incisive journalistic talent was exposed as unerringly flawed when he addressed us in a jovial, Sydney accent.

'You guys here for the cricket?' he asked, with a pep that indicated he had enjoyed a far more restful evening than either of us.

'That's right,' I replied, darkly. But he went on, unfazed, inquiring as to where we were from, how we were enjoying the West Indies, and what had led us to Kingstown. Upon learning we were cricket writers conscripted for all seven one-day internationals, his eyes widened.

'So you work for Rupert Murdoch? And he sends you off to places like this, to watch cricket for a living? How good is that? It's the best job in the world.'

I looked at my cereal-bespattered colleague, mentally flicked through a catalogue of the past twelve hours, and framed a short, pithy response that would be initially aimed at newspaper management, then broadened to take in global media magnates in general. But midway through my preparatory inhalation, our new friend interjected to take the wind from my sails. In the process, he possibly saved my career.

'Actually, I've got a bit of a media connection these days. My daughter just married your boss's son,' he announced, and checked our faces for any hint of recognition. All he got back was confused stares through dark-rimmed eyes, and a faint snap, crackle and pop as Crash distractedly stroked his chin.

'Lachlan Murdoch,' he pressed on through the silence. 'Do you guys know him?'

'So that would make you ...' I began, my voice floating away on the ocean breeze.

'Patrick O'Hare,' he announced with a wide smile, offering his hand.

I mentally shredded my script, and moved seamlessly instead to: 'Oh, of course, yes. The marriage. Right. Lachlan and Sarah. How great. That's super.' Fearing my drowning man routine was about to drag him under as well, Crash leapt to our rescue.

'It's just terrific, Patrick, we're so happy for them. Are they still on their honeymoon?' he said, while I just sat and blinked.

'As a matter of fact, they are,' Patrick said, seemingly relieved that at least one globe-trotting writer could construct a coherent sentence. 'They spent some time in New York, and now they're doing a bit of sailing ... out there somewhere.'

I looked past him as a huge yellow and orange spinnaker filled the window. Surely that couldn't be them, I wondered through fatigue and shock. And even if it was, surely my bitching couldn't have been audible on the deck of a passing yacht? Or, for that matter, in the far corner of the breakfast room?

'Well, if you're speaking with them, give them our best and tell them our tour's going really well,' Crash went on. 'I mean, how could it not be when we're being treated to places like this.' He waved his arm theatrically to indicate all that surrounded us.

'I'll do that, it's really good of you,' Patrick said, as he prepared to depart. 'And I'll keep an eye out for you at the ground on Sunday.'

As he made for the door, I stared blankly into my plate and made a mental note to confine any future steam releases and office bashing to the privacy of my own room. Or better still, my own thoughts.

Just as he disappeared into the day, Patrick O'Hare stopped and turned back to us, adding, without a hint of mischief, 'And good luck getting those bloody phones to work.'

5

West Indies, April 1999 (II)

Guyana's status as international cricket's sole outpost on the South American mainland is explained by the nation's former colonial name, British Guiana. Before that it was claimed by the Dutch, but in more recent times it's been synonymous with the 1978 Jonestown massacre, when more than 900 American cultists lost their lives to history's most infamous drinks break. These distinct cultural and geographical identities also help explain why it's only through cricket that the West Indies appears to the world as a single family unit. And from the moment we landed at Georgetown's Cheddi Jagan International Airport, a former US military base hacked into dense vegetation on the bank of the vast, mud-coloured Demerara River, it was achingly clear that Guyana was the Caribbean's poor relation.

Having departed the neighbouring island of Trinidad in pre-dawn darkness, the hour-long road trip from the airport to our new digs provided a welcome eye-opener. Tumbledown timber houses, many barely supporting badly rusted roofs and with rotting shutters that gaped open to the world, fought a losing battle against the encroaching jungle. Perhaps it was a product of sleep deprivation, but it was difficult to picture Georgetown's neglected buildings and infrastructure as relics of a once-buoyant centre that had enjoyed significant economic clout, and even greater aesthetic appeal.

The literal high point of the capital's distinctive timber architecture was the remarkable St George's Cathedral, which – according to our enthusiastic driver – was consecrated more than a century earlier, and proclaimed by all Guyanese as the world's tallest wooden structure. Rising more than forty metres above the Demerara flood plain, it looked to have been lifted directly from an architect's model of some ambitious Amish metropolis. I wondered aloud about the wisdom of constructing, from timber, a building that provides a home for a liturgy of naked flames. Which led our cabbie to point out that fire remained a constant threat to Georgetown's major public buildings – equalled only by the ever-present menace of flood, given that the original Dutch settlement had been built, as was their way, up to a metre below sea level.

In more recent years, however, those twin hazards had been surpassed by the modern-day scourges of kidnapping and drug-related gun crime. The Land of Many Waters' network of major rivers, most of which flowed across Guyana's borders with Brazil, Venezuela and Surinam, had helped it establish a frightening reputation as an operational centre for drug-trafficking cartels that were scaling up from traditional marijuana distribution to the more lucrative cocaine and heroin end of the market. The inevitable spin-off enterprises from this commercial growth were gang crime, extortion and violent death. So it was with dire warnings of potential conflagration, inundation and mutilation ringing in our ears that we were deposited at our hotel, which our taxi driver laughingly referred to as 'the stockade'.

It was a surfeit of water, largely the result of early morning rain, that created concern when we arrived at Georgetown's historic Bourda Ground on the morning of game five of the limited-overs series. The venue where, seventy years earlier, the loose outfit of Caribbean nations recorded their first Test match win under the united West Indies' banner, had not seen much remedial work since. Its majestic timber players' pavilion contrasted starkly with the rank, toxin-filled drainage channel that oozed its way past the stadium, emitting the stench of a thousand decaying animals. Heavily armed police astride unflinching white horses patrolled the streets surrounding the ground, where crowd numbers had swelled despite the delayed start, as astute hawkers set up impromptu food and drink stalls.

By the time play got underway, more than three hours late, the crowd far exceeded the ageing facility's ability to accommodate them in anything resembling comfort. Or acceptable safety. In addition to the packed bleachers and terraces, hundreds of fans perched in trees lining nearby Regent Street, clambered atop advertising billboards and the wall between the cricket ground and adjacent football field, and packed five-deep onto the rickety roofs of grandstands that already appeared too unsteady to hold the hordes beneath. Even though entertainment, in the form of migraine-inducing dance music, had been pumping non-stop during the delay, most of the crowd had opted to spend those hours on the drink. It was a debacle waiting to happen, and it happened shortly before game's end.

A scoreboard error meant that the penultimate over of Australia's run chase was incorrectly flagged as the last, which led spectators still capable of mental arithmetic to deduce the West Indies had triumphed by five runs. And those still capable of standing to storm the field, and make off with a majority of the six stumps. The match eventually restarted, but with hundreds of partially crazed, fully boozed fans poised inside the fence, as if awaiting the starter's pistol at a steeplechase, ready to reinvade the instant a result arrived. With one ball remaining and night all but fallen, Australia needed four runs to win. Stephen Waugh and Shane Warne were batting. And that's when the craziness scaled new heights.

West Indian spinner Keith Arthurton bowled, Waugh heaved ambitiously, and succeeded only in dribbling the ball to deep mid-wicket where two outfielders lurked. The crowd knew from the moment ball left bat that it would not deliver the boundary needed to deny their heroes victory, and they swamped the field like water flooding into a stricken boat. Amid the crush, Waugh and Warne fought the tide to complete a symbolic, but ultimately pointless second run.

Suddenly, I noticed through the thickening chaos that Waugh, unsure as to the ball's location or even the whereabouts of the West Indian players, began urging Warne to tackle a third run. Competitive even in the face of a stampede, the Australian captain saw the pandemonium as an opportunity to at least escape the game with scores tied. So he put his head down and charged through the mob like a demented shopper defying the flow at the Boxing Day sales. What I could also see, but was unknown to the batsmen, was that Arthurton had received the ball and was about to complete the run-out to formalise his team's deserved win. But no sooner had he lunged towards the bowler's end stumps than a fleet-footed young man clad in T-shirt, canvas jeans and sneakers uprooted the entire wicket and hot-footed it through the throng. Memorabilia had apparently become as lucrative for some locals as narcotics.

At that point, Stephen Waugh was halfway down the pitch and still intent on making his ground at the non-striker's end to level the scores. A metre or so behind him, and closing quickly, loomed a mob of more than fifty people in frenzied pursuit. It was a scene plucked straight from the closing credits of *The Benny Hill Show*. As Waugh extended his right arm to ground his outstretched bat, he was side-swiped from the left by a spectator who tried to wrestle the willow from the skipper's grasp. Waugh suffered mild whiplash as a result of that collision, but kept hold of his property, if not his cool.

So shambolic was the entire episode that the final result remained in abeyance while the match referee, former England Test batsman Raman Subba Row, convened a hearing. His refusal to cede the match automatically to the West Indies further agitated the already feisty crowd, members of which aimed angry threats at Waugh as he made his way through the crush to attend the post-mortem.

'We'll be after you, and we're gonna get you,' one wild-eyed fan threatened.

That was enough for the Australian captain. At his ensuing media conference, he launched into a tirade against the idiocy of crowds, and the impotence of authorities. He also speculated aloud that perhaps cricket had become a professional gamble not worth taking.

'You're risking your life,' he seethed, as we crowded around to hear him above the rising din outside. 'It only takes one guy who's had plenty to drink to run out there with a knife, à la Monica Seles, and it's over for you. It's not over-dramatising it. I genuinely feared for my safety.'

In total darkness, at 7.20 p.m. – an hour and fifteen minutes after play stopped and stupidity took over – Subba Row declared the match a tie. When news reached the crowd, it exploded into jeers, chants and shouted threats of recriminations. As an obvious out-of-towner, I baulked at wading through the angry gang gathered behind the pavilion and, instead, walked as fast and unobtrusively as possible away from the ground in the hope of finding a taxi driver who cared more for a fare than the negotiated settlement of a cricket match.

A small, maroon sedan with heavily tinted windows pulled alongside as I edged my way down an unlit street, guided by the poisoned moat that reeked and gurgled to my right. I instinctively threw myself into the taxi's back seat, recognising that the front was occupied by an amplifier obviously on loan from Chickie's Antiguan noise fest. As the car picked up pace through the grid of deserted back streets, I realised, to my alarm, that I had not been saved by a private cab operator, but simply a young punk cruising for cash. A young punk who was either very drunk, in the grip of hallucinatory drugs, or suffering from a medical condition that caused him to bleed heavily from the eyeballs. His appearance was not enhanced by the rhythmic flashes that pulsed, in time to a deafening soundtrack, from a string of red and gold lights that snaked over the dashboard and around the windscreen.

Fearing I was to become the latest kidnapping or murder statistic, and unable to make myself heard above the brain-rattling drum and bass thudding from the rear speakers, I dived into my emergency cash stash, produced a $US20 note and summoned all my available energy to scream the name of my hotel. At that point he turned, his head bobbing to the tumult, and his face took on a crazed half-smile of recognition.

Five minutes later we 'nnnchk, nnnchk-ed' into the driveway of 'the stockade', and I disentangled myself from the sub-woofers just as a small white van pulled up behind us, and unloaded a group of equally harried-looking match officials. Despite my hearing loss, I was able to make out one of the panel announcing he was headed straight to the hotel bar for a much-needed drink. I fell into step behind him, aware from my Perth experience that brimming resentment coupled with the lip-loosening properties of hard liquor were likely to produce a news story or, failing that, some sorely needed perspective. Accepting my opportunistic offer of a double whisky to help settle his distress, Raman Subba Row reciprocated by launching into a stinging critique of international cricket in South America.

'It's sad for Georgetown, being such an historic venue, and also for West Indies' cricket,' he announced, in his cultured English tones. 'But if they can't run a match properly, then they can't run it. It's bloody ridiculous. I could see what was going to happen before they even started the final over. And the security people just sat around watching it, doing nothing to stop it.'

I only stopped note-taking long enough to ask if he needed a top-up. Even though it was well past 9 p.m. – approaching noon in the land of the deadline – and I faced at least six hours of transcribing and writing before my pre-dawn departure for the airport, I had a spring in my step as I set off through the lobby towards my room. Until a bespectacled man in a sweat-drenched patterned shirt called out from behind a counter bearing a sign that showed humour far drier than Georgetown's surrounds.

'Mister Rumzeeee, you headin' buck to you room?' the alleged Customer Services Manager asked with an earnestness that immediately had me on edge. When I nodded, he began shuffling the sheets of blank paper that lay in front of him.

'There's ummm, a problem wit you room.' A brutal silence followed. 'It's been ... err, double-booked.'

'That's okay,' I said, with a dismissive wave. 'I'm on an early plane to Barbados in the morning, so I'll be leaving around 5 a.m. anyway. Then it's all yours.'

The ill-at-ease clerk searched the lobby's mildewed ceiling for his next line.

'No, sir. I'm meanin' it's been double-booked for too-night. Someone else already checked in there. So we had to move you tings out.'

I began to fear my hearing had been more severely damaged than I imagined.

'But it's okay. We got someone who's huppy to have you share his room too-night. So we taken the opportoonity to move you stuff in there.'

His bony index finger then traced the obviously redundant booking register and, without looking up, he announced, 'It's a Missah Craddock. Missah Robert Craddock. He's also from Australia.'

He peered up from the book, beaming. 'You know him?'

In trepidation, I made my way to Crash's room where the door was propped open by one of the metal hubcaps that pretends to keep room service meals tepid. From the corridor, I could see my hastily repacked suitcase lying open on a portable cot that had been squeezed between the wardrobe and an ancient air-conditioning unit. The items I had deposited in drawers, cupboards and bathroom shelves for safe-keeping spilled out of a plastic laundry bag that lay alongside.

'Hello, maaate,' Crash chirped as I pushed my way into the chaos, as if he had unexpectedly stumbled across a long-lost chum. He perched, in the Antigua souvenir T-shirt and board shorts that comprised his wardrobe in the continued absence of his luggage, on the proper bed with laptop on his thighs, and an armada of partially dismantled meals surrounding him.

'Make yourself at home. I ordered you some spaghetti bolognaise. I think it's here somewhere.' He searched half-heartedly beside the bed, before returning to his typing. His boundless bonhomie instantly helped defuse my frustration and self-pity.

'Don't think we would have got much sleep tonight anyway, Rams. That's the amazing thing about cricket. It just throws up big stories like this, without any warning.'

As I settled on to the saggy mattress that had become my makeshift office and home, I could only agree.

'But I don't reckon we'll be seeing another day like this for a while,' I boldly forecast, as I reached down for my notebook and plunged my hand into a plate of lukewarm pasta.

The phone call, when it arrived, came as a far greater shock than the events it interrupted. From the press box eyrie at Barbados's Kensington Oval and just days after escaping Guyana, I was surveying the latest outbreak of Caribbean churlishness that had brought the seventh and final one-day international of the increasingly brattish series to a halt. To show their distaste for a legitimate umpiring decision, a sizeable section of the 15,000-strong sell-out crowd lobbed bottles, fruit, half-eaten Johnny cakes and anything else within reach onto the playing field in another tiresome show of poor sportsmanship. Given the regularity of these public tantrums, I struggled to comprehend why an obscure Melbourne breakfast radio program would track me down for an eyewitness account of events to share with its handful of early morning listeners. Even more of a mystery was how.

That curiosity was shared by the unsuspecting soul who, on that sunny Sunday afternoon, answered the lone, unlisted telephone installed at the back of Kensington's media centre. Even though she dispensed desserts from the facility's makeshift kitchenette, Floriana was not a woman to be trifled with. Standing around 155 centimetres cubed, she was also distinctive for her ability to wheeze while remaining stock still. A low-pitched whistle accompanied each breath sucked through the sizeable gap between a pair of stunningly white, tusk-like front teeth. It was the whistling that betrayed her presence behind me as I peered through my binoculars at the rioters who had commandeered the game.

'You de man from de *Osstrayan* noospepper?' she inquired, before expelling a noise like a kettle on the bubble.

I nodded, at which point Floriana jerked her head towards the rear of the media box where a concrete walkway overlooked a car park's solitary tenant, an unoccupied police bus.

'Phone,' she snapped, before wheezing back to the servery.

I picked up the receiver not knowing who to expect, and was greeted by the excited voice of the radio show's producer, whose detective skills in finding the obscure phone number might have been better employed helping Interpol track wanted fugitives.

'What's goin' on over there?' he squawked. 'We're watching here on TV. Are they gunna have to call this one off?'

Trying to sound as off-hand as one can when nuzzling a brick wall while a major civic disturbance escalates on the other side, I was about to reveal I had not yet been able to work that out when he announced he was transferring me live-to-air to share my lack of insights with the show's host. Despite an acoustic echo that made the seven-second delay redundant, and the fact I could not see the playing field from the wall-mounted phone, I constructed a passable chronology of events that had prompted the ruckus.

The flashpoint arrived when local batting hero Sherwin Campbell crossed paths with Australia's taller and sturdier all-rounder Brendon Julian, while the West Indian attempted to scamper a single. The jockey-sized opener was sat on his bum mid-pitch as a result of the collision, and was duly run out. Campbell claimed his path had been deliberately impeded, in contravention of cricket's laws, and he shamelessly milked the moment by flinging his arm out and staring forlornly at the umpires to articulate his deep-seated sense of injustice. When it became clear his plea had moved neither the on-field officials nor the Australian captain, all of whom believed the contact to be accidental, his cause was taken up by the outraged mob.

The sight of the moping Campbell leaving the field, bat trailing behind him like Linus's blanket, egged them into action and their spirits took flight. Empty bottles of Mount Gay Rum, mainly. Although they were accompanied by a smattering of brandy and pre-mixed rum punch vessels, and even some soft-drink containers whose contents, from the general level of intoxication, had obviously been used as an alcohol mixer, rather than its substitute.

As the first projectiles thudded into the turf, the jaded Australian players formed a protective huddle near the pitch. With the bombardment becoming more sustained, Stephen Waugh opted to lead his men from the field. That was when it turned really ugly. A bottle thrown from the top deck of the Members stand flew dangerously close to Waugh's left ear. For the riot-weary Australians, their flight to London seven days hence could not depart soon enough.

With the crowd chanting 'Bring back, bring back, bring back my Campbell to me', the visitors slumped, disillusioned and dispirited, in their stifling dressing room. For forty-five minutes, the match was held to ransom as the two umpires and match referee Subba Row conferred as to the safest, not necessarily the most just, course of action. In a last-ditch bid to end the tomfoolery, officials persuaded local legend Sir Garfield Sobers, whose name adorned the VIP enclosure from where the most provocative missile had been launched, to make an appeal for calm. That was the point at which the least used phone in the eastern Caribbean had rung to life.

'What's Sobers going to tell them?' the radio host quizzed, assuming that the off-the-cuff service I was apparently providing extended to soothsaying.

'Er, I'm not exactly certain,' I fumbled. Even to such a select audience, it would not have reflected well on my professionalism to admit all I could see was a brick wall. So I resorted to subterfuge.

'To be honest, you've probably got more idea than me through your television pictures,' I boomed, in my best broadcast voice. 'That's because, after what happened in Guyana last week, the media has been warned to take every available safety precaution. As a result, we're all sheltering at the back of the press box. And I'm taking a big risk by venturing out to take your call. Lord knows how they'll react when an announcement's made, so I'm gunna have to dash off.'

With that, I hung up. Admiring my ingenuity and figuring it would also put paid to any further intrusive calls for freelance radio reports, I turned to head back to my desk and barrelled straight into Floriana's dodgem car bumpers. Hands on hips, head cocked quizzically, she fixed me with a look usually reserved for those miscreants who tucked into the lunchtime flying fish cutters without handing over their $5. Having overheard the end of my tale, she shook her chins disapprovingly. I eased guiltily past, advising her softly that I wasn't available to receive any more calls. And that the kettle appeared to be boiling.

In my absence, Sobers had informed the crowd that, during the lengthy interlude, the Australians had undergone a drastic change of heart and would allow Campbell to resume his innings. That was, I learned later, despite the match referee's belief there was nothing malicious or illegal in the Australians' actions, and that the West Indian batsman had been dismissed fairly, if not a little unluckily. Further soothing the crowd's temper, the home team's victory target was reduced because of time lost to the troubles.

So Campbell strode back to a hero's ovation and, in order to claim an immoral victory, the West Indies were set a perfunctory target, which they happily completed with three overs to spare. For their part, the Australians played out the final hour with all the zeal of forced labourers.

'The spirit of the game was gone,' Stephen Waugh later confessed.

Adding insult to misery, Campbell was named man of the match, and player of the tournament. Courtesy of the equally farcical tied result in Guyana, the teams were forced to share the tournament trophy with the seven-match series finishing 3–3. The crowd's hysteria had magically metamorphosed into euphoria, while the Australians were simply relieved there was no game eight.

I was starting to subscribe to the players' prevailing view that the stereotypical image of the West Indies as a collective of chillin', laidback cats who cared for little more than reefer and reggae was as fanciful as conspiracy theories that suggested Bob Marley was murdered by CIA operatives who jammed a length of carcinogenic copper wire into one of his boots. Evidence gathered over the previous week indicated that the Caribbean was, in truth, home to a lot of uptight, cantankerous types just itching for an excuse to chuck a drunken wobbly. Not just cranky, but litigious, as I soon learned.

Stephen Waugh was in no mood for diplomacy when he fronted the end-of-match media conference in a steamy annexe above the Kensington dressing sheds. The handful of glass louvres missing from windows that faced on to the choked street below ensured the celebratory whoops and songs from inebriates leaving the ground rang loudly in his ears. And suggestions from local journalists that the Australians had over-dramatised the afternoon's happenings got up his nose.

Waugh explained his decision to acquiesce and allow Campbell to continue batting was prompted by a thinly veiled threat. Prior to a meeting during the disruption with his rival captain Jimmy Adams and the match officials, Australia's team manager advised Waugh it might be best to get back out and play because 'the local Police Commissioner has told me that if we don't, they can't guarantee your safety'. Waugh was still shaken by the manhandling and the threats he copped in Guyana. And with his team due to spend the following seven days relaxing in Barbados before departing for England, the decision to let the crowd determine the match result was deemed prudent, even if it left a bitter residue.

'It was better than getting killed on the way home,' Waugh said, trying hard to raise a grin while at the same time airing his irritation. 'I don't think that's too dramatic.'

He might have held a dozen years' head start when it came to international cricket experience, but I was quickly coming to share the captain's weary view of cricket's very evident failings. This was not the same game I'd worshipped as a child, and as recently as the Antigua Test.

As a cricketer renowned for his coldly calculated methods, Stephen Waugh had few clues about how to keep a hotel room tidy. Unmitigated bedlam spilled from cupboards, drawers and kit bags that lay strewn around his Barbados beachside suite's barely visible floor. Bottle-green shirts and lemon-yellow pants were draped across most items of furniture. A pair of bright-gold batting pads stood to attention against a cane lounge chair, and next to them grew a pile of greying wool-blend cricket socks. It was a bedroom scene more befitting a lazy teenager, but I was not about to chide the captain for his domestic shortcomings. After all, Waugh had departed from accepted media protocol by inviting a couple of us to conduct an interview within his quarters at the team's hotel following the one-day series' undignified end.

Despite the lingering sour taste, the players had welcomed the week-long break that they planned to fill lazing poolside, hitting golf balls, or exploring the island on motorised scooters. Waugh, however, was spending this flawless afternoon seated at a desk that sprouted from the tangled undergrowth of garments. When Crash and I arrived, he was engaged in the modern cricketer's most repetitive chore, outside of travel and practising.

Waugh removed one sheet at a time from a stack of several hundred business-card-sized paper rectangles that sat in a pile on the desk, and scrawled his name in its centre with a felt-tip pen before transferring it to a similarly sized pile of completed slips. I asked where this heap of autographs was bound.

'Dunno, mate,' he answered, with a diffident shrug of his shoulders, which would have disillusioned any fan who believes their prized piece of memorabilia has been lovingly inscribed by their favourite player in a poignant act of dedication. 'Same place they all end up.'

If this was indicative of life in the inner sanctum of professional sport, I could understand why players fought so hard to keep it private. But as Crash and I rescued a couple of chairs from among the debris and posed our questions, he put the pen down, leaned back in his seat and, with hands clasped in his lap, reeled off a series of thoughtful answers. He had reached the end of a difficult debut tour as Test and one-day captain, and seemed almost grateful for a chance to debrief. Then, when the voice recorders were switched off and the notebooks closed, he added some even more revealing thoughts.

'I'm still new at this, and I'm learning more about relations with you media guys as we go along,' Waugh said, as he lifted himself from his chair and made a token attempt at clearing away some of the clutter. 'I'm happy to help you out with requests like this one, and I don't mind you coming to see me if there's something that you want to check, or clear up. But because of the nature of what we do, we can't be mates.'

'I want to treat all journalists equally while I'm captain,' he said, searching for the doorknob that was hidden beneath his yellow batting helmet, as our cue to leave. 'It's a professional relationship, and it can't be a friendship. I hope you don't have a problem with that?'

As we extricated ourselves from the mess, we indicated we not only understood, but agreed. I also ventured it was a symbiotic arrangement and that, if he wanted to clarify anything I had written or just share a few thoughts, I was always happy to listen. As he closed the door behind us, he wore the pained look of someone who had just been told the lamest of jokes. Next morning, our reclassified relationship entered unforeseen territory when I received a call in my hotel room from Tony Cozier, the unrivalled king of West Indian cricket journalists.

'Have you seen the local newspaper?' he asked, in his rolling Bajan accent. 'Man, you're being sued by the Commissioner of Police here in Barbados. You, and Steve Waugh.'

I bolted to the nearest grocery store to source a copy of Cozier's Barbados daily newspaper *The Nation*, which confirmed, in bold headlines, that the Commissioner had indeed issued an *ex-parte* writ against the Australian captain as well as *The Australian*'s touring correspondent. As co-defendant in an unprecedented litigation, I had achieved in the Caribbean press what had eluded me at home for more than a month. My name was on the front page.

Studying the article, I learned that the official who had informed Australia's team manager of the possible ongoing threat to the players during the riot was not the Commissioner of Police. In fact, as the aggrieved official pointedly spelled out in his affidavit, he was not even present at Kensington Oval when the drama erupted. For that reason, he viewed the assertion that the Australians' safety could not be guaranteed as 'extremely damaging' to his reputation as a law enforcement officer, and that such a suggestion was likely to cause him 'irreparable harm'.

Rereading the story, I struggled to understand why I had been singled out as the sole media representative in the writ, given that all newspapers in Australia, the Caribbean and beyond had carried the offending quotes. I also failed to see how my words had so seriously damaged his standing, especially given my newspaper struggled to reach its handful of readers in outposts like Broome, let alone in Bridgetown. But what troubled me most was why he chose to specifically sue me, a penniless journalist, rather than the significantly more substantial global media empire that employed me.

The fact that it had barely ticked over to Saturday in Australia also meant there was no point phoning the paper's unmanned offices in search of legal advice. Instead, I checked with the Australian team manager, who assured me that, as yet, no formal papers had been served. He also expressed doubt that they would be before we all departed for London in thirty hours' time.

I stewed until late afternoon, when I received a call from Clarence at the hotel reception desk to tell me I had a visitor from the firm of Finditt, Grabbitt & Runn, or similar, awaiting me in the foyer. Immediately I regretted not paying closer attention to those complicated media law lectures I had dozed through at university. Somewhere, amid all that Latin legalese about *habeas corpus*, *sub judice* and *quo vadis*, I vaguely recalled hearing that writs had to be directly handed to a defendant to be valid. And that some shifty types attempted to circumvent being served by refusing to physically accept the document. A cunning strategy formed in my addled brain. If the writ courier could not formally present me with the paperwork, I would not, technically, be a party to the legal action. And in just over a day, I would be departing testy Barbados for the home of English law.

I became further emboldened when Clarence pointed out my visitor, a nervous-looking lad in his early twenties whose polyester-blend grey suit and ill-fitting shirt collar spelled 'legal firm intern'. Regardless of the fact he had attended law lectures far more recently than me, and doubtless paid closer attention, I was confident my crafty plan gave me the upper hand.

'I am instructed to deliver you this,' the young man announced and produced a carefully folded handful of parchment pages from within the right breast of his oversized jacket. As he extended his left arm and the incriminating documents towards me, I calmly took two steps backwards to stand behind a wire rack laden with postcard pictures of Barbados beaches. I then fixed my predator with what I felt was a combative glare but, on reflection, more likely suggested the passing of a kidney stone.

'Sir, this is for you,' he continued, lunging at me in a half-hearted fencing manoeuvre complete with *papier* rapier. Again I parried, darting behind the coffee table as Clarence shook his head in bewilderment. The lad looked confusedly at the cardigan-clad staff member whose greying hair lent him an air of wisdom. It also confirmed Clarence was too smart to get drawn into this absurdist pantomime.

'You on your own here, son,' he muttered.

A further attempt to fell me with the legal kryptonite failed when I vaulted over the table and stood behind a lounge chair, arms folded defiantly across my chest.

'This is dumb,' the lad mumbled as he looked at his huge digital watch that confirmed it was verging on pub time on a Friday afternoon. 'You want me to leave it here on the table?'

His willingness to merely deposit the writ in my vicinity completely threw me. Maybe I had imagined the university lecture that dealt with serving summonses? Perhaps it only applied to traffic infringement warrants? What if neither of us knew the law in this regard? As we stared at each other and my adversary nervously tapped the fold of papers against his left thigh, I succumbed to defeat and embarrassment.

'It's okay,' I said. 'I'll take them.'

As I held open the glass door to grant the lad his escape into the waiting weekend, I'm sure I heard Clarence exhale, 'Well praise the Lord.'

Not having been sued before, I was not entirely clued up on company policy or protocols. It was one of the topics that would doubtless have been covered in my pre-departure briefing, had there been one. I knew enough to be sure I must urgently contact my newspaper's in-house lawyer, but was also aware that any Australian solicitor worth their salt would just be stumbling home at 7 a.m. on a Saturday. And tracking him or her down would be tough from the other side of the world, without access to salient details such as their name. I suddenly wished I hadn't blown off the radio producer who seemed so adept at finding pretty much anyone.

Instead, I again turned to Australia's team manager who confirmed that the legal had landed there as well, and that the first-named defendant would be represented by a local Queen's Counsel, as recommended by Australia's High Commissioner in Barbados. He asked if I wanted to be part of the defence team's meeting, to be held at the Australian squad's hotel the following morning. He then pointed out that, according to the terms of the writ, both defendants were explicitly forbidden from mentioning the proceedings, or the events that led to them, in any public forum. Therefore, I need not bother quizzing the skipper for his on-the-record reaction.

Stephen Waugh, the team manager, and a regally dressed elderly gentleman clasping a silver-tipped cane sat gathered around a poolside table when I joined the Saturday morning conference. The QC outlined the available legal options and each provoked the same reaction from the Australian captain.

'This is bullshit,' Waugh steamed. 'It's a simple mistake. I thought the bloke that told us about the safety problem was the police chief. I'll say, "Sorry, wrong bloke." End of story.'

Waugh held the strident view that this sort of impasse was no different to disagreements between cricketers, and that it was best sorted out face-to-face. By clearing the air, shaking hands, and moving on. The QC quietly explained that, in criminal law at least, that approach would likely inflame more cases than it settled. Besides, this civil issue had already progressed beyond the point of being redressed by an apology. The official in question was apparently up for re-election sometime soon, and this case afforded him some useful pre-poll publicity. The team manager calmly suggested to his captain that seeing as the QC's expertise had been enlisted, it might be wise to hear his advice. I sat silently throughout, pondering whether my employer placed a similar value on my wellbeing and reputation as the Australian Cricket Board did on its skipper.

While the lawyer indicated an out-of-court settlement was the most likely outcome, the cricketer's major concern, which I shared, was unhindered passage out of Barbados to London, where a World Cup campaign awaited. The legal expert had already indicated any court proceedings would be conducted at glacial speed, and the prospect of any of us remaining in the Caribbean while they dragged on was mildly terrifying. The QC then advised he saw no problems in us clearing immigration that night, though his conviction faltered somewhat when he added it might be prudent to have the High Commissioner present 'just in case ...' It all became too much for Waugh, who up and quit the meeting with a curt departing gesture.

'This is bullshit,' he fumed, as he stalked off.

Come Saturday evening, hours before we were due to depart for Gatwick, I finally established contact with my boss in Sydney to explain my predicament. Initially, he was more concerned about the stipulation in the writ that forbade me from commenting on the incident. He wondered how I could finally be gifted inside running on a cricket story of global interest, and yet be the only journalist on the planet expressly prevented from writing about it.

Eventually, he passed on the details of my bind to the paper's lawyer, who rang me shortly after as I packed in defiant hope of an imminent departure. I outlined the events leading up to the lawsuit, read him the relevant bits of the writ, and arranged to fax him all the accompanying documentation. When he asked if I had sought any local legal advice, I told him I had attended a preliminary briefing with a Bridgetown QC.

'Bloody hell,' he exploded down the phone. 'A Queen's Counsel. How much is that gunna cost us?'

Deeply touched by his commitment to my welfare, I explained that cost had not been discussed because I had not formally engaged the QC's services. I was merely an interested onlooker, invited out of courtesy because my name was on the writ. In multiple places. He sternly warned me about the ramifications of signing anything other than my hotel room account, and told me he would be in touch in coming days to provide further expert guidance. I still await that communiqué.

As we gathered at Barbados Airport, I made a point of maintaining visual contact with the skipper. I knew he was being accompanied everywhere by the High Commissioner, who seemed chuffed to have landed some sort of formal diplomatic role aside from bailing drunken Australian tourists out of the city watch-house, or its main hospital. In the absence of legal counsel, I resolved that, should another obstacle in a big suit try to prevent me boarding the flight, I would cling desperately to the ankle of my elected government's representative and scream diplomatic immunity. Or temporary insanity. But we cleared passport control without incident, the plane doors sealed shut and we left for London, relieved, and not a day too soon. Incongruously, it now seemed incumbent on England to restore the assignment's sunny appeal that had so unexpectedly clouded over in the Caribbean during the preceding couple of weeks.

Five years later, shortly after his final Test, I bumped into Stephen Waugh at a cricket function and took the chance to thank him for his good grace and cooperation during his tenure as skipper. I also passed on my gratitude for earning me the one and only defamation writ of my journalistic career.

'Me too. You reckon I've had one of those, before or since?' he shot back, not missing a beat.

I then asked him if he knew the outcome of that lawsuit, given I had heard precisely nothing since departing Barbados that May evening.

'Dunno, mate, I think it got settled,' he said. 'But I still reckon it was bullshit.'

6

World Cup, England, May–June 1999

London in May sits almost as far from summer as it does from Australia. The late spring welcome it turned on seemed even chillier for those who had spent the preceding five weeks in T-shirts, shorts and beachside resorts. Which is why none of us was displeased to hustle straight from immigration into a media conference, warmed to near Trinidad temperature by the tungsten lights of a dozen television news crews, and the more than fifty journalists in attendance. Throughout the series in the Caribbean, media events rarely drew a quorum sufficient to fill a cricket team, let alone an airport meeting room. And this was barely dawn on a Sunday.

While the warmth was comforting, the turnout from Fleet Street's finest also delivered a jolting reminder as to the increased level of journalistic rivalry the World Cup was to provide. For each of the twelve competing teams, there would be at least five times as many competing media organisations. Less than an hour into the six-week assignment, the professional pressure I felt was rising at a rate inverse to the outside air temperature.

Still traumatised by the threat of possible incarceration in Barbados, I had not slept a jot on the overnight flight to Gatwick. My stress levels were further heightened by the urgent need to file an immediate report of the team's arrival press conference, a task only achievable when I tracked down a suitable telephone point near the airport's main food hall that served briefly as my office. The ten-hour time difference was another enemy that identified itself early. As were the travelling logistics involved in up to fifty days criss-crossing a single island. Not for Crash and me the luxury afforded the cricketers, who simply stumbled aboard an opulent coach that waited in readiness outside the arrivals hall to whisk them direct to the squad's inaugural Cup base in Cardiff. Nor the convenience afforded rival reporters who had arrived direct from Australia hours earlier, and collected keys for a shiny new hire car from an airport desk.

Instead, for the duration of our stay we had been granted unconditional use of a company vehicle that awaited our collection from News International's Wapping headquarters in east London. More than an hour in the opposite direction from where we were headed. It also meant that, having picked up the car, we had to navigate a path back through one of Europe's most congested cities while simultaneously battling fatigue, frostbite and chronic unfamiliarity. Added to this was a pressing need, upon arriving in Cardiff, to find, write and transmit a story covering day one of the World Cup campaign, before sleep could be entertained. And as we hauled our weary selves on and off a commuter train to Victoria Station, then in and out of a black cab to Wapping, we realised that despite having visited London several times previously, neither of us had been silly enough to attempt any mode of transport more demanding than the Tube.

Arriving among the renovated and the rundown warehouses that fronted the narrow streets of London's Docklands, we presented ourselves to the parking lot gatehouse looking more like leftovers from the Notting Hill Carnival than eminent employees from the Down Under branch. Crash blue-lipped and shivering in his by-now heavily trafficked beachwear. Me still carrying the haunted fear of a wanted fugitive.

The keeper of the cars surveyed us with a scepticism that led to phone calls being placed, credentials triple-checked and, finally, an envelope containing a solitary key on an orange plastic tag being ruefully handed over. The only clue as to our auto's whereabouts on the vast lot was its registration number. No details as to its model, make, colour or map coordinates. Our twenty-minute grid search involved much stooping and cussing, before I struck gold. Or iron pyrites, as it turned out. Our gleaming chariot was, in fact, a dust-encrusted middle-aged Volvo station wagon with a sticky clutch, an irreparably damaged spare wheel, and a conspicuously absent *London A to Z*. I was left in no doubt as to my place within the empire's pecking order.

Forever willing to pull more than his share of the workload, Crash cheerily volunteered to drive the first leg. He also casually mentioned he did not boast much experience with manual cars but, already lapsing into semi-consciousness as the insipid morning sun tried meekly to find a way through the low-level cloud, I happily acceded. As we roared out of the car park, Crash kindly advised me to catch some rest. I quickly realised he was joking.

Sunday traffic was noticeably sparse on the northern edge of the Thames, and we made jaunty progress along Victoria Embankment. A little too jaunty, I began to suspect, as Waterloo Bridge flashed past and the face of Big Ben grew rapidly larger in the windscreen. In a blur of navy blue, we hurtled past a scattering of buses, taxis and disapproving cyclists, with Crash flailing the gear stick like an agitated gardener trying to uproot an unwanted sapling.

'Um, any idea what the speed limit might be along here, mate?' I inquired with forced nonchalance, as we veered violently right onto Northumberland Avenue and the Volvo took the south-west bend of Trafalgar Square on two wheels. I fought competing urges to grip the dashboard and leap for safety.

'Umm, not really sure, mate,' Crash replied distractedly. 'But I'm sticking to sixty ... to be on the safe side.'

'Ooh, okay,' I countered, pausing briefly to process that news and scan for police. 'You remember that, here in England, they still use miles? And miles per hour?'

In the instant he turned to face me, with eyes wider than the berth we had been granted by the city traffic, I glimpsed in the diminishing distance a large, instantly recognisable yellow-and-red advertising sign. I reasoned we were about to reach either a branch of an Anglo-Dutch oil franchise, or one of a chain of multinational drive-through hamburger outlets. Whatever it signified, it was somewhere we needed to stop. If that was possible.

'Pull in here,' I shrieked, a semitone shy of hysterical.

Crash fought the wheel with the intent of a sea captain trying to avoid a Newfoundland iceberg. We swung a fierce left off the roadway, over a kerb and squealed to a halt alongside a petrol bowser amid a plume of burned rubber and the stench of molten clutch. The car stalled. Beads of sweat glistened on the brow of driver and passenger, as if summer had suddenly arrived in SW1 with the same speed and lack of forewarning that we had.

'Umm, I'll take it from here,' I squeaked, lacking both conviction and facial colour.

The most striking element of the Australians' arrival in Cardiff was the absence of any hint that world cricket's showpiece tournament was about to emerge, blazing, from its four-year hiatus. That was largely due to the impending vote on Welsh independence which hogged the local headlines, and partly because of the weather that remained more suited to huddling on the terraces of Cardiff Arms Park than reclining in the open-air grandstands at Sophia Gardens, the city's community cricket ground plonked on the west bank of the River Taff. The Welsh skies remained as steadfastly bleak and threatening as the gangs of local girls shoehorned into tiny figure-gripping outfits that barely contained their bountiful enthusiasm, who hustled through the Trinity Street pedestrian strip on party nights. Which, as near as I could tell, was every night.

The only discernible glow of interest came when the Australians unveiled their World Cup playing uniform during their first full-team media function held in the contrastingly regal grounds of Cardiff Castle. Over the course of 2,000 years, the strategic stronghold has been occupied by a Roman garrison, Norman conquerors, local nobility, and even a nineteenth-century Gothic precursor to the modern theme park. But it's unlikely the historic landmark has seen a more conspicuous troupe of entertainers than the fifteen cricketers who posed for a memorabilia moment at the base of the castle's Norman keep.

The Australian playing strip was not just lurid, it was somehow luminescent. Like a canola crop blooming in front of the Tavern

Stand at Lord's, the cricketers stood out crassly against the deep green of the castle's lush lawn. Even the peacocks that loitered behind the photographer must have felt the visitors' livery overtly ostentatious. And it wasn't only the colour that prompted incredulity. The material from which the clothes were fashioned appeared, as I reported to readers back home, to be some sort of 'high-sheen fabric to which nothing but ridicule is likely to stick'.

The space-age garb emitted glare but no heat. And with the British conditions making a mockery of the term 'warm-up games', the Australians shivered their way from Cardiff to Worcester to Taunton searching for form that had been last seen in the Caribbean sunshine. The only warmth they could generate came from the small chemical hand-warming sachets they secreted into the pockets of their garish gold pants. When brought into contact with the air, these little chemical companions released sufficient heat to at least keep blood circulating and fingers flexible. Questions regarding the wisdom of staging a cricket tournament so early in the fickle English summer were gaining validity, and the only rationale organisers could provide was that they wanted to prevent one-day cricket's equivalent of the Olympics directly clashing with the All-England tennis championships at Wimbledon, due to begin in late June.

Reasons for the Australians' lacklustre early showings were less obvious. Rumblings about a touring party that was neither competitive nor cohesive began to surface. Former England captain-turned-journalist Michael Atherton predicted that not only was Australia unable to win the World Cup, it was unlikely to make it to the second stage of the tournament, when the twelve-team competition was reduced by half. Pressure was then applied from my superiors to be the first Australian newspaper to deliver a similarly stinging appraisal of the team's chances. My plea for circumspection, that we should wait at least until the meaningful games began before trumpeting imminent failure, were reluctantly accepted. But it was only a temporary reprieve. In the super-competitive world of modern media, being first is regularly preferred to being right.

That expectation meant investing even greater vigilance in my routine morning scan of England's national daily papers. Given they numbered roughly a dozen, this was as much a physical exercise as a cerebral one. With Google yet to celebrate its first birthday, my search engine was the Volvo, which was backed up to the nearest WH Smith newsagent each day to load the stash. It added an extra element to every morning – the scramble to update stories sent to Australia just hours earlier, in the ambitious quest to leave no morsel of news, from all available sources, unreported. And those items would invariably surface when least welcome. On the morning that Australia's Cup campaign proper began against the well-concealed cricket might of Scotland, in the famous Civil War city of Worcester, I was slapped awake by the first copy I hauled from my mountainous pile of Sunday papers. Through his weekly column in *The Sunday Times*, Shane Warne had decided it was an opportune moment to launch an unprovoked tirade against Sri Lanka's captain, Arjuna Ranatunga, who, at the time, was with his team in nearby Northampton.

'I don't like him, and I'm not in a club of one,' Warne wrote with trademark tact, apropos of nothing other than spleen.

The handful of Australian players I canvassed over breakfast dismissed the rant as simply 'Warney being Warney'. The Australian Cricket Board took a less phlegmatic view, not sharing their employee's belief that truth should stand as an absolute defence. They demanded an explanation and immediately implemented new protocols to ensure all future players' columns were carefully vetted by senior ACB staff prior to publication. Thus, the practice of players receiving cash for no comment was formally sanctioned.

Not only is Worcester's New Road ground – on the banks of the Severn River with its chestnut trees and stately twelfth-century cathedral as a backdrop – one of the world's prettiest cricket venues, its fame extends well beyond its white picket boundary fence. When a conga line of members, in their tweed coats and corduroy slacks, stood with backs to the cricket midway through Australia's afternoon pursuit of Scotland's modest total, I assumed it was a silent protest at the favourites' sluggish batting progress. It was only when two English journalists, well versed in the rituals of the county cricket circuit, jumped out of their chairs and disentangled themselves from the tiny press box shouting 'cake's up' that the truth emerged.

Worcestershire County Cricket Club's greatest charm resides in its home-made afternoon teas, dispensed from the Ladies Pavilion accessed via a wooden staircase just beyond the deep mid-wicket boundary. These are the real deal – orange sponges, apple and walnut slices, citrus cake encased in thick lemon icing, scones both fruited and fruitless – dispensed by serious women who understand that plastic and polystyrene are no substitutes for crockery and bone china. Up until the late 1970s, women patrons were confined to watching cricket from the Ladies Pavilion and were denied access to the mock-Tudor Members building, which housed the club's gentlemen, as well as the players' dressing rooms and the bulk of the amenities. In a shrewd countermeasure, the ladies fought back by providing more than just desserts.

Nowadays, men wait anxiously on seat's edge for the three o'clock chimes that announce the arrival of delicacies far more appealing than cricket. When the Australian team returned to Worcester for a tour match during the 2005 Ashes series, I closely monitored the queue that started forming around 2.45 p.m. My reconnaissance revealed Australia's coach, John Buchanan, installed in a prime position near the front of the line and facing steadfastly away from the game, even though his batsmen were pushing their claims for Test selection in the middle at the time.

Scotland's score was reeled in, but with no great conviction. In his post-match media conference, Stephen Waugh was uncharacteristically critical of his team's effort, confirming his frustration was on the rise. His demeanour also lent vague credibility to rumours that a rift had arisen between him and Warne. Its genesis, supposedly, lay in Warne's exclusion from the Antigua Test. Nobody in the team would ratify this whisper, but there was a palpable undercurrent of unease that seemed to explain the less-than-inspiring effort against a Scottish team better equipped to combat the cold than Australia's bowling and batting. Waugh scotched such talk by pledging all would be redressed in the upcoming game against New Zealand, back in Cardiff. But heaping fuel on these embers of discontent was Ranatunga's rebuttal of Warne's outburst.

'Warne's attack is more about Warne and Australian culture than about me, and I think we all know where the Australians come from,' Ranatunga thundered in his own newspaper column. This slur on his nation's convict past further rankled the Australian captain, who by then had started to resemble a man carrying if not the world's, then certainly a share of the World Cup's problems.

That was the impression I gained when I arrived late to the hotel breakfast room in Cardiff next morning and noticed only one other solitary patron in the all but empty restaurant. Stephen Waugh was hunched over a bowl of cereal, studying the top copy on a heap of newspapers. I briefly considered turning around and heading straight back to my room. I knew well the etiquette that covered dining, and its proximity to players. Several times since arriving in Britain, colleagues and I had entered eateries for an evening meal only to be confronted by icy glares from a group of Australian cricketers already ensconced. The players automatically suspected journalists were trying to inveigle themselves within earshot or eye-line of their private discussions in the hope of landing some gossip. In reality, we were just aiming for a quick feed before returning to work. But it was not a battle worth waging, so we would invariably offer our apologies to the *maître d'* and retreat in search of alternative venues *sans* cricketers.

In the moment that I hesitated to consider whether to take breakfast or flee, Waugh lifted his eyes from the newspapers and offered a vague nod, which I returned. Niceties completed, I set off for a table in the farthest corner of the room to let him know I wanted to neither cramp his style, nor force his friendship.

'Sleep in, mate?' he inquired, smiling at his quip, which incorporated his favoured pastime of lampooning journalists' work ethic. I smiled back, lacking the energy to point out I had spent the past few hours updating the latest skirmish in the Austro-Ceylonese war.

As I walked past, he added: 'You can sit here if you want,' and gestured to the five vacant places at his table.

I interpreted this to mean he either had a quibble with something I'd written, or there was a wider issue he wanted to air. Stephen Waugh was not a man to engage in idle breakfast-table chit-chat. Well, not to a newspaper journalist anyway. Having accepted the offer, I decided

I should take the opportunity to get on the front foot and tackle him about scuttlebutt of dressing-room divisions.

'Nah, mate, it's all bullshit,' he said between mouthfuls. 'It's a bloody rumour that Stumper's spreading to try and give 'em a leg up for Thursday.'

'Stumper' was former Australian Test wicketkeeper and Waugh's one-time New South Wales coach, Steve Rixon, who had gone on to coach New Zealand. I waited for him to expand further but was met with nothing more than the rhythmic crunch of cereal. Having scooped the bowl clean, he broached the issue that was really on his mind.

'Have you read Ranatunga's article?' he said, not awaiting a reply. 'It's bloody outrageous,' he continued, pushing his plate to one side and draining a glass of water. 'Imagine if I'd written something like that while we were in the West Indies. Havin' a go at them, talking about Caribbean culture and slavery. I'd be run out of the game … and rightly so. It's a bloody disgrace. How does he keep getting away with it?'

'Maybe he's not as scared of writs as you and me,' I ventured, not totally sure that humour was an appropriate response. Waugh tilted his head and the half-smirk returned. He pushed his chair out with a clatter, swept up the pile of papers and strode off.

'See you later, mate', he mumbled. Then he stopped, took a step back towards me and added: 'Don't write any of that.'

I raised the palm of my hand to show good faith. Our shared breakfast had been brief. Our moment of mutual trust even more fleeting.

Life didn't become any more straightforward for the Australian captain over subsequent days. The line-up that had misfired against Scotland in Worcester stalled utterly in the face of a New Zealand batting rampage. Australia's hopes of winning the prized trophy became less probable with every imperious strike that Kiwi all-rounder Chris Cairns launched against Shane Warne's bowling. A number of these cleared the long-on fence, as well as our makeshift press box, and splashed down in the shallow waters of the meandering Taff. As the sodden ball was retrieved and returned, Warne stood dumbstruck at the top of his bowling mark, wearing the look of someone who wanted to be somewhere else. In fairness, his mind probably was – in Melbourne, where his wife had given birth to their first son hours before the game began.

There were also members within the squad who felt the captain's strict players' midnight curfew for the tournament's duration, imposed because of what Waugh considered lapses of discipline in the Caribbean, was heavy-handed and inappropriate for grown men. For these reasons alone, it was an unhappy team that rode the M1 to Leeds in the wake of the New Zealand defeat, to prepare for their next match against one of the Cup favourites, Pakistan.

Headingley was clad in its traditional grey coat, with skies the colour and warmth of Yorkshire slate as the Australians battled to remain in the World Cup. Swaddled in every item of clothing I could wear without limiting my ability to type, I squeezed into my allocated seat in the press box, located incongruously between the players' viewing balcony and the historic venue's Members bar. The only details I could make out through the morning gloom were eleven brilliant yellow figures that trailed comet-like tails across the grass when they moved. The harder I strained to make sense of the picture, the darker it all became. I could not see how they could possibly play cricket in such dim light, largely because I was struggling to see anything at all.

Curiously, metres to my left where the Pakistan players sat on the balcony, the day seemed several lux lighter. It was only then I twigged that a thin film of black gauze had been stretched across the front window of the press box, which sat elevated only slightly above ground level. The screen's purpose was to prevent batsmen becoming distracted by movement among the media, directly behind the bowler's arm. Its effect was to prevent the media from detecting all but the most extravagant movement among the players. It was like watching television through the fine weave of a prawn net.

After straining my already heavy eyes for an hour, I surrendered my seat and moved to the 'overflow' media section – a line of bare desks in the equally sparse, open-air back rows of the Main Stand. Directly in front of the Yorkshire County Cricket Club bar, favoured by aged Leodensians, where the air was bitter by scent as well as feel. I reasoned hypothermia was a small price to pay for actually seeing what I was reporting on. But it meant my mood quickly grew as grim as the day.

That was reflected in the second-edition story I filed midway through the match. Another slipshod Australian bowling and fielding effort convinced me to abandon the iron-clad principle I'd been taught for writing 'live' copy. That is, pre-empting events that will take place after the presses rolled. As I battled exhaustion and exposure, prudence was tossed to the icy wind, which sliced across the ground from Kirkstall Lane and the aptly named Winter Shed.

'Australia's World Cup bid is essentially over,' I trumpeted, with a resolve fuelled by the countless cups of instant coffee I had nursed to keep my digits thawed.

'It is out of their hands, and has all but slipped through their fingers', I continued, employing a tortured metaphor that reflected my state of mind, but a premise that I believed would prove more or less correct. Hours later, that's how it panned out. Sort of. Australia's batsmen failed to overhaul their target, and a premature flight home now loomed barely a week away.

The only person not prepared to entertain that likelihood was Stephen Waugh, who stood defiant and bristling in the meat-keeper chill of the dour football change rooms that hosted his post-match meeting with the Australian media. The skipper cut a far more combative figure than had most of his teammates over the preceding seven hours. Hands plunged deep into his pockets, he didn't respond well to suggestions that Australia was about to be bumped out of the championship alongside other cricket lightweights Scotland, Bangladesh and Kenya.

'We just have to win our next seven games,' he retorted, displaying the bloody-mindedness for which he was renowned, and occasionally mocked. 'We're capable of doing that.'

Given his team's only meaningful victory of the past three weeks had come at the expense of a nation that could happily identify all variations of Glenfiddich but none of Glenn McGrath's, it seemed a laughably ambitious equation. Nonetheless, the captain's doggedness rattled me, as I harked back to what I had already written for the morning's paper. What if, unlike the *Titanic*, the campaign was not yet sunk? It wasn't only rival cricketers that Stephen Waugh was able to burden with self-doubt.

On returning to our hotel, and with the day finally abandoning any pretence of lustre, I spied a lone figure pacing the driveway. With his tracksuit collar upturned against the invasive northern cold, Shane Warne was sucking hard on a consolation cigarette. He had also endured a forgettable day. But while my impetuousness was confined to a few thousand newspapers, the failings in his efforts were broadcast to, and scrutinised by, the world. For that reason, I attempted to slip past him unnoticed. However, he looked up long enough to spot me as I slunk along the front wall. Warne's greeting extended no further than a fleeting raise of the eyebrows. In a clumsy attempt to bridge the awkwardness, I offered congratulations on the arrival of his son, Jackson.

'Seen any pictures yet?' I inquired, with forced familiarity.

'No, not yet,' Warne breathed, his words enshrouded in smoke. 'There's a problem with my email and I can't seem to open them.'

He took another deep drag, and I was about to bid him good evening when he unexpectedly continued.

'How do ya reckon I bowled today?' he asked.

I looked into his eyes and saw he genuinely sought a response. I dipped into my faltering mental archive, searching for any recollection of his unremarkable ten-over spell that had yielded fifty-odd runs and a wicket much earlier in the day.

'Um, okay, I thought,' I stumbled. 'I mean, not easy in those conditions. Cold day, seamers' pitch. And those Pakistanis really know how to handle spin bowling …' My assessment disappeared into the drizzle that was providing an appropriate full stop to the day.

Warne stood expectantly, cigarette poised near his recently repaired right shoulder. It was as much as I had to offer and, as a critique, it was neither insightful nor valuable. But it seemed to assuage him. In truth, the most gifted spin bowler of his time didn't really want a nobody from Nuriootpa technically deconstructing his current bowling form. He simply needed somebody, anybody, to articulate what he needed to hear. That he wasn't washed up. That traces of the old magic still flickered. And that he alone wasn't to blame for the team's dire predicament.

For all his bravado and cocksuredness, Warne was as prone to self-doubt as any of us when his world was not revolving as reliably as one of his leg breaks. His mood, his demeanour, his outlook on life were all enmeshed with his performance on the cricket field. He rose and fell on the quality of his bowling. But if he was turning to me for reassurance, then the immediate future did not bode well for him, or his team. Saving us both the embarrassment of more questions for which I had no answer, he took the cigarette from his mouth and scrunched it underfoot.

'Yeah, I thought they were coming out much better today as well,' he said, as if his personal fog, at least, was lifting. 'But it's gunna be pretty tough for us from here. Looks like we might both be back in Melbourne before we know it, mate.'

He headed indoors and I hung back in the damp to try and make sense of the exchange. I might have taken a gamble that afternoon by writing recklessly on what I had not yet seen, but I was fairly certain about what I'd just heard. Perhaps, after all, my pre-emptive World Cup obituary was not so wildly speculative.

7

World Cup, England, May–June 1999 (II)

If, as the coaches' cliché goes, defeat is infinitely more instructive than triumph, then the Australians should have been chock full of knowledge after the opening week of the 1999 World Cup. Instead, they appeared as bereft of ideas as they were short of time. Just as worryingly, the mood within the team had shifted from steely to edgy. The few players who were performing looked askance at teammates who weren't. Those who were blatantly underachieving turned their insecurities inward. As the Australian public sought answers, the players' frustration was increasingly directed against those posing the questions. And nobody more graphically illustrated the shift than Adam Dale.

A journeyman seam bowler forced to wait until his thirtieth year to win national selection, Dale had a more balanced appreciation of sport's vicissitudes than many of his more naturally gifted teammates. Unaffected and unfussed, he had seen a World Cup dream he fought so hard to realise almost snatched away by the untimely bout of pneumonia he contracted in the Caribbean. The diligence and good humour he had shown in recovering his place meant there was widespread empathy to complement the prevailing wisdom that his nagging bowling style would succeed in English conditions.

Prior to Australia's tournament opener against Scotland, our touring press corps convened at the Eagle Vaults Tavern, a 'real' English pub that's operated in the heart of Worcester since the nineteenth century in a building dating back to the reign of Charles II. As we raised a final pint to our forthcoming escapade, we noticed our party's number had grown to include the unobtrusive bowler. Dale had taken himself out to an early-evening cinema screening of a new release rom-com, and was pleased to spy a few familiar faces through the pub window on his way back to the team hotel because he felt in need of a quick drink and a chat. Not many of world cricket's opening bowlers would voluntarily confess to hardened journalists that they had just teared up during a PG-rated movie. Which made it tough, even for the most flint-hearted among us, to publicly question his place in Australia's starting line-up after he captured a solitary wicket and uncharacteristically bled runs in the first two Cup games.

He was overlooked for the loss to Pakistan at Headingley and, upon reaching Chester-le-Street in County Durham for the next game, Dale was clearly of the mind that unkind media assessments were succeeding where pneumonia had failed. On the eve of the team's tournament-defining match against Bangladesh, as the Australians undertook their pre-training stretching exercises, a handful of travelling scribes wandered across the Riverside Stadium's expansive outfield to cast our inexpert eyes over the pitch. Catching sight of our collective, Dale drifted away from the playing group and barged towards the press pack. Even across such a vast distance, it was clear he bore little of the good humour we had enjoyed in Worcester. He sought out the member of our team whose copy had wounded him most deeply and began his own heated inquisition.

'What gives you the right to question my place in the team?' he demanded. 'I mean, have you ever played the game at this level?'

I thought of the standard refutation of this evergreen criticism taught to me by a wise older colleague during my cadet days. 'You don't need to have killed anyone to report on a murder.' But simply grateful that I'd been spared the outburst, I confined my attention to the strip of rolled dirt at our feet.

Dale was not the only squad member who believed the team's batting and bowling shortcomings stemmed directly from, as opposed to being accurately described by, words arranged on newsprint. That evening, on a break from my writing, I took a short stroll across the Elvet Bridge to the centre of Durham city, where I popped into a cheap and cheerful *trattoria* in search of a quick spaghetti supper. No sooner had the waiter donned that pitying look reserved for solo diners accompanied only by a paperback than I became aware of six pairs of eyes burning into me from the back of the room. A sizeable portion of the Australian cricket team made it silently, but abundantly, clear they did not want me seated anywhere nearby. I made it equally plain I got their message by seeking a table by the window. Of a curry house, in distant Silver Street.

In between biryani and DeLillo, I attempted to deconstruct why the world's best job had rapidly begun descending, day by day, into an unending chore. The boss might have been in another hemisphere, but there was no escape from the pressing weight of sourcing, producing and delivering a selection of daily newspaper stories. Forget rest days. Or even mental health days. There were, as warned, only playing days and non-playing days. And the toughest moment of each of them was prising open the laptop, at whatever time duty called, to be taunted by yet another blank page. After fifty consecutive days of filling three or four of those empty sheets at a time, my inspiration was badly overdrawn.

To compound my growing sense of isolation and subjugation, each subsequent Australian defeat saw the cricketers withdraw deeper into surliness, thereby increasing friction and reducing cooperation. This only served to further prick the interest of a newspaper industry that revels in conflict and failure, which in turn meant heightened competition between rival journalists previously united as travelling companions. And that had started to manifest itself in occasional bouts of secrecy, jealousy and paranoia.

Having mulled over these issues in brooding silence at dinner, I took a reflective evening walk along the banks of the River Wear and through the hushed grounds of Durham University to try and clear my clouded mind. I needed to unearth a means of reawakening my initial enthusiasm for the job that I had somehow misplaced between riots in the West Indies and the chill that had descended in England.

Slowly, it became clear that it was the constant heavy presence of the next deadline that had come to weigh most oppressively upon me. Opening my eyes each morning after too little sleep, knowing I was already under pressure to hit an edition just hours away. Then the next one, a few hours after that. I needed to find a definable point in each day where the job ended and reality began. It didn't reside in my endless blur of hotel rooms, which also served as my de facto offices. Likewise in the press boxes, the decrepit Volvo, or even at our touring media team's regular and thoroughly enjoyable collegiate dinners, because in all those places the conversation rarely strayed from cricket. And cricket, for so long my passion, had now come to represent work. The answer, as it came to me on a gentle Durham evening breeze, was to rediscover the world's best job by escaping from it every chance that arose.

Among the lengthening shadows cast by Durham's haunting Norman cathedral and the ghosts of scholars and powerbrokers dating back to the prince-bishops, I was awakened to the richness and diversity of experiences that were drifting distantly past while I rigidly fretted over the inanities of selection permutations, batting averages and telephone connections. I swore a silent oath that night that on subsequent tours I would make time to immerse myself more completely in my surrounds. To keep sight of the fact that cricket made for an interest, not a life. All predicated on the shaky assumption there would be other tours.

The salve for the cricketers' ills lay simply in winning. Seven games out of seven, as the captain had audaciously declared. The first of those was predictably ticked off against Bangladesh, not in a canter but at a furious gallop. Which led to a rematch with the West Indies and, more pointedly, with Brian Lara in Manchester.

Among the motivational methods the Australians had adopted to revive their campaign was to, in jargon let loose from a public-sector training seminar, give the players greater 'ownership' of the team's plans. More specifically, each member of the starting XI was assigned an individual opponent and asked to explain to their teammates pre-game how they would go about reducing their target man's impact. The job of quelling Lara, fresh from his routine dismemberment of

Australia's bowlers in the Caribbean, was handed to Glenn McGrath. His strategy, revealed to an expectant Australian team meeting in their hotel not far from Old Trafford on match eve and subsequently leaked to the press, was as economical and incisive as McGrath's famously frugal bowling.

'Get him out,' he scrawled on a sheet of paper.

At face value, McGrath held little claim to the title he would rise to secure – cricket's most successful pace bowler. He boasted neither the raw speed of Dennis Lillee, nor the steepling bounce generated by Curtly Ambrose. His weaponry did not extend to the unplayable new-ball swing imparted by Richard Hadlee, nor an ability to somehow bend the old one like Wasim Akram. Where McGrath excelled, however, over fourteen years of cricket's most attritional art, was in his unrivalled capacity to land the ball precisely where he wanted to. Over after over. Day after year.

Like most so-called champions, his talent was a gift fashioned from ambition and dedication, employing the universal tools of patience and repetition through a childhood of single-minded practice conducted on a rural property at Narromine, in north-western New South Wales. The McGrath academy was a home-made pitch scratched out of the rocks and dust behind his dad's machine shop. Having completed his daily chores, he would trundle in and bowl repeatedly at a forty-four-gallon oil drum positioned twenty-two yards away. He came to know the location of every pebble, every contour on that rudimentary strip. And not only did he understand exactly how the ball would behave upon striking the various grooves and the gravel, he could put it in such a place as to achieve his desired outcomes more often than not.

Their proud place in Trinidadian heritage aside, Brian Lara presented a far different proposition to a steel drum. But on a bitterly grey morning in one of Britain's dampest cities, it took McGrath just six deliveries to calibrate his radar against the world's pre-eminent left-hander. Then, with his seventh, he coaxed Lara to lean marginally forward by pitching on an immaculate length – full enough to commit the batsman to a stroke, but short enough to prevent him smothering any movement. And move it did. Sufficiently off the raised seam of the white Duke ball to deviate past the bat pushed speculatively towards it.

Lara's back leg twitched instinctively into line as he anticipated contact that never occurred. Instead, the ball kissed the top of his off stump before skewing off to an elated slips cordon.

Having kicked the door to victory number two of seven ajar, the Australians then showed an unseemly lack of intent to amble through it. In a nakedly cynical, though entirely legitimate, attempt to lift the West Indies into the second stage of the tournament at the expense of the New Zealanders (who would carry points from their Cardiff victory through to the subsequent 'Super Sixes' round), the Australians understood their cause would be best served by labouring as long as possible over their pursuit of victory.

Which is why Stephen Waugh and Michael Bevan took the best part of twenty overs to accumulate the final twenty runs. After suffering through the inhospitable Manchester weather, the crowd was justifiably miffed by this artificial outcome, and showed their displeasure by booing, slow hand-clapping, and walking out en masse before the final run was scored – precisely how public displeasure should be aired. Had the game been played in the Caribbean, they would have rioted from the instant Lara's stumps were rattled.

The newspapers that had decried the Australians' lack of success in the tournament's initial stages immediately reacted to their most meritorious victory by complaining loudly about the evils of contrivance, some even floating the spectre of collusion. It served to stir greater antipathy between the press corps and Waugh's team, which now surmised it was not only expected to win, but should do so in a caring, sharing kind of way. But if the touring journalists were doggedly refusing to play cheerleader, at least the Australian public was rapidly getting on board.

Consecutive wins in the group stage meant back-to-back Super Sixes fixtures in London, where McGrath repeated his form of Manchester to destroy India's celebrated batting line-up at The Oval. Then Mark Waugh found form with a characteristically deft century to secure a hard-fought win over a Zimbabwean team neither overawed nor over-shadowed by its historic first outing at Lord's.

During our welcome ten-day burst of semi-permanence in London, players from all World Cup squads were invited to a slap-up reception at Buckingham Palace. Members of the media were not. The Australian players emerged from Her Majesty's, not so much bowled over by the spread she laid on, but intrigued by the overt air of tension exuded by the South African entourage. Expectation clearly sat as comfortably with the tournament's outright favourites as egg and cress sandwiches. It also allowed a revealing glimpse into their fragile mindset, the sort of detail the Australian captain was known to exploit ruthlessly. And in the days leading into his team's return to Headingley to tackle South Africa on the same patch where the low ebb had been reached against Pakistan three weeks earlier, he didn't decline the gift. Whether prompted by obliging media questions or simply by addressing it unprompted, Stephen Waugh took every opportunity to point out there was no international cricket team Australia admired and respected more than South Africa. The sting in this tale was sharp, and toxic.

'That's why we get such great enjoyment out of beating them,' he taunted.

He was acutely aware that, player-for-player, South Africa fielded the most complete team in the game at that time. And that those same individuals had failed to win any major international cricket trophy in the eight years since their nation returned from sporting isolation, which carried with it a crushing weight of hope. Happily adding to that burden, Waugh also pointed out that his team always performed well against South Africa in matches that mattered.

'They know that, so this will be a pointer to who'll win the World Cup,' he said prior to the Headingley match. As a street fighter, Waugh knew the value in wielding any weapon that lay within reach.

Other, seemingly less plausible, items were added to the arsenal. At a team meeting on match eve, Shane Warne – not for the first or last time – prompted sniggers and muttering among his teammates when he presented his 'ownership' offering.

'If you're batting and Herschelle Gibbs takes a catch, then stand your ground,' Warne announced, before being forced to explain further by a room full of puzzled looks.

'He doesn't hold it,' he continued, becoming more insistent. 'He shows off, and flicks it straight up into the air.'

More eye-rolling ensued, but Warne went on to reveal that he had discussed this very issue with other international players and that on the West Indies' recent tour to South Africa Antiguan Ridley Jacobs went so far as to inquire of the umpires whether Gibbs had shown sufficient control over a catch, such was the fielder's enthusiasm to rid himself of the ball in the interests of showmanship. On that day, Gibbs blamed the mishap on a painkilling injection that had left him with no feeling in the middle finger of his right hand. He was to experience even greater discomfort at Headingley.

The danger with dishing out trash talk is that deeds will always have the final word. To that end, accusations of mental frailty seemed wrongly apportioned when Australia's bowlers let South Africa post a hefty 271, and then their top-order batsmen wilted in reply. The South Africans gathered in high spirits at the fall of the third wicket when, under thinning Yorkshire clouds and past the black-cloaked sight screen, Stephen Waugh all but gate-crashed the game, his normally brusque walk to the centre taking on additional urgency – as if he intended to individually put the entire opposition XI to the sword. Expecting a tense, introspective Australian skipper, given the circumstances, the South Africans were stunned when Waugh arrived, all gums blazing.

'I'm going after you today,' he goaded rival captain, Hansie Cronje, who had not even contemplated taking the ball himself at that stage.

'I want a piece of you,' he snarled at other South African bowlers, his demeanour fuelled by an overdose of adrenalin and a pathological disdain for defeat. Despite their unquestionable position of strength, Cronje's men suddenly felt under siege.

But the most memorable remark attributed to Stephen Waugh on that history-shaping afternoon was one he never made. Having faintly raised Australian hopes on the back of his own fighting half-century, Waugh flicked a ball off his pads and floated a waist-high catch to mid-wicket. Gibbs accepted the straightforward offering, but – as if reading from Warne's fantastic script – he inexplicably went to celebrate the decisive breakthrough by flicking the ball casually over his shoulder. Only this time, instead of launching skywards, the ball dribbled from his grasp and on to the Headingley turf.

As per the team talk, Waugh defiantly stood his ground. The crowd of more than 15,000 caught its breath. Cronje lodged a half-hearted, and ultimately futile, appeal, arguing that his fielder had actually controlled the ball. Unlike the Australian captain, it was summarily dismissed. It was then, as the South Africans silently moved through the field to begin the next over, that the greatest sledge never made was supposedly uttered.

Legend maintains Waugh deliberately placed himself in Gibbs's path, and heaped salt into an already gaping wound by growling, 'How does it feel to drop the World Cup?' With his team still requiring 120 runs from nineteen overs simply to remain in the tournament, it would have been a remark dripping with the sort of hubris that had just indelibly marked Gibbs's career. But the fact that Australia ultimately got there, with two deliveries to spare and Waugh unbeaten on 120, gave the fabrication lip-smacking appeal.

In truth, Waugh said something along the lines of 'That's going to cost your team today, Hersh', in keeping with the earlier lip he had dished out. But the more incendiary version was tailor-made for newspapers. Or, in this case, made up by them. Nobody has owned up to fathering the falsehood, just as there was a fraternal unwillingness to expose it as a fib. And for once, Waugh did not mind being misquoted. After all, he had just compiled what he long regarded as the best century of his career, under unimaginable pressure, against the world's best all-round bowling attack, on a lively Leeds track. And despite reeking of arrogance, the fake quote fitted the Australians' broader goal snugly. Especially when it was revealed that their semi-final opponent, four days later in Birmingham, would be South Africa.

The team's audacious run at the prize had snapped the Australian public, sports fans and otherwise, from their slumber. Television sets that had sat cold and unused during the wee hours of the Antipodean winter were suddenly being switched on and kept on until the approach of dawn when games in England reached their climax. The interest of newspaper editors had been similarly stirred, heralding the first of a string of all-night writing shifts after Headingley in a draining attempt to do justice to what was already being billed as 'Australia's most memorable one-day triumph'. It was a title that survived for all of ninety-six hours.

That night's labour through until daylight, in order to cover every conceivable angle of Australia's coup, meant there was bugger-all fresh material left to fill the insatiable demand leading into the next game. The listless, heavy-lidded eyes uniformly worn by the Australian press corps as we embarked on the two-hour drive down the M1 to Birmingham told their own story. The trip was completed in abject silence. Nobody was prepared to float an idea, or discuss a potential yarn lest it be snatched up, like a discarded jewel, by a competitor.

By the time we dragged ourselves along to Australian training the next day, so desperate was the quest for any line that might be spun into a story and draped beneath a headline that I buttonholed the team's consultant psychologist. He had been drafted into the squad early in the tournament when things weren't travelling so well, and had received coverage in some Australian papers after he was overheard chatting with Shane Warne, as they alighted the team bus, about their appointment later in the day. That exchange had then dubiously morphed into proof irrefutable that Warne was teetering on the edge of insanity, and that secure ties were being fitted to the sleeves of his tracksuit top.

In my similarly fragile state, I had hoped the shrink might detail the clinical tricks needed to rouse a team basking in the afterglow of their win, given they were tackling the selfsame opponent in the next encounter. Initially reluctant, he eventually agreed to a guarded chat, and we found a quiet spot on the periphery of training. No sooner had I turned on my voice recorder and framed my opening question than a giant paw loomed over my shoulder, snatched the machine from my hand and whisked it beyond my reach.

'Don't answer any questions about me,' Warne demanded of the perplexed psychologist. 'That's an invasion of privacy.'

Warne then took a couple of steps backwards and held the recording device above his head, like a parent who had successfully intervened in a playground dispute. He then stood silently, shifting his defiant glare from one dumbstruck onlooker to the other.

'Er, Shane, we weren't even talking about you,' the head doctor shot back. 'And even if I'm asked about individual players, I don't answer.'

If the leg-spinner was embarrassed, it didn't show. He silently handed back the machine, mumbled something about the trouble that would ensue if any of that exchange appeared in the newspaper, then turned to rejoin his teammates. The psychologist shrugged apologetically and trotted off after him. The interview never took place.

Increasingly desperate, I abandoned the Australians and resumed my search for a story inside Edgbaston's main stadium, having been drawn by a series of hammer blows that echoed chillingly across the vacant seats. Settling into what I hoped was the safety of the Eric Hollies Stand, I watched South Africa's coach, Bob Woolmer, who stood a quarter-way along one of the central pitches, and repeatedly threw badly scuffed off-white cricket balls at the feet of a batsman I recognised as Lance Klusener.

An Afrikaner as muscular as he was humourless, Klusener had emerged as the undisputed player of the World Cup. Over the previous month, he had brutalised every opposing bowling attack by wielding his hefty 3lb 2oz bat with the menace and effect of an executioner's axe. From my vantage point at extra deep mid-wicket, I counted seven consecutive strikes that sent attempted yorkers screaming over the fence. Each swing was accompanied by a distinctive 'crrrack … crrrack', not unlike the report from a .22 rifle. I made a note that should the semifinal come down to a shoot-out between Klusener and Australia's bowlers, I would back the bloke nicknamed 'Zulu'.

As the match unfolded, that scenario became more and more unlikely. The Australian batsmen again faltered early, but this time there was no miracle mid-innings rescue, or fielding *faux pas* to save them. Consequently, Stephen Waugh's team finished their innings at least twenty or thirty runs shy of a total that press box wisdom deemed satisfactory. As the Australians prepared to return to the field, lifting themselves to once more defy expectation and a buoyant opposition, it was Warne who again grasped their attention.

This time he served to confuse, rather than inspire. Curiously, he challenged his comrades to summon up a mighty collective effort because 'this might be the end for some of us'. For the benefit of anyone who might have missed the subtlety of his pre-emptive retirement announcement, he repeated it. Those who took the field with minds troubled by the leg-spinner's timing found no comfort in the cricket. The South African batsmen, led by a chastened Gibbs, began at a sprightly clip. Then Warne took the ball and history arrived.

With his eighth delivery, Warne defeated Gibbs with a leg break that would have held claim to 'ball of the century' had the spinner not already secured that honour with his inaugural Test delivery on English soil, six years earlier. This one appeared to be drifting harmlessly down leg side before it dipped alarmingly towards the batsman's left ankle, and compelled him to poke at it like someone trying to scotch a snake with an umbrella tip. Upon landing, the ball changed direction so fiercely that Gibbs had no option but to limply follow it with his bat. He was unable to catch it up before it clattered into his off stump. For the second time in as many matches, the South African stood stunned, unable to comprehend what had just taken place.

Warne simply exploded. Months of pent-up frustration, self-doubt, anger, humiliation and defeated ambition surged out of him as he pumped his fists furiously and exhorted his teammates to believe. The huddle that formed was part celebratory, part protective custody as the Australians tried to restrain the frenzied leggie lest he lose the plot he had just rewritten. When he repeated the sorcery to remove the other opener five balls later, Warne's reaction was even more bullish. He was back where he belonged – in the spotlight. And through sheer strength of character, reawakened belief in his ability, and an extraordinary capacity to deliver his unique skills amid the most demanding circumstances, he was dragging his team, and his country, into its warm glow.

The next three hours showcased the thrust and parry that only top-level sport can conjure. With deadline well and truly past, my privilege was to sit back and watch it unfold, jotting semi-regular notes to help jog my foggy recollections when typing much later in the evening. South Africa threatened to once more implode, then rallied to nose in front. Australia clawed back and panic gripped the South Africans yet again. Eventually, it boiled down to a basic equation. One over to bowl. Nine runs to win. No spare batsmen remaining. Klusener versus Australia.

Back home, millions of pyjama-clad night owls sat transfixed to their televisions, wide-eyed and white-knuckled even though it was closing in on 3 a.m. on a frosty mid-June Friday. But in the Edgbaston press box, despite the knife-edge drama approaching its denouement not 200 metres in front of me, I found myself battling to stay awake. The day had reached that gorgeous transition, the onset of an English summer evening, when the intensity of light drifts languidly from glare into gloaming. Filtered through the gossamer fog of a weak Midlands' heat haze, I was being warmed to the point of unconsciousness by the watery sun. Unable to face another cup of instant coffee, I yearned for fresh air to breathe some life into the stifling media enclosure. But as I had learned from seven weeks of professional confinement in equally airless hotel rooms, England's windows were rather like their pubs. Never open when they needed to be.

Having watched Klusener prepare for this very contingency, I also felt I had entered a dreamlike state of *déjà vu*. I fought to stave off any hazy preconception that our entire assignment was just minutes from completion. Because once my brain locked on to the prospect of imminent down time, I feared there was no chance of jump-starting it back into life should reality suddenly change. I focused, instead, on a simple truth. If Australia fluked a wicket, I soldiered on. If South Africa scored nine runs, I went to bed.

The dull throb I became aware of as Damien Fleming began the final over was not, as first suspected, a cry from my oxygen-deprived brain. It was Klusener, jaw squared, eyes narrowed, bludgeoning his enormous bat into the pitch. It sent an unmistakable message of intent, even before he sent the first two balls Fleming served up scorching to the boundary rope. Scores were level. The journey was all but over. And with our collective fate finally apparent, relief began to swamp fatigue.

I stole a glance at my Australian colleagues. They wore a uniform half-grin, half-scowl. The absence of obvious disappointment helped ease any guilt I wasn't feeling. Sure, Australian defeat heralded crushing disappointment for the players who had spent years preparing and planning. And it would unleash frustration, even desolation, among the thousands of Australians at the ground, and countless more tuned in around the world. But I remained determined to see the smaller picture. And Crash seemed to be thinking along similar lines.

'Whaddya think you'll do, Rams?' he asked vaguely, colouring in a small stick figure in the margin of his tattered scorebook, as the work benefits of a South Africa–Pakistan World Cup final began to crystallise. 'Do you reckon you'll go to London for the final?'

I half-heartedly suggested I probably would, safe in the knowledge the decision was not mine to make. Although, on further contemplation, there was no way I could see the newspaper stumping up for accommodation and travel costs for a final act that featured no Australian actors. In truth, I expected to be on the first plane home. Suddenly, Crash swivelled to face me and, betraying a level of excitement last seen when his long-lost suitcase was delivered to his hotel room in Cardiff, he frothed: 'You know what would be really great? A couple of quiet days in London before we leave. And we could take in a West End show. Maybe *Phantom of the Opera*.'

I didn't let on that I was already plotting a lengthy season of my own one-man production of *Sleeping Beauty*. But his mention of forward plans sent my brain spinning out of control. The sudden collapse of the retaining wall that had been successfully blocking out all thoughts of an Australian loss set free a torrent of urgent, competing thoughts.

An exhaustive wash-up of the semifinal would have to be written overnight, covering the usual angles – where the campaign went wrong, apportionment of blame, whose futures were now clouded etc., etc. If I was to return home immediately, I would also need to cancel my existing accommodation bookings in London, rebook airline tickets, and check the team's movements so our photographer could get the obligatory snaps of forlorn faces boarding the bus or the plane. Then again, if I had to return to London to catch the homeward flight, I might be asked to stay and cover the final. That would require revalidating my media accreditation, because press box seating at Lord's would be rightfully allocated to Pakistani, South African and English journalists. That, in turn, would impact on my ability to access a telephone line, thereby meaning I might not be able to file live copy from the ground, even if I was present. Oh, and for Christ's sake watch the game. Fleming's running into bowl.

What happened in the next ten seconds has been replayed enough times on YouTube, in highlights packages and on programs devoted to memorable sporting moments for me to retain an enduring image despite my acute brain fade. The footage etched into my subconscious shows Klusener winding up for another almighty blow, the ball dribbling off a hefty bottom edge just past the bowler's-end stumps, where it was scooped up by Mark Waugh. Klusener took off for the winning run. His batting partner, Allan Donald, responded, then opted to head back to the safety of his crease, dropping his bat in the process. Both batsmen were by now heading in the same direction. To ignominy and disaster. South Africa's reputation for choking in big games was assured for perpetuity in a single act that was part kamikaze, part comedy capers.

The match was a tie, but that remains a semantic detail. By dint of earlier results, Australia was through to the final, via a game still regarded as the benchmark against which all one-day cricket matches are measured. And in the space of one botched attempt at a single, my workload had quadrupled. One night without sleep had suddenly blown out to three, possibly four. Through glazed eyes I tried to focus on the Australian players as they leaped into each other's arms in celebration. The terraces erupted. Non-partisan journalists squealed like teenagers at a sleepover in response to the knife-edged drama. South African reporters sat silent, gutted and disbelieving. I searched my soul for any response at all. But amid the pandemonium, I was an empty shell.

I slumped back in my chair and turned slowly to my left to gauge Crash's reaction. He stared, drained of emotion, through the glass. Australia's World Cup dream remained alive. The unthinkable was now distinctly possible. The grand finale awaited. And in a spontaneous moment of mutually unrestrained jingoistic fervour, we muttered in chorus, 'Awww shit.'

8

World Cup Aftermath,
Australian Summers 1999–2002

Given the preceding week's drama and intrigue, there existed a nagging fear the World Cup's final might turn out to be a fizzer. As it happened, that was the only expectation the tournament showpiece met. Australia was ruthlessly flawless. Pakistan totally clueless. The game's saving grace was that it finished two hours ahead of schedule. Bad news for those who had forked out upwards of £100 to be there. Good news for those of us hoping to neatly wrap the result into Australian newspaper deadlines that had been stretched to 2 a.m. Sydney time to accommodate an event of such magnitude.

With the result apparent long before then, interest was provided by the game of whimsical chairs being played out on the Australian team balcony overlooking Lord's. Making the most of the telegraphed outcome, photographers trained their long lenses on the team's viewing platform where group scenes of elation would be far more expressive than any two-man celebration involving batting pair Darren Lehmann and Mark Waugh.

Front row centre sat the captain, in full batting gear and torn between wanting victory without any further setback and the tantalising chance to finish the job himself should a wicket fall. But next to him, inexplicably installed in position B for the upcoming memorabilia moment, was the team psychologist. While a case could be mounted to suggest he had performed vital work in mending the team's broken mindset after those difficult early weeks, his Cup statistics showed only that he had been caught in a scandal and run out of an interview without facing a question.

Prominent through his absence was Shane Warne, who had all but secured the trophy earlier in the day with another inspired bowling effort. He had opted to keep himself, for the time being, away from the intrusive gaze of the world's photo media, although his preference for the refuge of the dressing room was more likely to meet his regular need for cigarettes. But with the World Cup just a handful of runs out of reach, there was sudden movement on the balcony. Accompanied by a cloud of freshly exhaled smoke, Warne edged his way along the front row, and his counsellor did not need any of his professional skills to interpret the vice-captain's non-verbal message. His stint as seat warmer was over now that show time had arrived.

If Warne's timing was typically spot-on, then his ability to irritate also remained intact. In contravention of a team directive that everyone in public view was to don their full playing kit, to show solidarity as well as pictorial uniformity, Warne appeared in the dull light of a grey and chill London afternoon rugged up in his training tracksuit. Then, at the moment Lehmann nervelessly stroked the winning boundary and the balcony stood as one in triumph, Warne leaned so heavily into his captain to place himself squarely in centre frame, he almost caused Stephen Waugh to topple into the crowd. And it wasn't the leg-spinner's last bid to hog the spotlight that afternoon.

The world's cricket media waited patiently inside the Lord's Nursery Pavilion that doubled as home to the post-match press conference. Warne and Stephen Waugh took their places behind a laminated table with the gleaming trophy, like a gilded roll-on deodorant, occupying the space between them. It was then, to the apparent discomfort of his skipper and the surprise of assembled journalists, that Warne chose to purge himself of innumerable demons accumulated over the previous months. In doing so, he consciously ensured the next day's worldwide headlines would not dwell on his team's triumph, but rather on Warne's own speculation about his playing career.

'I'm going home to have a good think about what the future holds for me,' he announced to a synchronised raising of eyebrows. 'I don't go out and play cricket to try and prove the critics wrong. I go and play cricket because I love playing for my country. But it's been a pretty hectic six months, and a lot of things have happened in my life that I didn't expect. So over the next couple of weeks I'll be having a good chat about what's going on, and having a good think before I make a decision. Hopefully whatever the future holds, I'll be happy.'

That Warne, reaffirmed as a genius and a national hero with consecutive man-of-the-match honours in the World Cup's two most crucial games, should immediately veer from superstardom to self-pity provided another telling insight into his world view. Which was, essentially, that he was the world. Aggrieved by what he considered a lack of respect afforded his untrammelled talents when success briefly eluded him, he was making sure those who had doubted him, most notably his captain, endured the uncomfortable prospect of trying to win future games without him. It was his unyielding belief that every event under the sun should be evaluated in terms of the benefit or detriment it yielded Shane Warne that drove dressing rooms and committee rooms to distraction.

'Typical Warney,' one bleary-eyed teammate groaned when our paths crossed in the hotel lobby late on the morning after. 'Our theme of the whole tournament's been the importance of sticking together. That the team always trumps the individual. And what happens when we achieve what we set out to? It's all about how he feels, and what impact the whole journey's had on him. Like none of the rest of us have copped some stick, or made some sacrifices along the way. I'll tell you, some of the boys are spewing.'

Not as a result of over-celebrating, although the party had raged in the Australians' beloved visitors' dressing room at Lord's until well past dark and culminated in a nocturnal pilgrimage to the pitch where the team song was delivered with a gusto that would have drowned out any orchestra of 'drums, whistles, klaxons and fire rockets' that are expressly forbidden from the historic ground, as per a sign at the Grace Gates. The residents of St John's Wood are as intolerant of loud noise as one would expect from a suburb that sounds like a retirement village.

Then, around midnight, the festivities flowed from Lord's into the lobby of our posh Kensington hotel. Hunched over a full night of work in my room, I recognised the cacophony of drunken voices from the moment the team bus pulled up in the driveway, led by Tom Moody's expletive-laden battle cry that bounced off the foyer's polished marble floor.

As the party crashed its way up to the establishment's normally genteel mezzanine bar, I briefly contemplated slipping the yoke and joining the champions for a congratulatory glass. We had, after all, shared an arduous crusade, stretching back to Antigua and encompassing almost ninety days, more than twenty hotels, two riots, several near-death experiences and a lawsuit. But persuaded by a workload that acted as gaoler, I soon dismissed that thought. We may have jointly negotiated the triumphs and adversities of an ultimately successful campaign but, at day's end – which, in my case, remained several hours away – I was as much a part of the players' accomplishment as all the other sleep-deprived who had watched the glory unfold from their couches in Australia.

The inescapable conflict between our respective roles was laid bare when the phone jolted me from my coma at 7.30 the next morning, just hours after I had collapsed into bed. It was the Ideas Factory in Sydney, bursting with a fresh angle. Ending a twelve-year quest to reclaim one-day cricket's biggest prize was all very admirable, but news of Australia's win was already sixteen hours stale and would be positively fetid by the time the next paper hit the streets.

What wasn't so widely known was that the Waugh twins' paternal grandfather had died just hours after the winning runs were scored. Somehow, I was told, my newspaper had come into possession of a 'terrific photo of both of the Waugh boys, taken years ago with their grandpa'. It had been pencilled in for the front page but needed suitably poignant quotes from one or both of the bereaved brothers. Which was where I came in.

It wasn't only fatigue-induced delirium that churned my stomach when I twigged that I was being instructed to gatecrash their victory party and deliver a death knock. My immediate instinct was to flat-out refuse. Even through semi-consciousness, my mind recognised the words 'insensitive' and 'inappropriate'. But as was regularly pointed out, the people who made these decisions were also the ones who paid my salary. So I had no choice but to drag myself from hibernation, through the shower and back down to the lobby.

Attempts to contact either twin in their room were predictably fruitless. My only chance of jagging a quote or two rested on a chance encounter in the foyer, so I planted myself strategically on a sofa, between a pair of Armani-clad Yemeni businessmen. Through a fog of their cologne and my exhaustion, I spied an equally weary team manager who claimed to understand the urgency of my request, and honoured his pledge to phone me with a response inside the hour. In all likelihood, he composed it himself. The words were certainly sufficiently benign. But I was grateful beyond caring. Within ten minutes, the quotes were in the paper and I was back to bed.

The imperative to acquiesce to every dubious whim dreamed up on the Factory floor had always been silently inferred, but never definitively spelled out. Until the following year. In its oft-flouted wisdom, the paper decreed that the Sydney Olympic Games of 2000 were not, as the world believed, a sporting event. Rather, the newspaper brains trust maintained, it was a nation-defining, socio-political celebration that just happened to wear lycra. This must have come as a rude shock to the Australian Olympic Committee, which had spent numerous years and the GNP of many competing nations to win the planet's pre-eminent sporting competition only to learn they had, in reality, secured some sort of Davos Summit on steroids.

It was an even greater setback for the newspaper's dedicated sporting journalists, many of whom had spent their careers aspiring to this very opportunity, only to be told that coverage of such a watershed could not be trusted to mere sports hacks. The Olympics called for the specialist skills of political commentators, economics experts and incisive columnists, even though most of them freely admitted they could not tell a javelin from a J-curve. As a goodwill gesture, a handful of sports correspondents were hand-picked to fill cameo roles on the paper's 'Olympics team'. And when one of those chosen few had to unexpectedly surrender his berth, several months before the opening ceremony, I received a phone call that carried all the gravity of a royal decree.

'I'm ringing to inform you that you've been added to the paper's Olympics team,' the paper's Games tsar sermonised. 'You'll need to come to Sydney and spend a month here before they begin. During that period, we'll decide what role you'll play in the coverage.'

It wasn't the sort of offer that required deep consideration. Not in my case, anyway. So I offered profuse, obsequious thanks, and then politely declined. The Olympics had long struck me as an unsightly show of institutionalised flag-waving. And while I didn't want to appear ungrateful for the chance to be a part of the historic Aussie, Aussie, Aussie-a-thon, I also acknowledged that I was something of an oddity – a sports reporter whose passion for sport extended not much beyond cricket. It certainly had no intention of making the lonely trek to archery, rhythmic gymnastics or skeet shooting.

'I'm not sure you quite understand what's going on here,' came the response, with a disbelief verging on outrage. 'This is a big deal. It's an honour to be on the team, and knocking back this assignment could have serious implications for your career. I strongly advise you to think about your decision. Talk it over with anyone you have to and I'll call you again tomorrow.'

So I mulled over my original thought process, discussed it with nobody and, when the following day's call arrived, I rejected it again. Not to be obstreperous. I just reasoned that if it was such a prestigious reward, it would be better in the hands of someone who desperately wanted it. Better for that individual, and for the paper's coverage. I even imagined I might gain some professional kudos for my selflessness. Instead, I was seen as intractable, and possibly insane. It took just minutes for my sports editor to jump on the blower.

'What do you think you're doing?' he bellowed. 'This is not a job you knock back. Your card's already been marked. Not a smart move. I hope you know what you're doing.'

Perhaps not, but I had a clue about the sort of corporate repercussions I might be facing. Early in my Adelaide cadet years, an administrative error saw me receive written notification of an upgrade and salary rise I'd been verbally guaranteed, but was not yet technically entitled to receive. Whisked in to meet urgently with the editor, it was clearly explained the offer had been issued in error and would not be honoured. It was also very pointedly articulated that, should I choose to challenge this decision by enlisting union support or industrial law remedies, I stood a good chance of winning.

'But by doing so, you'll lose the goodwill of the company,' was the blunt threat.

For a budding print journalist, being ostracised from the organisation that operated the vast majority of the nation's newspapers represented a sizeable problem. So I shut up, copped the pay cut and, within weeks, was mysteriously offered an interstate bureau posting that came complete with not inconsequential remuneration and career benefits. I learned early that newspaper culture was a contradiction in terms. But turning down the Olympics was not the only accepted wisdom at which I was thumbing my nose. Despite the overwhelming historical evidence tendered by most of my peers and predecessors that the notions of 'touring cricket writer' and 'long-term relationship' were mutually exclusive, I was getting married. A week before the Olympics began.

Kindly recognising the pressure that lengthy overseas travel might exert on my new domestic arrangements, the Factory absented me from the national cricket team's subsequent visit to Sri Lanka. Then its trip to New Zealand. Both tours to South Africa. To England. And to Zimbabwe. In fact, the only time I was required to take my cricket writing skills back on the road was during the long, dry Australian season, when the political commentators, economic experts and incisive columnists were, coincidentally, on summer holidays and their collective absence left gaping holes in the paper.

Having successfully convinced itself, if not the nation, that the Olympics amounted to a nation-building exercise rather than a fortnight of pharmacologically enhanced sports, the newspaper also sought to capitalise on the swollen appetite for sports coverage they left behind. Consequently, in the Games' backdraft, the paper's decision-makers became tricked into believing every day should deliver stories of Olympian significance. And if events weren't sufficiently seismic to justify a full broadsheet page, or numerous think pieces from the in-house thinkers, then they would have to be confected.

That was the landscape in which Stephen Waugh's world champion one-day outfit found itself in the home summer of 2001–02. The annual limited-overs tri-series was up and running, but the Australians most definitely weren't. Outgunned by a motivated South Africa, and outfoxed by an innovative New Zealand, the home side lost three games in succession, which was more than enough to spark a national crisis in the otherwise barren news period that follows New Year. Sights were trained on the diminishing returns of the thirty-six-year-old Waugh twins, and I learned what the conference-room opinion shapers were discussing when I took a Friday-morning call, while queuing at a Sydney Airport coffee counter following another late-night end to an SCG one-dayer.

'I've got a great idea for the cover story on tomorrow's lift-out,' the sports editor enthused, as my instinctive reaction was fortuitously drowned by the background howl of milk being frothed. 'After last night's debacle, it's obvious the old guys have to go. Steve and Mark Waugh. Shane Warne. Michael Bevan. They're all past it. We need to be the first to call for a full clean-out. Bring in this Shane Watson. The young tyros. Generation next.'

I wondered whether demanding the heads of a majority of the talent that had secured a World Cup eighteen months earlier just so we could air that string of musty clichés was perhaps a little contrived. But having well learned a lesson, I offered nothing more obstructionist than 'okay'.

'I'm already getting the artwork done up,' the boss went on. 'The headline's going to be ... "Sea Change".'

That's why it was known as the Ideas Factory. Your average lowbrow publishing enterprise could never aspire to the sort of creative wizardry that lifted the title from a popular television series of the day, and slapped it effortlessly above a tenuous, page-filling feature that called for a handful of veteran cricketers to be given the chop. I gestured to the barista to whack in an extra couple of shots.

'I know you're about to jump on a plane to Brisbane, but you've still got five or six hours to get that to us,' the boss ploughed on. 'You'll need to make a few calls, so I suggest you get cracking the minute you land. Be good to get a few voices of former players in there as well.'

'Voices' is the accepted euphemism for those all too freely available contacts who obediently echo whatever line a paper chooses to push.

In this case, it referred to that group of ex-cricketers who jump at every opportunity to ridicule contemporary players who they believe carry half the old-timers' ability, but several hundred times their earning capacity. The more florid and outrageous the assessments from these partial observers, always recognisable by the descriptor 'former Aussie Test star [insert quote mule's name here] yesterday called for …', the more often their opinions are sought. This manufacturing method, known as the 'Phone Five Former Players and Get Them to Sack Someone' template, was once a tool reserved exclusively for slow news days. It's now as commonplace as it is inane.

That's because the trouble with routinely fabricating sensation to feed the short-term need of the daily news cycle – with loud-hailing every modest success as a 'dazzling triumph', with shrieking that every slight stumble plunges 'a dagger through the heart' – is that when something really extraordinary happens, there's no levers left to manipulate. Massive setbacks, stunning upsets, miracle victories, crushing losses now arrive with all the regularity and wonderment of lunch. Getting stories noticed requires stoking contrived conflict. Screeching the loudest. But when you run the scream-meter flat out seven days a week, people just tune out. Or go deaf. In trying to seize the attention of a market that can now scour a world's worth of alternative 'voices' with a couple of keystrokes, mainstream media has become the boy who cried werewolf.

The 'Sea Change' ran across the front of that weekend's sports lift-out and duly called for the Waugh brothers to be culled. Embracing the view that if you're going to kindle a flimsy argument you may as well ignite it with an absurdity, I also floated the notion that Warne should inherit the one-day captaincy. And while Matthew Hayden (age thirty), Andrew Symonds (twenty-six) and Darren Lehmann (almost thirty-two), weren't exactly 'the young tyros of generation next', they had been confirmed in my off-the-record chat with a selector as the most likely to win promotion should changes occur. Even fiction needs a passing nod to fact.

Predictably, Stephen Waugh's bunch of washed-up old farts comfortably accounted for South Africa in Brisbane the next day, and I approached his post-match press gathering with all the enthusiasm of someone prescribed an iced-water enema. It was obvious from the moment the skipper entered the claustrophobic storage-cum-media room beneath the 'Gabba's grandstands that he was spoiling for a fight. So I decided we should get it over and done with.

'Are you disappointed that some commentators questioned your place in the team coming into this game?' I asked, in a pathetic attempt to diffuse culpability. He narrowed his eyes and gave a dismissive snort.

'You should know, mate, you wrote it,' he shot back. A reasonable assessment, but not a quote I could use in the next day's paper. So I waded back in.

'Yes, but are you disappointed the issue was raised?' This time it was met with a painfully long silence.

'You should know, mate, you wrote it,' he said. Then more silence.

I knew this couldn't go on all night. I had a story to file and he had a bus to catch. So I tried again, and at the third go, as colleagues shifted uncomfortably in their chairs, he obviously felt he'd made his point.

'We're not used to losing three in a row, and obviously a lot of other people aren't either,' he sneered.

When it was over, he stormed from the room muttering something incomprehensible beneath his breath. I consoled myself with the knowledge that, as per our conversation in Barbados, we did not share a friendship to terminate. And that at least somebody was reading the paper. As I slunk out in his wake, I met the South African team's media manager who had taken in the event from a safe distance against the back wall.

'Glad that was you and not me,' she whispered sympathetically. 'That look of his could peel paint.'

By summer's end, the world champs had finished bottom of the tri-series ladder, missed the tournament's finals which cost Australian cricket a packet in gate takings, and the Waugh brothers' one-day international careers had been terminated. The ensuing 'sea change' saw Ricky Ponting inherit the limited-overs captaincy, with Adam Gilchrist installed as his wing man.

Shane Warne's aspirations to captain his country were officially dead. He had been stripped of the deputy leadership in the wake of another tawdry scandal involving a lady friend who was not his wife. The nation's cricket administrators had made it clear that vice was no longer a prerequisite for the vice-captaincy. It did not stop Warne taking a swipe at Gilchrist's appointment, confirming the uneasy personal relationship that percolated for years beneath the pair's productive on-field union. Warne caustically suggested his flamboyant character held far greater public appeal than Gilchrist's family-friendly nice-guy image.

'Australian cricket needs the Fonz, not Richie Cunningham,' Warne retorted, his reference to the dated sit-com spelling out his view that cool was a more valuable commodity than common sense. It also explained succinctly, although Warne remained oblivious, why the Australian Cricket Board had made its decision. The leg-spinner never did grasp that the game had moved on from the lager and larrikin days of the 1970s to an era when marketing wielded far greater influence than machismo.

Sea change had also swamped the national broadsheet. Newly promoted bums filled the high-backed managerial chairs. And two years after my Olympics boycott, I was asked to once more dust off the brown suitcase. Although I was under no illusions as to why.

9

Kenya Tri-series, August–September 2002

Even Kenya Airways flight KQ-461 was unsure about going to Nairobi. As the Boeing 737 emerged from a shroud of thick cloud, granting its passengers a brief sight of the National Park that's separated from Jomo Kenyatta International Airport by a few strands of electrified wire, our pilot apparently decided this was not at all where he wanted to drop us. Instead, he throttled into a steep climb and we returned to the enveloping whiteness.

'Sorry about that, folks,' a distinctly English voice buzzed through the cabin. 'Just a slight change of plans to our approach. So we'll complete a circle and have another go. Should have you on the ground in around ten minutes.'

From my aisle seat, I craned forward in an attempt to see if the rethink was purely aeronautical, or the result of something more apposite – like herds of blue wildebeest straying onto the runway as part of their annual southward migration to the Serengeti grazing lands. But a 'slight change of plans' had been the recurrent theme running through our impending nine-week venture, which potentially spanned three continents, from well before we almost landed in the Cradle of Civilisation. It was therefore no great shock that our pilot seemed reluctant to put down in the Kenyan capital. After all, the fourteen members of Australia's one-day squad, its six support staff and the five-man touring press contingent were technically not supposed to be in Africa.

The triangular tournament to which we were all headed had been initiated to celebrate the golden jubilee of Pakistani cricket. It was 1952, four years before its formal birth as an independent republic, that the partitioned Muslim state first engaged its former master, India, in a Test match at Delhi. The neighbours' uneasy relationship has been on the slide ever since, so the Pakistan Cricket Board decided the next-best way to commemorate this important milestone was to lock horns with Australia in a series of one-day internationals and Test matches.

That plan unravelled faster than an iffy Rawalpindi rug, in the wake of the September 11 terrorist strikes. Even though the PCB wanted to push ahead with the series, grave concerns bubbled through the Australians' playing ranks. An even more influential pressure group – the players' wives and girlfriends – was far more trenchantly opposed. And all further debate was ended by a suicide bomber who, in May 2002, detonated a massive charge just fifty metres from the front doors of Karachi's Pearl Continental Hotel. Inside at the time was the New Zealand cricket team, due to begin a Test match against the host nation later that morning.

The bomb killed fourteen people, severely injured a further twenty-two, and blew the glass from all of the 300-room building's street-facing windows. It also destroyed the oft-peddled diplomatic line that international cricketers were somehow exempt from terrorist threats. Pakistan suddenly held less chance of hosting a gala jubilee bash than it did of unearthing Osama bin Laden.

Protracted discussions throughout the middle of that year failed to yield a mutually agreeable alternative venue. The obvious compromises – England and Australia – held limited financial appeal to the cash-strapped PCB, which hoped to flog the lucrative fixtures to a hefty subcontinental prime-time television audience. Pakistan's other left-field suggestion, an almost-completed cricket stadium in the Moroccan city of Tangier, was ruled out because it was in the Moroccan city of Tangier. With the entire proposal dangling in the balance, it was eventually decided the limited-overs component (which also included New Zealand) would be staged in Kenya. Details of the subsequent three Tests were not simultaneously inked in, but it seemed they might be played in Sri Lanka. Or even Sharjah, in the United Arab Emirates. Or split between the two.

This announcement, just weeks before the first game, could scarcely have been less reassuring if it had been penned on a slip of paper and waved skywards by Neville Chamberlain. Instead of insurgent-wracked Pakistan, we could all look forward to a fortnight in one of Africa's most notoriously dangerous cities, known among its own residents as 'Nairobbery'. And where, four years earlier, an al-Qaeda terror attack levelled the US Embassy in the city's heart at a cost of 213 lives. Not surprisingly, the bomb-shy Kiwis greeted this decision by immediately pulling out of the tournament altogether. They were replaced by the only other vaguely international-standard team prepared at such short notice to spend two weeks in Kenya – that being Kenya.

From Nairobi, our entourage would then head to the International Cricket Council's biennial cash-raising event the Champions Trophy tournament, being held in Colombo. Where the Liberation Tigers of Tamil Eelam continued to wage a bloody civil war against the Sri Lankan Government, and which had resulted in almost 100,000 deaths over two decades. When that assignment was complete, we potentially faced three weeks of Test matches against Pakistan in the desert emirate of Sharjah, strategically located on the shores of the Persian Gulf and the Gulf of Oman, and a mere 1,400 kilometres from Baghdad, which global political wisdom accepted was ripe for a US-led invasion any day. And this configuration was deemed the safe option.

If first impressions count, then Nairobi quickly revealed itself to be innumerate. Even before reaching the passport police at Kenyatta Airport, we were confronted by a sign that confirmed all our preconceptions by warning, in large black letters, 'NO BRIBES SHOULD BE GIVEN OR ACCEPTED WHETHER DEMANDED OR NOT'.

At least passage to the city in a rusting *matatu*, which belched noxious blue smoke, was not encumbered by luggage. In another worrying portent, my belongings had been mislaid somewhere between my home and my destination. And while the cricketers' short ride into town was decidedly more grandiose, with fringed blinds drawn over the windows of the team bus to shield them from the realities of a poverty-ravaged city of around three million, which was also home to more than seventy disparate tribal groups, it was no more triumphal. The handful of curious onlookers gathered out front of the historic New Stanley Hotel when the players pulled up seemed decidedly unimpressed by the line of unsmiling white folk uniformly dressed in dark-blue polo shirts and fawn slacks, who shuffled silently into the lobby. The small crowd had clearly been hoping for real celebrities when the police motorcade swept in – Manchester United, the Brazilian national football team, or possibly Michael Jackson.

Cricket's lack of profile in Kenya did offer some benefits. The world's leading players were unlikely to be ambushed in a lift or harassed by insistent autograph hunters while tucking into the exquisite tomato and basil soup at the hotel's streetside Thorn Tree Café. But that was where the freedom afforded by daily life in east Africa started and finished. Reg Dickason, the sharp-eyed ex-policeman and counter-terrorism expert retained by Australian cricket as its security advisor, delivered a no-nonsense safety briefing that left the players wondering if Pakistan really had represented such a risk.

The rules were as unambiguous as they were incontrovertible. Don't walk anywhere beyond the hotel after dark, and even in daylight hours, avoid leaving the hotel on your own. Advise members of team management of your movements at all times. Everywhere other than the hotel and the secured confines of the Gymkhana Ground, where matches and training were held, was deemed an unnecessary risk unless accompanied by a security officer, a police detail, or a death wish. No such life-saving advice was provided to the press pack before, during or after arriving. Our self-administered preparatory regimen consisted of a round of jabs from a travel doctor, the purchase of a reliable guide book, and perusal of the Australian Government's relevant travel advisory bulletins. The only warning from the office, albeit implied, was that mugging victims should obtain a tax-compliant receipt from their assailants to help in reconciling corporate expenses at tour's end.

An unexpected by-product of the involuntary curfew was the camaraderie, born of a shared predicament, that grew between the players and the press. Our evenings invariably began and ended around the Exchange Bar at the New Stanley, a dark-panelled room furnished with sumptuous leather chairs and a row of palm-leaf ceiling fans, which whirred constantly even though August evenings at 1,500 metres above sea level carried a distinct wintry chill.

Rather like cricket, our setting was a charming relic lifted straight from Kenya's colonial past. It was at the New Stanley that Hemingway had undergone a lengthy, and very public, recuperation to rid himself of the litany of ills he had bagged, seventy years earlier, while hunting beneath the snows of Kilimanjaro. The room that now housed the bar had also served as Nairobi's stock exchange for almost four decades. However, by 2002, the only commodities being traded on the floor were the bullish prostitutes who lurked in the dim recesses and announced their availability by rattling ice cubes in tumblers of tonic water.

The downside of such strict personal safety measures was their potential to render my Durham vow, to immerse myself fully in any new surrounds, about as meaningless as the tournament I was covering. So I decided that if I was not party to the cricketers' privileges, then I was in no way bound by their security restrictions. Having previously outwitted such eminent street bandits as the gypsy kids of Rome's Spanish Steps, the mustard-bottle-wielding tricksters of Buenos Aires, and Bangkok's limpet-like gemstone peddlers, I confidently told myself Nairobi held no fears. And that I would explore daily life in the capital to the fullest, work commitments permitting.

Fortunately for my personal welfare, the demands of journalism severely curtailed the joys of sightseeing. Not the punishing workload of my earlier overseas stints. My newspaper showed about as much interest in the tri-nations challenge as they did in pre-departure planning. The problem in Kenya was drumming up stories from the daunting lack of news. Not just an absence of revelation or intrigue, but days totally devoid of action, context, even movement. The tournament was proving as quixotic as its planning. Two established world cricket powers tackling a glorified club side through six preliminary matches in order to decide which pair would play in the grand final. Not even Pakistan could orchestrate an outcome other than the bleeding obvious.

The inequity of the premise was exposed in the Australians' opening game, when they plundered 332 from their fifty overs, then dispensed with their hapless opponents for less than a third of that total. And that was against Pakistan. Results threatened to be even more lopsided the following week when the world champions shaped up to Kenya. It was hardly surprising that half the Australian squad then opted to spend the intervening weekend at a luxury safari lodge, around 300 kilometres away in the Masai Mara National Reserve.

Even if seats on the team's charter flight had been offered to the press, there's no way the Ideas Factory would have sanctioned the trip. It was enough of an extravagance to be forking out for a fortnight in Africa on such a dubious exercise without suggesting the budget be extended to take in the indulgences of wildlife spotting. Keeping track of the team might be a fundamental touring rule, but only if it can be achieved without an additional splurge of company cash. However, with half the cricketers out of town and the other half safely holed up in their rooms watching US cable television, or kerbside poking down another bowl of soup, there was nothing to stop the intrepid among the press gang braving a closer look at our surrounds. Using our own funds, of course.

So a colleague and I signed up for a pseudo-safari to the nearby Lake Nakuru National Park, a trek that took us beyond Nairobi's Soviet-style concrete skyline and through the surrounding townships – acre upon acre of galvanised iron ghettos, where hope somehow found a foothold between the bare mud streets and the dingy shacks. That sobering landscape was soon replaced by breathtaking views from the rim of the Mau Escarpment, where the world dramatically dropped away to the floor of the Great Rift Valley. This vista alone was worth enduring the trauma inflicted by our impatient *matatu* driver, who believed the wrong side of the road was the right place for his van. Which meant the terrifying descent to the Valley floor was almost as memorable as the awe-inspiring glimpses it provided into the heart of Africa at each hairpin turn.

As we closed in on Nakuru's shimmering soda lake, it appeared to be buttressed by a wall fashioned from coconut ice. It then became clear the pink and white bank stretching to infinity was in fact hundreds of thousands of flamingos foraging among the algae treats that thrived in the warm shallows of the lake's perimeter. During our day trip, we were also able to tick off, from our African fauna checklist, black and white rhinoceros, giraffes, gazelles, monkeys and Danish backpackers, all in proliferation. The non-appearance of hippopotamus, as we interrupted the return journey for afternoon tea in the refined waterfront grounds of the Lake Navasha Country Club, left but one box unchecked. But having learned from my guide book that the 'river horse' was reputedly even more aggressive and dangerous than a Nairobi elephant-hair bracelet salesman, this was not an unwelcome omission. By the time we rolled back into Nairobi, I was secretly wishing our stay could be extended.

The playing group was eventually reunited, and the cricket resumed, but my desire to explore remained unsated. Nightly drinks provided an opportunity to swap intelligence on places to visit and avoid. Included among the travellers' tips were the inner-city Masai Market (fascinating but infuriating; best avoided if you suffered from tout aversion), the main produce market (take a deep breath before negotiating the fresh meat section, unless you possessed a cast-iron gag reflex), and the City Stalls near the Ring Road traffic island (not a visitor attraction; the only thing you were likely to get there was maimed). Handy hints on dining experiences, happy and sad, were also swapped over the Exchange Bar. One of those, we were assured by a couple of adventurous batsmen, offered a true taste of Africa.

In its early days, Carnivore restaurant carved a reputation for serving spit-roasted hunks of most animals that roamed Africa's interior. It pitched itself unashamedly at Western tourists who wanted to not only observe the continent's unique wildlife, but to sample a plateful of it as well. Sensibly, that charter was rewritten when someone realised most of the eatery's exotic game meat was being illegally killed and supplied, thereby threatening the very industry it was trying to cash in on.

By the time we arrived at the famous dark brick-and-timber dining barn, Carnivore's menu had been restricted to those animals that were legally farmed. But it was immediately obvious that its proud reputation as a joint-joint remained untouched. A fire pit replaced a bandstand as the restaurant's feature piece, and the cooking was conducted behind floor-to-ceiling windows that showcased a large circular *parilla*, ensuring everyone could see what was being tossed onto the griddle. Hovering around it were furiously sweating men wearing oversized straw boaters, heavy aprons and bow ties, who resembled forge workers masquerading as extras for a Swahili barbershop quartet.

We were seated on zebra-print chairs at a bare wooden table, the only adornment on which was a three-deck central carousel which contained assorted petri dishes of glutinous salad and, above them, a selection of mystery sauces. The top deck was reserved for a pyramid-shaped ornament bearing our table number, with a hole in the top from which a tiny white flag attached to a toothpick stood at attention. It was explained that until such time as we lowered the flag, counter-intuitively signalling our defeat, the meat would continue to arrive.

With that, one of the wandering minstrels appeared, wielding a traditional Masai sword onto which a roasted hindquarter of an unidentified beast had been threaded. Brandishing a machete, he sawed off a hefty slice for each of our group, then announced to nobody in particular, 'Hartebeest.' As he turned to leave, he glanced back to see four faces staring uncertainly at the wedge of light-grey flesh before us, and added, by way of translation, 'Antelope.' That ritual was then repeated with lamb, crocodile, pork, beef, zebra, chicken, ostrich and eland, as the best part of an hour passed in a haze of protein, smoke and Audubon roll call. The growing ache in my groaning stomach was part dyspepsia and part suspicion that each new offering differed little from the last. Dry, stringy meat is dry, stringy meat, regardless of which hoof it's harvested from. As a bowl of gazelle balls was thrust towards us, I made a desperate lunge for the flag.

Our group left the restaurant feeling slightly guilty and more than a little unwell. The air of collective biliousness we carried into the hotel foyer pricked the curiosity of a couple of players loitering near the safety of the reception desk. Our critique of Carnivore surmised that if its culinary appeal were to dwindle, it could always diversify as a torture camp for vegetarians.

'I've never really understood vegetarianism,' mused Glenn McGrath, who years later was to release his own book of barbecue recipes. 'I mean, if God didn't want us to eat animals, why did he make them out of meat?'

The next night we limited ourselves to the comparative humdrum of an Italian *trattoria*, just a few blocks from our hotel but still deep in the dark heart of Nairobi. A light meal enhanced by a couple of glasses of imported Lesotho lambrusco left us feeling sufficiently fortified to chance a walk back to our lodgings. Stepping out into the brisk, still night, we scanned the terrain along an apparently deserted Kaunda Street and stuck firmly to the footpath that ran opposite the menacingly dark Holy Family Cathedral and its concreted, consecrated grounds. Even though visibility was restricted due to the lack of street lighting and a smoky haze that had settled over the inner city, we soon distinguished half a dozen formless figures up ahead. The gang had materialised from somewhere under the cathedral's grey perimeter wall, and then noiselessly crossed the street to make steady progress towards us.

Our pace slowed. Hands were thrust deep into pockets, and the conversational pitch rose by a nervous half-octave. We countered by tacking to the blessed side of the street and the mob confirmed we were in its sights by mimicking the movement. Our group then came to a dead halt. Theirs continued to advance. The only available path to our hotel took us directly through their ranks. Our sole cause for hope lay in the fact that, as a collective, we appeared to be decidedly taller. And thanks to the previous night's meat frenzy, significantly heavier.

The reason for our physical superiority became clear when the leader of these brazen *wezi*, an eight-year-old boy huddled beneath a fraying blue blanket, strode up to us and thrust out a tiny pink palm, and then followed his Swahili greeting of '*Jambo*' with the equally traditional request for cash. Bravely eyeing off his even younger cohorts, I hurled loose change of various currencies from my pocket onto the street and, while the crèche of criminals was busily scooping up the booty, we made a dash for the hotel, where we congratulated ourselves on our valour over a steadying tipple.

Any complacency about the brutal reality of Kenyan violence was excised the following morning when the Australian team bus and our dilapidated taxi were stopped at a traffic snarl near the Gymkhana Ground. A *matatu* with all its windows smashed stood abandoned in the middle of Muran'ga Road. Its dozen passengers and the driver sat trembling and bleeding on the roadside, awaiting the arrival of medical help to treat head and facial injuries of varying severity. Word filtered back that the van had been ambushed by agitated students hurling rocks in protest against Kenya's upcoming presidential election, due later in the year. The level of concern shown by the cricketers was significantly less than that exhibited by those of us forced to travel that road each day without a security detail. But the depth of feeling inflamed by local politics was noticeably absent at the cricket.

That was because the overwhelming majority of cricket fans in Nairobi came from the city's huge *Wahindi*, or Indian, community. Which meant they attended matches with the sole motivation of barracking for whichever team was playing against their bitter subcontinental rivals, Pakistan. They also showed a determined reluctance to watch games that involved the home team, probably because the Kenyans were never going to win anything bar the occasional coin toss. It was therefore slightly surreal that, of the tournament's three competing teams, it was the Australians who garnered the strongest crowd support. Not only was the Pakistan Cricket Board forced to stage its jubilee carnival 5,000 kilometres from Islamabad, it was hard pressed finding anyone prepared to turn up and yell for its team.

That lack of interest wasn't restricted to local fans or Australian newspapers. Nairobi's daily media carried barely a word about the event, which partly explained the anonymity the Australian players enjoyed in and around their hotel. The only issue to excite one strident commentator was the disgraceful lack of respect being afforded touring journalists by Kenyan cricket authorities. In a stinging editorial, a writer for the *East Africa Standard* lambasted officials for their failure to provide complimentary beer in the press box. Given that alcohol consumption during working hours was as much a part of modern journalism as typewriters and paid overtime, the column did not reflect the demands of a disgruntled Australian press corps. Indeed, our only request to the organisers was for the provision of a scorer so we could drop the occasional statistical nugget, such as a batsman's score, or the final margin, into our copy.

As it eventuated, both appeals were answered by the start of the second week. Not only did we arrive at the ground one morning to find a makeshift timber bar, complete with gleaming keg of Tusker beer, installed at the back of the press box, but a young man with a pristine scorebook and a year's supply of sharpened pencils was camped immediately in front of it. Unfortunately, in addition to being our scorer, he was also the only patron of the new boozer, and sadly lapsed into a lager-induced sleep during the third over after lunch.

Frittering away the days before the inexorable Australia–Pakistan final, we yanked all the usual chains to try and dislodge a story. In-depth profiles of new players such as Nathan Hauritz, who – until that point – were justifiably unknown, were prepared to a chorus of 'who cares?' from inside the newspaper and beyond. Inconsequential twaddle, such as Glenn McGrath trimming several paces from his run-up, was passed off as legitimate news. But it was the yarn splashed across one of Melbourne's Sunday papers that stood as the touring media's equivalent of lowering the white flag.

After the 'Phone Five Pensioners' charade, the next-most transparent admission of a story vacuum was an airing of Shane Warne's perennial declaration that he had perfected yet another 'mystery ball'. This was purely a publicity routine that nobody, least of all the famed leg-spinner, credited with any legitimacy. But journalists were happy to write it because it represented a win for both parties. Warne was able to sustain the nonsensical belief he could defy biomechanics and credibility by inventing new ways to make a cricket ball travel on a straight path. The zooter, the slider, the gazunder – all novel titles for a delivery squeezed from the front of his bowling hand and distinguished by its lack of spin. Newspapers similarly loved it because it filled column space and gave everyone a giggle whenever it was mentioned by gullible commentators. It was Australian cricket's equivalent of the April Fool's prank. And for days, in response to pointed queries from the Factory, I had to feign annoyance that my travelling companion, Martin Blake from Melbourne's *The Age*, had, in concert with Warne, played it before the rest of us thought of it.

A couple of nights before the final, I made the familiar trek to the Exchange Bar where I had arranged to meet Adam Gilchrist. The vice-captain was employed as a paid columnist for my paper, and had suggested we catch up for a meal before the next leg of our world adventure kicked off. He was standing among a group of his teammates when I arrived, so I opted for a quiet corner not tenanted by hookers until he was ready to break ranks. Before we could depart, he also had to report our intended movements to the security boss. Reg, in turn, wanted to know exactly where and how we were headed. I assured him the friendly *trattoria* I knew was no more than three minutes' walk from where we currently stood. He initially suggested he make the journey with us, but eventually seemed satisfied with the thoroughness of my scouting, and gave us the okay to tackle the short trip unsupervised. We had moved barely five steps when McGrath piped up from the bar.

'Hey, Gilly. You guys heading out somewhere for dinner?'

Upon learning we were bound for an Italian gourmet experience, the fast bowler quickly invited himself along. As did a number of his hungry teammates. Which explained how I came to nervously lead Gilchrist, McGrath, Jason Gillespie, Andrew Symonds, Shane Watson, Andy Bichel and Nathan Hauritz out through the front doors of the New Stanley and into the night.

As I wheeled the party hard right into Standard Street, I wondered briefly if I should have checked with Reg to make sure he harboured no upgraded qualms about me suddenly being entrusted with fifty per cent of the Australian touring party on the potentially lethal streets of Nairobi. But I pressed on and, despite the fact we were the only visible pedestrian presence on the inner-city strip at 8 p.m., there was no discernible concern among the group as we reached the intersection with Wabera Street. At least, not among the players. As tour leader, I found it mildly disconcerting that this was the corner that should have housed the promised land of pasta and pizza. Yet there was no trace of anything other than a couple of metal grilles that guarded darkened shop windows.

Must be the next corner, I convinced myself. By the time we reached that point, I was inwardly panicking. Not even the busted street lamps ventured this deep into town. The cracked concrete footpath had given way to bare dirt underfoot, and the reassuring chatter of the cricketers had petered out. I froze, accepting that leading half of my nation's cricket team toward an uncertain fate represented a far greater travesty than admitting I was lost.

'Umm, Rambo. Are we in the right place?' McGrath asked, employing a measure of equanimity that belied his unjust reputation as surly.

'It should be here, er, somewhere. Perhaps it's just...' My voice thinned to nothingness as I scanned the pitch black in every direction. 'I reckon we must have walked past it.'

I knew that not even I could have missed a brightly lit two-storey Italian restaurant occupying the corner of a major city intersection. But it bought me some time. And by that stage, my currency was trading pretty low. So we silently retraced our steps at a more urgent clip, and gathered outside the first premises we saw that offered an open door, an electric light, and a staff member. It was the sort of scurvy diner that would cause greasy spoons to sue for libel. As it was devoid of clients, it was also fair to assume it remained open out of blind hope rather than economic practicality.

McGrath couldn't resist. 'So this is it, eh? Looks nice.'

A heavy-set woman in a navy-blue cleaner's smock, who appeared to be deep frying lumps of offal in what smelled like formaldehyde, moved out from behind the barren shop's counter and motioned towards four uninhabited battle-scarred tables.

'You here to enn-joy the food or the view?' she snapped, hand resting at an awkward angle on an enormous hip that rose almost to her armpit.

Condemning the bowling component of the squad to amoebic dysentery was no more appealing than having them mugged in a dark alley. So I trawled the remainder of my dignity and bravely inquired as to the location of 'that lovely Italian *trattoria* I understood was in this vicinity?'

With arms now folded defiantly, the plainly insulted proprietress barked: 'And woss wrong wid diss place?'

As I grappled for a diplomatic response amid audible unrest on the footpath behind me, a deep voice caught both of us off guard.

'Honest, we'd love to. Unfortunately, we're meeting other friends at the Italian joint. But we'll definitely be back here tomorrow night. Absolutely. Reserve a table for ten of us.'

Cynics who believe all fast bowlers lack subtlety and smarts have never been hauled out of a tight spot by Jason Gillespie.

'Well I look forward to seein yoo wall then,' she replied, in a tone underpinned by a generous dollop of suspicion. 'You turned a block too soon comin' out of the hot-ell. The place you lookin' for is right ah-cross there,' she explained with a flourish of her hefty left arm, the tricep of which dangled pendulously downward like an over-subscribed hammock.

As one, we turned in the direction she was pointing and could just make out a well-lit, heavily populated restaurant. By the time the *trattoria* manager ushered us to a specially selected table upstairs, menus were distributed and the first bottle of Soave Classico ordered, my appetite had left me. I knew the dinner conversation would be far more relaxed if the journalist were removed. The trust that had built up in the hotel bar over the preceding fortnight had all but evaporated on the dark streets of Nairobi, and I felt my pariah status had been reconferred. So I proffered a lame excuse about sudden work commitments, checked to make sure the cricketers could safely find their way back to the hotel without my expertise, and made a hasty exit. By taxi, just to be safe.

The tournament final was then rained off before a result was reached. Nobody much cared, in Kenya or further afield. Even the helpful café owner didn't score her return booking. There were, apart from a handful of happy tour operators and a small gang of street kids, no winners from the entire Nairobi escapade.

10

ICC Champions Trophy, Sri Lanka, September 2002

Not only did the Kenyan tournament fail to produce a victor, its soggy anti-climax also meant it finished similarly bereft of the one story the fortnight had promised. And with the next thirty-six hours destined to deliver travelling journalists nothing more than in-flight meals and waiting, the rumblings of disquiet from the Ideas Factory were clearly audible in east Africa.

Which was why, as rain tumbled on the deserted Gymkhana and hopes for a yarn that would tide me over a travel day and a half appeared just as bleak, I bailed up Pakistan's team manager who stood glum-faced outside his players' dressing room. The jubilee series had proved anything but, and during our chat he dejectedly confirmed that the schedule for the three celebratory Tests due to begin a month later was still not finalised. The games planned for Sharjah remained in the hands of a much higher authority than cricket administrators or God – the United States military. And if any further rescheduling was needed, the manager confided, the entire Test series might be staged in Sri Lanka. In terms of finalising any onward travel plans, it was not especially helpful news. But it at least delivered a story that bought me a day's grace.

Colombo's heat and humidity attached itself like clingwrap the moment I stepped out onto Bandaranaike Airport's tarmac. We had landed in vastly different climes, obvious not only by the sultry, sub-tropical weather. Heavily armed guards patrolled the terminal corridors and stood sentry at every doorway to ensure nobody except bona fide travellers and more security personnel gained access. The fortified guard post set up where the airport spur met the main Colombo Road, with its sandbagged look-out turrets and high-powered artillery, resembled a war-zone checkpoint. Which is precisely what it was. Barely a year earlier, the Tamil Tigers' feared Black Tiger suicide squad had stormed the airport, murdering seven people and destroying military and commercial aircraft. For all its malevolence, at least the threat of violence in Nairobi was reasonably discreet. In Colombo, guerrilla conflict was out and proud. But during the lengthy taxi ride to the hotel that would be home for the next month, maybe longer, it was my senses that bore the most brutal assault.

The highway into town was a crush of trucks, cars, motorised tri-shaws, motorcycles and foot traffic. Beside the road, every spare metre of space was filled by some sort of enterprise – auto repair shops, mobile phone sales centres, family-run cafés. Walls were covered in hypnotically sculpted, but utterly indecipherable, swirls of Sinhala script. And every doorway was adorned by seemingly aimless folk, most of them perched in the obligatory Asian squat. Bums balanced inches from the ground, arms folded around knees, staring blankly ahead as if waiting for a bus. To try and reduce the overload of noise, smog, heat and humidity, I shut my window and asked my taxi driver to crank up the wireless to compensate for his absent air conditioning. Just as I began to stop fretting about my missing suitcase and drifted into a doze, the lead story on the English-language station's noon bulletin jolted me fully awake.

'A report in *The Australian* newspaper this morning claims that all three upcoming Tests between Australia and Pakistan might be played here in Sri Lanka,' chattered an excited announcer, as if Colombo had just pipped Beijing to host the 2008 Olympics. Bad news travels fast but, in the days of instant global communication, no news can be just as speedy.

Doubts that lingered over the upcoming Tests also extended to the logic behind all of cricket's Test-playing nations, and a couple of also-rans, gathering in inter-monsoonal Colombo for a limited-overs tournament when they were to repeat the entire exercise less than six months later for the World Cup in southern Africa. At its genesis, four years earlier, the Champions Trophy was a noble concept aimed at raising funds for, and the profile of, developing cricket nations. But after the first couple of biennial championships in Bangladesh and Kenya, world cricket's officials judged the tournament had become far too valuable to be entrusted to the sorts of places it was designed to benefit. The penny had dropped that cities sorely in need of decent cricket infrastructure and facilities could not viably host major international games, because they lacked decent cricket infrastructure and facilities. So the Champions Trophy was to be farmed out among the game's existing powers and, not for the last time, Colombo was deemed the best compromise option.

Evidence that the Champions Trophy had devolved into nothing more than expedient television fodder to swell cricket's coffers could be found by simply perusing the playing schedule. The whole tournament offered just fifteen games of cricket across the best part of three weeks, with the most compelling of those preliminary matches programmed into the opening days to blatantly whip up instant viewer appeal. All it achieved was to render the second week about as suspenseful as a Zimbabwean election, with blockbuster games such as New Zealand v Bangladesh, and Pakistan v Holland ensuring global audiences switched off in droves.

The lack of cricket also meant another worrying dearth of news. The game's elite had landed in Colombo, but none of them were doing anything much, apart from shuffling glassy-eyed around the competing teams' hotel. To try and justify my existence, and the newspaper's investment, I offered to broaden my coverage by daubing colourful vignettes of life in the Sri Lankan capital to try and illustrate the Champions Trophy had a pulse, if not a point.

That proposed package included chronicling activity on the vibrant Galle Face Green parade ground, the town square for a town of around a million. All but vacant during the day's heat, come evening it seethed with promenading families, courting couples, children wrangling kites, teenagers playing cricket, and a brave few squealing as they waded ankle deep into the adjacent surf. It also served as an open-air market that dispensed grilled chicken, roasted nuts, ice cream, balloons and donkey rides.

I suggested reflective essays about the evening sippers who settled behind outdoor tables in the main garden of the dowager Galle Face Hotel and, over a few frosted glasses of Three Coins lager, watched the papaya-orange sun slowly disappear behind the fuzzy outline of India, which spanned the western horizon.

And to document the ritualised mayhem that was morning trading at the Pettah markets, or the ancient, bureaucratic rituals involved in sending an overseas parcel from the hilariously officious main hall of the city's General Post Office. All sketches that I found utterly fascinating as I became part of daily life in my new home. But all were impolitely refused by those in charge.

'If people want travelogues, they'll read the travel section,' came the gruff response. 'Just tell us about the cricket.'

However, the first probing cricket interview I scheduled quickly descended into such a farce it would have proved far more revealing, and certainly more productive, to have reviewed The Terrace buffet at the famous Mount Lavinia Hotel. In addition to his standing as one-day cricket's most effective batsman, Michael Bevan was also a legend throughout the game for being volatile and moody. And he had arrived in Sri Lanka in especially volcanic form. Word filtered out that, on the first night in Colombo, he phoned a startled member of team management in the morning's wee hours to demand a first-aid adhesive strip be sent to his room. The crisis was caused by the red standby light on the in-room television set that could not be extinguished, and whose glow prevented Bevan from achieving the total darkness he needed to sleep.

A few evenings later, one of the Australian team's sponsors held a celebratory barbecue for the players on the hotel's pool deck. A number of the cricketers attended begrudgingly, fulfilled their commercial obligations and then resumed their free time, leaving the party in the hands of grateful house guests and freeloading tourists. As the music cranked up and the sponsors' product slipped down, an irate Bevan suddenly reappeared and stormed the music desk, threatening to hurl the speaker stacks and the startled DJ into the deep end if he didn't appreciate that guests were trying to kip. Stumps were drawn forthwith.

So it was with trepidation that I awaited the batsman's appearance in the hotel lobby, and that unease grew when he declined to start our interview until the front bar barista delivered a suitably hot *café au lait*. He had slowly begun to thaw over a few introductory questions when a lone figure appeared, unannounced, at table's edge. It was tough to figure how we had not seen him earlier, given his gaudy green and orange checked seersucker shirt, grey woollen slacks and dust-encrusted rubber sandals that displayed a set of dust-encrusted toes. But we were not alone in failing to detect the moustachioed man, who the hotel's specially hired security staff had not pegged as a professional autograph hunter, even though he carried a meticulously drawn-up A4 page with rows of vacant boxes, each one assigned to a member of the Australian squad.

'Bewaaan,' he announced in a voice remarkably similar to a truck's air horn, as he thrust the document in front of the bewildered cricketer. He then stood proudly at attention, as if reporting in from a successfully completed espionage mission. Bevan studied the interloper's aquiline features, turned quizzically to me to gauge if this was part of the interview and, accepting my confused look as confirmation it wasn't, glanced over his left shoulder in the hope of locating a nearby staff member. Our new friend remained undaunted and unmoved.

'Bewaan,' he honked again. I wasn't sure if a famous 'Bevo attack' would make or destroy the planned story. All I knew was it couldn't be far away.

'Mate, I'm doing an interview. Just leave us alone,' Bevan said, the muscles in his strong jaw line clearly straining. 'I'll sign it for you when we're finished.'

He leaned further across the table as if to continue our chat. The shadow didn't budge.

'Bewaaaan,' the man trumpeted, edging his paper closer and threatening to up-end the cricketer's coffee in the process. That was when the drama climaxed. Bevan jumped to his feet. I followed his lead, but with far less intent. If a fight ensued, I was unsure whether to weigh in or call a photographer.

'Mate, I'm telling you now,' Bevan hissed. 'Leave us alone or I'm not signing anything.'

He spun towards the coffee counter, waved his arms agitatedly and demanded a security officer intervene forthwith. Moments later, uniformed guards attached themselves to each of the nuisance's arms, and he was led away still staring maniacally at the cricketer and clutching his clipboard. Sensing the curious crowd in the foyer might feel he had overreacted to an assailant packing nothing more lethal than a ballpoint, Bevan called contritely after him.

'Mate, I tried to be polite. I would have signed it later on,' he shouted, more for the benefit of the onlookers than the captive. 'But you guys just have to learn.'

As he reached the hotel's front doors, the unrepentant memorabilia man switched his plaintive gaze from one security guard to the other and, in a futile explanatory gesture, wailed simply: 'Bewaaan.' The batsman drained his coffee, the interview was terminated by mutual agreement, and my hunt for that day's story began afresh.

The fugitive was nowhere to be seen the following morning when I returned to conduct my first one-on-one interview with Ricky Ponting since his elevation to the national one-day captaincy. My first one-on-one interview with Ricky Ponting, full stop. I had never held a meaningful conversation with the new skipper, and knew little about him other than what his official biography, batting statistics and Australian cricket charge sheet revealed.

His appointment, ahead of Gilchrist, and even Warne, had come as something of a surprise. It was a decision founded on the certainty he offered for another decade or more, rather than the leadership skills he possessed. A strength of Australian cricket over preceding decades had been its stability and dependability at the top. Allan Border, Mark Taylor and Stephen Waugh could be relied on by selectors and supporters alike. Ponting had shown a willingness to curb his wayward off-field tendencies in a manner that Warne had not, and was therefore deemed the safest pair of hands. Gilchrist was thought to have enough on his plate, combining wicketkeeping with match-changing batting exploits. It seemed Ponting's only glaring shortcoming as a captain was an almost complete absence of captaincy experience.

Recognised as a batting genius from almost the time he could bat, the boy from Mowbray – Launceston's working-class northern suburb, which boasts, instructively, sports grounds, a golf course, and a horse and greyhound track – progressed so swiftly through junior cricket that he was forever the youngest player in his team. He prematurely learned the ways of adults, but was never in a position to lead them. By the time the national job beckoned, his only captaincy experience was a couple of games in charge of the Tasmanian team, when State selectors belatedly realised they might have the next Australian skipper in their midst.

His decision-making acumen, therefore, developed by closely observing his mentors, Taylor and Waugh, as well as other ex-officio team leaders – Mark Waugh, Tom Moody, Warne, Gilchrist and McGrath. But the experiences of his first-class upbringing had also left an indelible mark. All those influential peers had enjoyed regular and sustained success in dominant teams at domestic and international level and, accordingly, adhered to a philosophy built around relentless attack. Keep blazing with the heavy artillery until the opposition inevitably crumbles. Ponting's Tasmania, however, had long been the poor sibling of Australian cricket, experiencing few individual or collective successes. And perennial disappointment breeds self-doubt and caution, not swagger and confidence. He was happy to unleash his big guns early, but if they failed to decide the battle, he preferred strategic withdrawal to continued bombardment.

'There are times in a game when partnerships might be developing and bowling changes have to be made, just to go on the negative side a bit more,' he confirmed during our lobby chat.

His penchant for retreating into all-out defence when the wheels looked set to wobble loose was to become the most criticised element of his captaincy. Especially as the ill-fated 2005 Ashes series unfolded. During our half-hour meeting, he also showed he had clearly come to the captaincy with no agenda other than to win games of cricket. He did not aspire to becoming a statesman or a crusader, as Taylor and Stephen Waugh before him. Instead, Ponting was dogged in his unwillingness to broach anything beyond the obvious and the necessary.

Attempts to coax him from his comfort zone were treated like the initial overs of a previously unseen bowler. Eyed cautiously, before being patted safely back. Across a squat wooden coffee table in a secured recess of the hotel lobby, I introduced the subject of his recent marriage to Rianna Cantor in an attempt to uncover a hint of his character. Even the fact that, following a decade of occasional lessons, he had recently sat and passed his driver's licence. All failed to turn up anything approaching an insight. Like so many trundlers before me, I learned there was no easy way through Ricky Ponting's defence.

'For all his swashbuckling as a batsman', I was compelled to write that evening, 'deep down beats the heart of an accountant'.

Chasing the one major international cricket trophy that had thus far eluded Australia, Ponting's men made an impeccable start to their Champions Trophy campaign with easy wins over New Zealand and Bangladesh. But having quickly earned a berth in the semi-finals, the Australians suddenly faced a yawning eight-day gap in their playing schedule. The diabolical fixture meant a number of other teams were likewise lacking anything to do, and staring at more than a week in which to do it. So they went on holidays.

Half of India's squad made the short trip across the Gulf of Mannar for a few days at home. The Kiwis booked themselves into a quiet retreat in the Sri Lankan hillside, away from the heat and the hustle of Colombo's baking cityscape. And a majority of the Australians packed their bags and headed for a long weekend of snorkelling and beach volleyball in the tranquil honeymooners' island refuge of the Maldives. All smack in the middle of a major international sporting tournament. It was hard to envisage Pete Sampras sneaking away for a night or two in the Hamptons, having won his way past the round of sixteen at Flushing Meadows.

More remarkable was the missive that came from an Australian player announcing that a couple of seats were available on the team's charter flight to Malé, and that the press was welcome to come along if we could come up with the necessary cash. Initially, it appeared that traditional enmities had been cast aside. But it soon became clear the vacancies had been created by the late cancellation of several tightwad players who balked at the prohibitive cost, and that the olive branch was more a 'kiss and make up … the shortfall'. Thus, the offer was respectfully declined.

By the time the Australians took to the field for their semi-final against Sri Lanka, our party had been on the road for precisely a month. In that time, the players had managed six completed days of international cricket. That, and a glaring inability to handle Aravinda de Silva's friendly off-spin, explained why Ponting's team lost comfortably to the host nation, and thereby failed at its third attempt to win the Champions Trophy.

The tournament final, between neighbours Sri Lanka and India, generated a level of local hysteria that was as easy to foresee as each evening's spectacular pre-monsoonal rainstorms. Which made the fixturing of the showpiece as a day–night game even more nonsensical than the original tournament schedule. Any fool, save for the fools in charge of world cricket, could see that evening events held in Colombo in late September would be deluged. And so the final was abandoned due to flooding rain, eight minutes into India's run chase. It was rescheduled for the following day, in the same playing hours with the same result. This time, forty-five minutes into the evening innings. With the likelihood of history repeating itself until the dry season arrived, and after a month dawdling to a conclusion that never arrived, Sri Lanka and India were declared joint champions. Which, in turn, meant three of the past four overseas one-day tournaments I had witnessed had failed to deliver a victor.

Greater Colombo is divided into fifteen numbered precincts. Rather like Paris, but also rather not. And it was only after touring most of them with a taxi driver who spoke no English and cared even less for cricket that we understood that our destination, Paikiasothy Saravanamuttu Stadium, was as difficult to find as it was to pronounce. For more than an hour, the increasingly agitated Australian press corps was taken to a selection of half-baked playing fields, suburban parks and livestock holding pens, none of which bore the remotest resemblance to the sort of venue that would host the upcoming first Test against Pakistan. At every location, we asked if anyone among the curious crowds that gathered out of thick air knew of Paikiasothy Saravanamuttu Stadium, or could point us in the rough direction of where a Paikiasothy Saravanamuttu Stadium might hide. Until, eventually, some kind and wise soul cracked the code, laughing that everyone in Colombo knew where the clandestine ground was located, provided we used its 'good' name – P Sara.

As it turned out, P Sara was a quaint almost English-style cricket ground set among clutters of shanty-style dwellings that hugged the Cota Road train line, and sat in the shadow of Colombo's notorious Welikada maximum security prison. Its timeless scoreboard fought a losing battle against the aggressive deep-green ivy that clung to three of its sides, and behind it stood a regimented four-storey block of Air Force flats whose saving grace was their uninterrupted, front-door views of the cricket ground. Between the northern end sight screen and the perimeter fence lay a roped-off section of soil, on which grew several immaculate rows of lovingly tended lettuce and cucumber plants, as well as an array of local herbs. This plot was tended by a group of middle-aged women wrapped in brightly coloured saris who, when the game got underway, would emerge from the garden at the close of each session and innings to diligently sweep away the loose turf and dislodged dirt from around the batting creases with their stiff straw brooms. A local journalist explained they were the destitute wives of long-term inmates of the neighbouring gaol.

Along the ground's western flank ran a single-level grandstand, covered by a low roof of corrugated iron, which sloped towards the verdant outfield. The end of our harrowing ninety-minute taxi journey to training coincided with the Australian team's post-practice cool-down drill. And while their teammates packed up equipment and dragged gear to the welcome chill of the dressing rooms, Glenn McGrath and Jason Gillespie amused themselves in a crude derivation of real tennis.

They took up positions twenty or so metres apart, just inside the playing arena where the pavilion grandstand was separated from the turf by a thigh-high cyclone wire fence, and took it in turns to lob a cricket ball onto the overhanging roof where it would bounce haphazardly on the corrugations. They would then challenge one another to guess where it would roll off the roof line, with the added complication of catching it before it hit the ground. It was like watching a pair of ten-year-olds fighting summer holiday boredom. This pastime kept them occupied for fifteen minutes or more, and infuriated members of the support staff who were deployed to recover the practice balls that bobbled into the car park behind the grandstand. It also served to distract the normally vigilant rifle-toting security staff.

Taking advantage of their inattention, I jumped the fence and made for the centre of the ground to cast an eye over the Test pitch that had been freshly rolled and left to bake. Or more likely steam. I could no sooner read a cricket pitch than I could fathom Saqlain Mushtaq's *doosra*, but this was my first overseas Test match as the paper's solo correspondent, and I wanted to at least create the impression I knew what I was doing. And standing around, staring at strips of mowed and flattened grass has long been an accepted part of the serious cricket ritual. Like an obscure chapter of horticultural freemasonry, learned cricket folk endlessly analyse and debate the latent power of a twenty-two-yard stretch of shaved, rolled turf to dictate the march of history as if it's a living Rosetta Stone. To help me decipher the secrets of the P Sara deck, I felt it wise to tap into the expertise of the one man who stood between me and the wicket block. After all, Gillespie's bowling skills had already netted him almost 150 Test wickets more than I was going to claim.

'I'm not following you anywhere, not after Nairobi,' he replied, straight-faced, when I asked him if he would join me for a pitch viewing. Ignoring the cheap shot, which McGrath found hellishly funny, I reframed the question to gauge his informed thoughts on how the strip might behave come the start of play next morning.

'Dunno, mate, haven't even bothered looking at it,' he said candidly. 'I never look at it before a game. I mean, what do I know about grass? I just run in and bowl. If the deck's green, I pitch it up. If it's brown, I bang it in. Don't really need to know anything more than that. I've never quite got my head around this obsession with the pitch.'

So the venue was a state secret, the pitch an enigma, and the opposition, not atypically, was in disarray. Through a combination of injuries, lack of interest and internal politics, four of Pakistan's best players had opted not to be part of their nation's golden celebration. Furthermore, inconsistent performances in the preceding one-day tournaments had cost coach Mudassar Nazar his job, and many of the players donning Pakistan's baggy green cap for the first Test were barely known to cricket fans in their homeland, let alone in Sri Lanka. Little wonder there were more people crowded into the northern market garden than in the public grandstand when play began.

Those who did brave the draining humidity and held more than a passing familiarity with world cricket might well have wondered as to the identity of the lithe, suntanned Australian parked at first slip. In response to being overlooked for the one-day captaincy, Shane Warne had undergone a transformational exercise and weight loss program. Just as profound was the image make-over that accompanied his svelte new figure. He took to wearing a bandana when at training, and was happy to tell anyone who cared, as well as those of us who didn't, that he'd embraced the full-body wax. What's more, rumours had filtered through from Australia that he was poised to reinvent himself as a connoisseur of life's finer things by launching his own wine label. Given his culinary preferences extended little further than spaghetti, pizza and toasted cheese sandwiches, and that his preferred evening tipple was sickly melon liqueur mixed with lemonade, it was a difficult stunt to take seriously. Even by Warne's standards.

However, my Australian sources confirmed that not only had Warne discovered wine, but two reputable drops made by a family winery in Victoria's Riverina were to be launched under his name within weeks. It wasn't exactly a smoking gun leading to the instigators of world cricket's corruption, but it was a story nobody else had. And, as I discovered when I approached Warne in the lobby of the team hotel after the Test's opening day, he was keen for it to stay that way until the label's upcoming publicity launch back in Australia.

'I don't know where you heard that from, buddy,' he said, as he made his way to a waiting taxi in the hotel driveway. 'Might have your wires crossed there, I reckon.'

So I played the reporter's standard bluff, telling him I already had sufficient information to write the story regardless of whether he chose to take part or not. I threw in gratuitous details of the grape varieties in question – a chardonnay and a blend of cabernet, merlot and petit verdot – just to make sure I had his full attention. He sized me up as if I were a clueless tailender.

I then added that if it was going to be announced in the national newspaper, he might as well aim for as much coverage as possible. And the best chance of getting it near the front was for him to participate in a photograph. Having weighed the relative merits of this deal, he agreed to a brief interview, near the foyer door, while his driver waited patiently.

'I want people to judge the product, not the bloke whose name is on the label,' he explained, using lines lifted directly from the Shane Warne Collection's back labels. 'I'm not pretending to be a wine buff, but I enjoy a glass of wine. And I know the basics of why it tastes good to me, or why it doesn't. In the last twelve to eighteen months while I've been on the fitness kick, I've gone off beer and got on to the whites and reds.'

It was obvious Warne's epicurean epiphany was about as genuine as his most recent 'mystery ball'. But what the leg-spinner didn't know about 'woin', as his teammates unkindly claimed he called it, he certainly understood about publicity. And as he jumped into the waiting cab, we agreed to meet at P Sara an hour before play the next day for our photo.

Even for a journalist, phoning room service before 8 a.m. to order a bottle of white wine is a touch tragic. But in the absence of a sample of Warne's eponymous plonk, we needed a prop. And I guessed the world's leading sommeliers would be hard pressed to correctly identify a stand-in glass of South African gewürztraminer from a newspaper photograph.

Armed with laptop bag, wine bottle, glass, corkscrew and a photographer, I arrived at the ground as the Australians were beginning their morning warm-up. It was a ritual Warne vehemently opposed, which explained why he was its conspicuous absentee. As the players filed back towards the dressing room at session's end, I asked Brett Lee if he could check on Warne's availability. The fast bowler looked at me, at the opened bottle of wine I was gripping tightly, and smiled sympathetically. I couldn't bring myself to explain it was part of an important national news story and not a cry for help.

Minutes passed before the team manager appeared and reported the request had been logged, but that coach John Buchanan ruled it was not a good idea because Warne was the next batsman in if an early wicket fell. I protested that he was only required to pose, not swallow.

But it was dismissed without consideration. The whole story looked bound for the spittoon until Warne made a fleeting appearance outside the rooms to complete his own preparatory exercise regime. A cigarette and a yawn. I signalled to him it was now or never for our snap.

'How long's it going to take?' he asked, looking nervously askance. I reassured him we had the optimum location in the grandstand worked out, the wine was poured, and all we needed was a leg-spinner to hold it. Two minutes, absolute maximum, I fudged.

He stubbed out the fag against the umpires' room wall and, looking every inch a male model in his plastic beach sandals and oversized training shirt that hung loosely over a pair of white lycra shorts, he padded gingerly to where we waited. He lifted the cheap hotel glass of nasty African wine up near his right cheek, smiled obligingly, and in the time it takes an SLR motor drive to fire off half a dozen frames, the job was done.

'That's it. Gotta go,' Warne said, slopping gewürztraminer on his shirt, and the concrete path where it met the morning sun and released a sickly sweet vapour.

'So what's the caption gunna say?' he asked distractedly as he walked past. It's not often that the world's best leggie tosses up such a generous gift.

'Probably something like "Australian leg-spinner Shane Warne prepares to bat on the second day of the first Test against Pakistan in Colombo",' I said, po-faced, as I emptied the remainder of the glass into a nearby bin.

Warne's green eyes opened wide, and he looked suddenly stricken. 'You bastard,' he wailed. 'After everything I've just done for you.'

11

Tests in Sri Lanka and Sharjah, October 2002

The excess of spare time in Colombo was useful for more than sightseeing. On the days I wasn't exploring the coastal fort city of Galle, visiting the turtle hatchlings in Hikkaduwa, marvelling at the high-wire coconut collectors who traversed the network of aerial ropes along the Galle road, fawning over the glamorous 'Cashew Girls' of Cadjugama, mingling with the pachyderms at Pinnewala's elephant orphanage, or prostrating myself before Lord Buddha's holy molar at Kandy's Temple of the Tooth, there was the other staple of touring life – bureaucracy – to attend to.

When we departed for Kenya, none of us knew where our mystery tour would end. That meant I arrived in Sri Lanka clutching travel documents that granted me passage no further than Colombo. Once the final two Tests of the peripatetic series were confirmed for Sharjah, I passed on this information to my employers in the belief the appropriate onward arrangements would then be made. Instead, I learned the complexities of international airline ticketing meant it would, apparently, be easier if I took care of those contingencies from on the ground in Sri Lanka. Easier for them, anyway.

It all sounded so straightforward in theory. In practice, it made sense like integral calculus. A prolonged wait in an overcrowded airline office in central Colombo yielded nothing other than frustration. It was explained that, because the other components of my travel itinerary had been organised outside Sri Lanka, the best the airline could do was sell me a Colombo–Dubai return fare. This solved my professional dilemma, enabling me to at least cover the last two Tests. However, it did nothing to help me secure safe passage home. Appeals to the office to help find a resolution met with deafening uninterest.

'The company will pay for a ticket to Sharjah,' I was told, 'and then the remainder of the details can be worked out when you're there.'

It was the same glib response I had received to similar queries upon arriving in Sri Lanka a month earlier. A course of action that had, in that time, not delivered a single tangible result. My unease grew, aggravated by another two-hour stint in the simmering human soup of the airline office days later. I eventually emerged with a ticket to Dubai, and a foreboding as to how long I would be marooned there. For all of the Arabian Peninsula's doubtless appeal, it was not high on my preferred locations for indeterminate exile.

Incomplete travel arrangements were but one concern as I boarded the four-hour flight to the Middle East. It wasn't only ambient air temperatures that had been steadily climbing in the Persian Gulf. President George W. Bush had issued a direct challenge to the UN General Assembly that it should hold Iraq to its promise to disarm. Shortly after, the Bush Administration further toughened its stance and flagged a number of possible resolutions stretching as far as military intervention, and stressing that Saddam Hussein's regime would be given 'days and weeks, not months' to comply. Sri Lankan friends who knew a thing or two about war assured me I was flying from one combat zone into another.

I attempted to push aside the prospect of conflagration and to focus, instead, on the cricket. But when I checked into my sixth-floor hotel room in Sharjah and stood at the double window that faced west across the still waters of Khaled Lagoon, on which the occasional passing fishing *dhow* created the only obvious turbulence, I found myself staring directly down the Persian Gulf. Off in the heat haze, roughly the same distance that separated Adelaide from Melbourne, was the Iraqi coast.

* * *

Having spent childhood backyard summers toiling off my long run in the unrelenting sunshine and hot, dry winds funnelled into South Australia from the nation's desert interior, I was confident I could handle the Emirates' prevailing conditions. But the Arabian Peninsula takes the same approach to daytime temperatures as it does to urban construction – the higher the better. From the first step outside Dubai's refrigerated airport, I became aware that the heat didn't just suck out your breath. It scorched the cilia in your respiratory tract and drew a reflexive rasp from blistering lungs.

While lingering in the last moments of airport air conditioning before being initiated into the afternoon inferno, I sidled up to Stephen Waugh at the baggage carousel. If nothing else, it killed time until I made myself known to another baggage services staff member to talk lost luggage. It also allowed me to check his availability and interest for the interview I had planned to mark his upcoming milestone – 150 Test match appearances. As the only player other than Allan Border to reach this lofty mark in more than a century of international cricket, I reasoned it was an achievement of such significance that the Factory might relinquish its monopoly on ideas and accept my submission for a detailed testimonial. If the skipper agreed to participate.

'Yeah, mate, let me know when you want to do it,' Waugh said brusquely, without shifting his eyes from the conveyor belt. On the basis of that feeble commitment, my pitch for a feature story was accepted.

The opportunity to reconfirm our meeting did not arise until after the Australians' necessarily brief mid-afternoon training run on Test eve. The official verdict on conditions they would face the next day ranged from 'ridiculous' to unprintable, and the players were as drained of humour as they were bodily fluids as they prepared to hastily depart at session's end and return to the refuge of their hotel pool.

I took up a position in the barren corridor outside the dressing room door, the sweat engulfing me only partially due to the ferocious heat. My stress levels were peaking along with the mercury as it became clearer my chat with the skipper was becoming as likely as a cool change. That gnawing fear was confirmed by the Australian team manager who reported back, after yet another grovelling plea for my promised audience, that Waugh was in no mood to talk. Furthermore, the captain had thoughtfully suggested our get-together be rescheduled for an evening over the coming weekend, after play had finished. And days after the paper I had pledged to help fill had been printed.

As countless rivals knew well, Stephen Waugh was tough to budge once his single mind was set. But from where I was melting, he was not nearly as intimidating as an aggrieved sports editor who had sketched in a 1,000-word feature for the Saturday lift-out. I had no option but to toss dignity in the puddle forming at my feet, and forlornly threaten public pouting, sulking, even tears if the skipper reneged on our agreement. The official justifiably retorted that Waugh had completed his media obligations for the day when he held a fifteen-minute conference prior to training. Which, he pointedly observed, I had attended.

'But, but … he promised,' I blubbered, bottom-lip quivering like a short-changed five-year-old's on Christmas morning. To my amazement, and to almost bladder-emptying relief, the ploy worked.

'He said he'll do it for you,' the manager said sternly after another brief discussion with the captain behind closed doors. The first group of ruddy-faced players had already begun pushing past and hauling themselves aboard the bus that waited with motor running and fans blasting. 'But only because you reckon he made a deal. And only for five minutes. He's in the rooms.'

He motioned to the glass doors immediately behind him, and I charged headlong through the oncoming tide of lightly roasted players lest he suddenly change his mind.

Past the litter of adhesive strapping, piles of painkilling and salt tablets, massage benches, sopping towels, insulated tubs in which sports drinks would be mass mixed, makeshift plastic-lined ice baths, mounds of cricket equipment and a carpet of discarded water bottles. Then, hunched forward on a plastic chair in a dark corner, I found Stephen Waugh. Sitting in solitude beneath the hem of his candy-striped team blazer that hung from a bare hook on the white plaster wall. In his shorts, training shirt, thick woollen cricket socks and ever-present sponsor's cap, he was sweating like a defendant in a murder trial.

'The bus is ready to go,' I said by way of greeting, clumsily trying to lighten his mood that was as patently gloomy as his surrounds. 'You're gunna be unpopular.'

He looked briefly up at me and then back to the new, blue rubber grip he was diligently unrolling over the handle of one of his prized MRF bats.

'Nah, mate,' he said, implacably. 'They'll know why I've stayed behind. And if it goes longer than a few minutes, *you'll* be unpopular.' When it came to media relations, Waugh was strictly a front-foot player.

With half an eye on my watch, we rattled through most of the questions I had painstakingly prepared, and he fired off a series of answers that were nowhere near as rehearsed. Asked to nominate who he believed was best qualified to follow him as Test captain, he could easily have deflected such obvious speculation by pointing out that he had no say in choosing his replacement, or even when that handover would take place. But shirking wasn't in his nature.

'I think Ricky's got the stomach for the job,' he said, after pausing momentarily and studying the bat that twisted in his hands while he framed his words. 'You have to want this job, embrace it, and take it on because it's not always going to be easy. But he's a tough sort of character, and I think he can handle what it throws at you.'

He also articulated his plans for life after cricket: 'I won't stand back and wait for somebody to hand me a job.' His thoughts on reaching 150 Tests: 'The greatest thing about a longevity milestone is you've obviously got through and dealt with adversity, which says a lot about a sportsperson.' And the legacy of his tenure as captain: 'More people are watching Test match cricket now, which I think is a direct result of how Australian sides have played over the last few years. We've played very aggressively and gone all out to win ... so if that's the legacy this Australian cricket side leaves, then I'd be very happy to say I was part of that.'

In six minutes and forty-eight seconds, he delivered more interesting material than many of his contemporaries managed in their entire careers. No sooner had I snapped off the voice recorder and thanked him for honouring his word, than he leaned the bat carefully against the wall, slung a grey day pack over his shoulder, and stalked off towards the idling bus.

'This weather's bullshit,' he muttered to nobody in particular, even though I was the only one there. 'Buggered if I know what we're doing here.' He lazily kicked at a ball of spent sticking plasters on the floor, and was gone.

The stomach and the steel extolled by the captain were called on from the moment he lost the coin toss the following morning and, to the undisguised irritation of his players, the Australians were forced to field in heat that would have cowed rattlesnakes. As early as our arrival in Colombo, team medical staff had expressed fears that mid-October in Sharjah could present a serious health threat. Constant daily temperatures well above forty degrees, coupled with ninety per cent humidity, meant players were likely to lose up to three kilograms of body weight through fluid loss over the course of a two-hour session.

On that Test's first day, a thermometer placed on the pitch during the lunch break showed forty-eight degrees. But so intent was Stephen Waugh on showing the Pakistanis that his team was mentally and physically stronger, he instructed his men to run between their fielding positions at every rotation of strike and each over's end. It was strategy ruthlessly lifted from Erwin Rommel's desert playbook, and likewise produced its share of casualties.

After bowling three overs, Andy Bichel, the raw-boned Queenslander who boasted commando-level fitness and endurance, became so disoriented he wandered, dazed, in the opposite direction to his assigned fielding location. Two overs later, he was helped to the dressing room and immediately placed on a saline drip. Brett Lee was mystified by the muddy pool that started to form on the popping crease soon after he began his stint with the ball. It turned out that sweat was being squeezed from his sodden socks, and out through a hole cut in the toe of his left boot to ease foot pressure as he hit his delivery stride. Having bowled his three overs, he strapped an ice vest under his shirt and, from then on, he and Glenn McGrath operated in one-over spells. And most of their teammates wore towelling collars stuffed with ice cubes around their necks, in a throwback to the wetted neckerchief sported by Douglas Jardine during the equally intemperate Bodyline summer of seventy years prior.

As an exercise in human endurance, it bordered on lunacy. But as a test of wills, it was a no-contest. Spooked by their superhuman opponents, it was the Pakistan batsmen who wilted. The team was bowled out for fifty-nine, in just over a session. It would have sent shockwaves of disbelief through the crowd, if one had bothered to show up. Even allowing for play beginning on traditional Muslim prayer Friday, the banks of red plastic seats radiating beneath towering Bedouin-style canopies sat tellingly vacant. But the Pakistani surrender had suitably fired the imagination of a more remote audience.

The working week was drawing to a close at the Ideas Factory, and the carpet strollers who gathered around the sports department's television were indulging in the celebrated journalistic tradition of knowing everything about everything, while exhibiting zero comprehension of what it is they manifestly don't know. Every workplace harbours folk like this. But, for some baffling reason, at newspapers they're taken seriously. And often promoted to middle management.

'We need an urgent piece on Warne's new mystery ball,' the boss shrieked down the line during the change of innings. 'The one he's getting all the wickets with. It's unplayable.'

I clawed at the hotel hand towel spread out next to the laptop, to reduce the risk of sweat dripping into my keyboard, and briefly contemplated knotting it around my throat.

'What mystery ball?' I replied, straining not to sound as steamed as I felt. 'There is no mystery ball. Who on earth told you that?'

'Nobody told us, we can see it for ourselves on the TV,' came the response. 'It's the one that *The Sunday Age* had a story on months ago. I'm sure you remember that.'

I flashed a look at Blakey that, had it translated into deed, would have seen me publicly beheaded at sunrise. As patiently as I could muster, while screwing the towel into a sopping sphere, I attempted to politely challenge the interpretation by a person sitting at a desk 12,000 kilometres away, of events that were unfolding on a cricket field a few hundred metres in front of me.

On a slow, dry, first-day pitch, I began, sounding like a preschool teacher beginning a fairytale, Warne understood he would be able to extract neither turn nor variable bounce. And so, he opted to bowl flatter, straighter and from close to the stumps. Instead of expelling needless energy ripping huge leg breaks that would only turn slowly and be easier to score off, he squeezed the ball from the front of his hand, imparting only backspin to ensure it stayed low upon bouncing.

This was, I explained, regulation fare by the great bowler's standards, but had netted him four wickets in next to no time because Pakistan's novice Test batsmen, like the folks around the TV in Sydney, had no clue what he was doing. Therefore, they propped speculatively forward in expectation of vicious spin that was never going to arrive, and simply stood there waiting to be adjudged leg before wicket. Upon finishing this dissertation, I found I was pinching the bridge of my nose so hard I had almost drawn blood.

'So there is no mystery ball,' I finished, exhausted. 'He's bowling straight breaks. And just for the record, that story out of Kenya was more spin than anything Warne's managed here. I'm guessing the only person stupid enough to fall for that is the same person who's providing expert commentary in the office.'

It was a rush of smart-arsedness I'd been fighting to tether, and one that I instantly regretted. Under normal circumstances, I would have quietly acquiesced, sworn under my breath, and set about typing up whatever banal request was issued. But these, from where I sat in the relative discomfort of an *al fresco* typing pool within a convection oven, were far from normal circumstances. The distressing heat was compounded by the nauseating effect of sickly sweet, but oddly satisfying, cardamom-infused tea that was steeped with condensed milk and dispensed ceaselessly to the meagre press corps by smiling Korean tea ladies. Throw in the fatigue born of a long and gruelling three-month assignment, and the angst created by its still-unresolved final act, and it led me to breach my own golden rule. To never give anyone in the office the impression I was at all fussed. In the silence that ensued, I draped the soaking towel over my head, just as a small, round-faced lady cheerily bowed and placed a steaming plastic cup beside my right elbow.

'It just so happens that person is the editor of the paper,' the boss eventually answered, in a voice usually reserved for 'and if you don't let me have it, I'll tell mum'. 'He requested it and wants it for page one.'

What ran across the front of the weekend edition next day made no mention of 'mystery deliveries', or Warne's supposed sorcery. Just an oblique reference to 'killer balls delivered from the front of the hand to mesmerise his inexperienced opponents'. And a small kicker, in bold type, pointing to an exclusive interview with Stephen Waugh somewhere much deeper in the paper. My obduracy, someone in the organisation let slip, had been noted. I devoted the remainder of prayer day to silent entreaties for the match, the series, and the tour to be over.

The Pakistanis, or the higher authority manipulating their fate, did their best to hasten the finish. Suggestions that their vapid first innings marked the low-point of the Islamic republic's fifty years in Test cricket were re-evaluated next day when they were bowled out for fifty-three in less time than it takes to watch a Hollywood blockbuster. Anyone looking to blame the hostile conditions for such spinelessness was pointed towards Matthew Hayden who, in the period between Pakistan's twin humiliations, not only batted three hours longer than his eleven opponents managed across two innings, he outscored them by seven runs.

A Test victory achieved inside two days would normally unleash wild celebrations among players and press alike. But mitigating the joy of some unscheduled free time was the fact we were all stranded far from normality. We were in Sharjah. Where setting foot beyond the hotel was as enticing as climbing into a kiln. Where the only discernible shadow was that cast by the spectre of war. And where anyone contemplating a party faced being stoned before they could get stoned. It may be the third-largest city among the federation of fiefdoms, but Sharjah is to the United Arab Emirates what Jan was to the Brady Bunch. In contrast to its flashy and flirty nextdoor neighbour, Dubai, Sharjah's dowdy, conservative image was reflected in its pre-eminent features – stately mosques, spacious *souks*, a huge shipping port, and a sleepy waterfront development.

A place of commerce and contemplation, it takes seriously its reputation as the Emirates' cultural and education capital. It is also subject to strict Islamic law. Non-married couples are forbidden from meeting in public, and face the lash if found cohabiting. Anyone flashing too much flesh can be hauled off the street by police and questioned. And alcohol is strictly, expressly banned. Not really the sort of place you need to be stuck for a week between Tests. There's a finite number of ice-cold peach juices one can ingest to wash down the desert dust and quell the heat of Hades.

Conditions meant the Australians abandoned all notions of training before the final Test, restricting themselves to swimming, and organised tours. To Dubai's Burj Al Arab, the world's only seven-star hotel, and aboard the Australian warship HMAS *Arunta* which was part of the Persian Gulf blockade of Iraq. None of these outings included the press. Consequently, my dwindling reserves of energy and enthusiasm were channelled into restorative, explorative walks, strategically scheduled to avoid the heat of the day. Which meant roughly the hour either side of dawn and dusk.

For fear of being spot-seared when the sun's rays bore down from much above the horizontal, these hikes were restricted to localised attractions. The Blue Souk was the city's premier market and hideout for much of Sharjah's Arab population at any given hour. All outdoor construction and menial work was undertaken by imported, lowly paid labourers, mainly from Bangladesh. The Souk's high vaulted ceilings, spotless marble floors and industrial-strength air conditioning meant it offered respite to the privileged, as well as 600 or so shops dispensing reams of delicate fabrics, rivers of gold jewellery, prayer rugs and antiques, and, naturally, imported designer-label clothes, fragrances and cosmetics. Western morality might be a crime, but Western extravagance remains an essential status symbol.

Marginally further afield lay the fruit and vegetable *souk*, where trays piled with dates stood taller than the bearded men selling them. The fish *souk* was a gut-covered terrace along the wharf where the *dhows* tied up, and was best avoided once the sun took effect. And the bird *souk* was where majestic falcons occupied pride of place, alongside the elaborate accoutrements of their sport – leather hoods inlaid with intricate gold trimming, vellum gauntlets, swivel-topped wooden perches to which the birds of prey could be safely tethered in the evenings.

Falconry engenders infinitely greater interest and respect than does cricket throughout the Arab world, as reflected by the Emirates' founding father, Sheikh Zayed bin Sultan Al Nayhan, who philosophised:

Stuart MacGill bowls to journalist Robert 'Crash' Craddock at a beach in Barbados during Australia's 1999 tour of the West Indies.

In the 'press box' during the 2000 West Indies tour match at Alice Springs: (L to R) Michael Horan (*Herald Sun*), Andrew Ramsey (*The Australian*), Michael Crutcher (Australian Associated Press), Mark Ray (*Sydney Morning Herald*).

Matthew Hayden appears unfazed by the presence of one of Africa's 'big five' while fielding on the boundary during the 2002 tri-series in Nairobi.

Adam Gilchrist interviewed by a local television reporter in Colombo during Australia's 2002 Test series against Pakistan.

Drinks cart on standby during the Australian team practice session prior to the first Colombo Test against Pakistan.

Australia batting against Pakistan in front of a virtually empty stadium during the 2002 Test series in Sharjah.

Adam Gilchrist provided with table, chair, wet towel and drinks during a break while batting in Sharjah's extreme heat.

The Australian media touring party in the Abu Dhabi desert during the 2002 Test series in Sharjah: (L to R) Michael Donaldson (Australian Associated Press), Martin Blake (*The Age*), Glenn Mitchell (ABC Radio), Mike Coward (*The Australian*), Andrew Ramsey (*The Australian*).

With the Frank Worrell Trophy following Australia's 2003 Test series victory in the West Indies: (L) Trevor Marshallsea (*Sydney Morning Herald* – complete with crutches) and (R) Andrew Ramsey (*The Australian*).

Capacity crowd at the world's largest cricket venue – Eden Gardens in Kolkata – during the TVS Cup tri-series tournament in India, 2003.

The Australian team training at Newlands Cricket Ground, Cape Town, during the 2006 one-day series in South Africa.

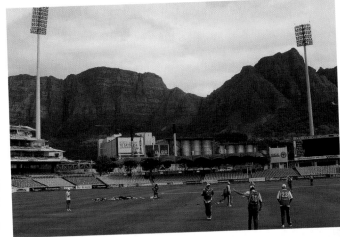

Brett Lee bowls to Andrew Symonds at a training session in Durban during Australia's 2006 tour of South Africa.

Michael Kasprowicz and Shaun Tait (back to camera), atop Table Mountain, Cape Town, during the 2006 South African tour.

At Dubai airport en route from Johannesburg to Dhaka in 2006: (L to R) Brett Lee, Stuart Clark, Stuart MacGill and Phil Pope (media manager).

Young boys playing cricket on a barren field in Dhaka during Australia's 2006 tour of Bangladesh.

Australian batsmen practise in the nets alongside a temporary spectator shelter prior to a Test match in Chittagong during the 2006 tour of Bangladesh.

Scoreboard attendants recover name plates dislodged by a violent storm in Chittagong.

Adam Gilchrist chats to the crowd during a rain delay in the Chittagong Test match.

Ricky Ponting at the Chittagong ship-breaking yards.

Filing an urgent update in front of an attentive crowd during Australia's 2006 tour of Bangladesh.

A cricket match on the Mumbai maidan during the 2006 ICC Champions Trophy tournament in India.

Traffic snarl in the heart of Old Dhaka, Bangladesh; and (R) a juice vendor at a market stall.

A resident of Soweto, South Africa.

The author as an aspiring (and delusional) cricketer in the backyard, aged twelve.

'Falconry teaches endurance, strength, and patience.' Which explained why I was sorely tempted to buy one to help me negotiate the coming week. At least one of us then stood a plausible chance of flying home.

Despite my daily harassment of the newspaper's travel consultants and sympathetic administrative staff, come the start of the final Test I was none the wiser as to when, or how, I might get back to Melbourne. My feeling of isolation was heightened by another of Sharjah's draconian restrictions. Local internet servers allowed the transmission of emails, but access to web pages was blocked lest they inflame subversion, or loins. A couple of times, I dared to dial into a rogue server hosted in neighbouring Qatar, but fears as to the impact it might have on the company's phone bill, and potentially on my liberty, meant the risk far outweighed any benefit. Consequently, our window to the world was the CNN feed piped through the hotel room televisions.

'Heard any news about the war?' Adam Gilchrist asked sombrely one morning as our paths crossed en route to the breakfast room, a facility the media and players had shared until some of the cricketers complained about the press's proximity during their morning meal, at which point we were shunted off to a scungy buffet set up to cater for loudly dressed, loudly spoken Russian tourists.

'Last update I saw was that US Congress had authorised Bush to use force against Iraq,' I reported, trying to sound like the authority on world politics that I wasn't. 'But I'm pretty sure that's come from the same sources you're tuning into.'

'You're right,' he lamented. 'I think I'm watching too much CNN. And it's made me even more depressed. I'm not sure if things are especially bleak at the moment, or if the world's always in this shape but I'm just not aware of it because I don't usually have time to sit around watching twenty-four-hour news.'

Next day, our collective feelings of apprehension and vulnerability escalated immeasurably when suicide bombs tore apart two nightclubs at Bali's Kuta Beach. The non-stop CNN coverage focused largely on the implications of the al-Qaeda connection, and devoted scant attention to details of the eighty-eight Australians among the 202 lives lost. Nonetheless, it was instantly apparent that this event carried major implications, both at home and in the Gulf. Suddenly, history was on the gallop.

Conflict in Iraq was now touted as days away. The Australian Government ramped up its security warnings for its citizens in, or heading to, a long list of global hot spots. Politically, not meteorologically. The need to get out of Sharjah had become critical. My own sense of unease was exacerbated by sketchy reports of a potentially dire health crisis that was afflicting my wife at home. Rational fears that, should an invasion be launched, the cricketers would be whisked to safety and journalists left to fend for ourselves only added to the desperation of my travel inquiries. And if, as was likely, the final Test took as long to resolve as its predecessor, time to secure my escape was already running out.

All I needed was an airline ticket. I wasn't asking to be carried across south Asia in a sedan chair. But by Test eve, I had nothing other than windy assurances that travel arrangements would be taken care of. So in another act of imprudence, I fired off an angry email to my superiors, composed on a belly full of peach juice, which bluntly spelled out my disillusionment. I boldly suggested that if nobody in the organisation was able or inclined to organise my passage home, then I would be forced to turn up at Dubai Airport come Test's end and use my emergency-only issue corporate credit card to purchase any available one-way fare. Economy, business or celebrity class. I figured the only guaranteed way to elicit a response from a global media monolith was to use the language it understood above all else – money.

The fact there was a response awaiting me when I logged on next morning confirmed I had, indeed, struck a nerve. Unfortunately, it was a self-inflicted wound. The email from on high was as acerbic as it was self-explanatory.

'You may think you are the most important person in the world, but you are not,' it read. 'Our resources are stretched to the limit dealing with the horrific events in Bali. Not that you seem to care. You will be brought home when we are ready to do so and not before. Should you act on your threat to purchase an airfare using corporate funds, it will be viewed as a fraudulent transaction. The card will be confiscated, you will be required to reimburse the company for the expense incurred, and the appropriate action will be taken.'

I fumed with indignation, self-pity and panic. I felt abandoned as well as admonished. My job was apparently now in peril simply because I had sought, over the course of many weeks, to organise safe passage home from a work assignment to a selection of the world's foremost trouble spots. I was not so delusionally self-important to demand the newspaper abandon the biggest story of the decade in order to fly me across the globe. I merely wanted a travel agent to purchase an airline ticket on my behalf. Or provide me with the authority to do same. By that stage, I would have been more than happy to pay for it myself. What's more, the slight about my disregard for the Bali victims was unkind and uninformed. The atrocity was a significant reason for my urgent need to get home because the lack of information available in Sharjah meant I had no idea if the dead and injured included any of my relatives or friends. These issues were all addressed in a provocative reply I typed in a blind rage, then wisely opted not to send. Instead, I closed the laptop having reread the initial missive over and over, and prepared to head to the cricket.

The Test's predictable result was completed early on the fourth morning. The next day, I caught a cab to Dubai Airport where I handed over a sheet of telex paper I had received that morning that was decorated with sufficient booking numbers, airline codes and travel industry jargon to stump the code breakers at Bletchley Park. I had been assured, in an accompanying note from an apologetic travel agent, that it could be swapped for a valid plane ticket.

A day later, I returned to the same desk dragging my suitcase, and even less hope. But after forty-five minutes of negotiations, hollow threats and international phone calls, I was gifted a boarding pass to get me as far as Singapore, where I camped overnight, before finally slumping into a seat that was bound for Australia. As I touched down at Tullamarine, sixty days after arriving in Nairobi, I was again convinced that I had completed my final overseas cricket tour. And, at that point, nothing could have pleased me more.

12

Australian Summer 2002–03

England's cricketers landed in Australia to begin preparations for the 2002–03 Ashes series while Stephen Waugh's men were still engaged in their Middle East campaign. The game's oldest rivalry stoked fires in many bellies, but none more fiercely than the media's. As well as tradition and folklore, the battle for the tiny terracotta urn lent itself to those trusty circulation-boosters, jingoism and hyperbole.

In the weeks leading into the opening Test in Brisbane, acres of newspaper space would be devoted to exhaustive reasons why this series could be different to the seven that had preceded it, most notably because England appeared to have unearthed a means to be competitive. Then, when that was revealed as a pipe dream, even more space was allocated to pour scorn on the Old Enemy because it was just as laughably poor as before. It was this yawning need for content that saw me included in the paper's starting line-up for the summer, just weeks after my acrimonious return from the Emirates. Even recriminations took a back seat to the Ashes.

The early signs for a close-fought series were promising. England emerged from all three of its first-class warm-up matches undefeated though, in fairness, none actually earned them a victory. And speculation arose that, for reasons of jet lag, sunstroke and shellshock, the Australians were likely to be off their game when hostilities began at the 'Gabba. But to nobody's genuine surprise, the Poms were whipped in the first Test, flogged harder in the second and reduced to a punchline for a routine of well-worn jokes in the third. The Ashes had been decided on summer's first official day and, as if anticipating the need to randomly throw some element of contest into the schedule, the Australian Cricket Board wasted no time getting stuck into the series that really mattered – the annual three-sided limited-overs tournament, featuring the much-awaited return of the litigious Sri Lankans.

Sneaking in five one-day internationals between the Perth and Boxing Day Tests might have appealed to those groups interested in gate takings and evening television ratings, but for the game's purists this was rather like plating up the *petits fours* just as diners were polishing off their *entrée*. Then, out of the blue, the tut-tutting of serious commentators was drowned out by the stifled whoops of daily journalists as a Christmas–New Year silly season that threatened to be denuded of meaning and news gifted a story that would sustain us to season's end and well past.

It arrived on a cool Sunday evening, a week or so shy of Christmas, with England on course for another shellacking. Shane Warne was nearing the end of a fruitful ten-over bowling spell when, reacting instinctively to a firmly hit straight drive, he flung himself to his right, bowling arm outstretched. As his full weight crashed on the pitch, the top of his humerus was violently forced upward, popping it clean out of the shoulder joint. A hush fell over the MCG as the local hero willed himself to sit up, cradling his right arm against his chest and grabbing at the damaged joint as his face contorted in agony. Even before he had been lifted on to a stretcher, I phoned the boss to flag that we might need to consider rejigging the front page for the second edition. Then, as four support staff and a couple of concerned teammates helped carry him from the field, I block deleted the words I had already composed, and furiously began work on the latest Warne episode.

Even I recognised this was more than a routine sports injury yarn, and not only because it involved the game's walking circus. In two months, the Australians would arrive in South Africa to defend their World Cup, and a mainstay of that campaign now faced a minimum of six weeks to recover. That was if, at thirty-three, and having already undergone one full reconstruction of the over-used joint, he was able to recover at all.

But Warne had worked hard to modify more than his palate over the previous year. After undertaking a fitness regime that saw him shed a dozen kilograms and trim ten centimetres from his waistline, he wasn't about to let a mere anterior dislocation fast-track him into retirement. Not only did he make good his promise to return to international cricket, he did it after just twenty-six days recuperating. And true to the soap opera plot that he often admitted doubled as his life's narrative, his comeback coincided with the start of the one-day finals, which offered the Australians one last chance to humiliate their historic foes.

He stood tanned, trim and revitalised at training on the day before the big comeback game in Sydney and, at session's end, he was one of four players approached in the SCG dressing room by officers from the Australian Drugs Sports Agency to provide a routine, random urine sample. Even then, all seemed well in Warne's world.

That afternoon, Warne fronted a prearranged media conference in a meeting room filled to bursting at the team hotel, and positively glowed through his announcement that, while he would be fit to spearhead Australia's bowling at the World Cup, the tournament would also serve as his swansong from limited-overs cricket. The decision, he explained, had been made to extend his longevity in Test matches. Minds were immediately cast back to the previous World Cup in London, where Warne had last floated the retirement scenario and successfully hijacked the spotlight by doing so. And just like last time, his news caught teammates on the hop.

Having reclaimed his rightful place in the nation's one-day team and on its newspapers' front pages, Warne departed the press call in exuberant spirits. So cheerful, in fact, he voiced no objection to a journalist tagging along with him later that evening to a promotion of his new wine label at Sydney's Watsons Bay Hotel. I was invited by a mate who was also the brand's public relations flack. And the leg-spinner, clearly chipper about the way the day's events had panned out, voiced no reservations when confronted by the 'leech' that lurked in the back seat of the event photographer's car as all four of us took off from The Rocks and into the night.

Under regular circumstances, Warne would rather break herb bread than share a confined space with a journalist. He wasn't quite as anti as Mark Waugh who, as the players' minibus edged past a group of press men following training at Adelaide Oval one afternoon, shouted loud enough at the driver for all of us to hear: 'Speed up and run them down. Bloody cricket nuffies.' Or Andrew Symonds who, when the team bus passed me as I waited for a taxi outside Bellerive Oval one evening, responded to a suggestion from one of his teammates that they stop and offer me a ride, given we were all staying at the same hotel, with a snarling: 'Piss off, he's a journalist.' To which one of the crew bravely suggested: 'Yeah, but he's one of the trustworthy ones.' Prompting Symonds to spit back: 'Maybe, but he's still got a fuckin' pen.' By contrast, the only baggage Warne was carrying when he jumped into the front passenger seat was the ham and pineapple pizza that had been freshly delivered to his room.

'You guys want some?' he asked breezily, in lieu of traditional pleasantries. 'Good,' he laughed when we all declined, ''cos I'm starving.'

He spent the twenty-five-minute drive through the eastern suburbs to South Head juggling dinner, running us through the log of calls and text messages he'd already received from wellwishers around the world, finalising a ghostwritten column that was to appear under his name in an English newspaper the next day, and, in the few spare minutes in between, making easy conversation with his fellow travellers.

'So how do you think today's announcement went down, Rambo?' he quizzed me, as he poked down the final slice. 'Thought I'd better give you guys something to write about,' he continued, turning to face me over his right shoulder, the oncoming headlights causing the grease on his chin to glisten. I smiled back, pretending to convey gratitude as a couple of pineapple chunks dislodged and fell *thud, thud* into the cardboard container.

The entourage that awaited in the hotel's function room was largely made up of wine and food connoisseurs, the sorts who ordinarily wore their reluctance to be impressed like a merit badge. But the hubbub died to hushed adulation when Warne, freshly towelled down by a paper napkin, made his entrance. Some gawked unashamedly. Others forcibly kept their eyes lowered until he had moved past, lest their stares appear too adoring. If Warne was intimidated by mingling with a group that understood far more about his new product than he did, he showed no outward sign.

For an hour or more he chatted and backslapped, posed for photographs and signed bottles that immediately became more valuable for their packaging than for their contents. Citing impending cricket commitments, and in keeping with the team's pre-match curfew, he departed at the civilised hour of 9 p.m. In transit and in situ, he had been relaxed, effusive and totally charming, which flew in the face of subsequent conspiracy theories that he knew all along he was harbouring a dark secret.

News that Warne had, on the basis of the urine sample collected that day, tested positive to a banned diuretic broke the day before Australia's opening World Cup outing in South Africa. His explanation – that he had innocently taken tablets recommended to him by his mother to help him appear leaner during his triumphant media conference – was dismissed by most as either laughably naive, or ham-fistedly devious. Others gloated that it was fitting that a man who so openly embraced style over substance should be brought down by vanity. And some took the remarkable speed of his rehabilitation from the shoulder injury, added it to the use of diuretics, and came up with a circumstantial sum that indicated a bare-faced attempt to mask more sinister substances in his body. After all, that was the reason diuretics were explicitly banned by sporting organisations, including the International Olympic Committee. But it was the case tendered by Warne himself that was the most compelling.

As recent years had regularly borne witness, Warne was far less accomplished at masking his emotions than he was at disguising the apparently infinite array of deliveries in his bowling repertoire. It was easy to tell when he was on a biorhythmic upswing. He was gregarious, charismatic and craved attention – the bloke who impressed everyone at his Watsons Bay 'woin' event. When things weren't turning his way, he quickly became brooding, self-absorbed and withdrawn – the guy found skulking outside a hotel in Leeds, or confronting the team psychologist in Birmingham. If he had knowingly used illicit means to fast-track his recovery, the realisation that his career was in tatters would have hit him like a Lance Klusener cover drive the moment he was asked to pee in a bottle. Putting on a brave face in front of your captain and coach during a low spell at an Antiguan restaurant was admirable, but feigning the levels of enthusiasm and humour he managed to generate at a full-blown media conference and then an upmarket groupie gig required the sort of artifice only a gifted actor could hope to carry off. And anyone who endured the television chat show Warne was to host in retirement knew that his capabilities as an *artiste* were strictly confined to cricket.

Warne's reappearance in Australian one-day colours on the day after his Sydney soiree was typically fairytale. He bowled serviceably for all but one delivery of his ten-over spell. The exception, naturally, was the final ball that left the sell-out crowd hollering his genius, and his teammates shaking their heads. Though this time, in admiration.

His last offering was a perfectly looped leg break that lured England's Paul Collingwood out of his crease, as he scampered to meet the ball at its bounce. But the revolutions Warne imparted through his rebuilt shoulder meant it dipped sharply before the wide-eyed batsman could quite get there. Upon pitching, it then spun sharply away from the bat that had been thrust forward in desperate hope, and into the gloves of wicketkeeper Adam Gilchrist, who completed a straightforward stumping. The Australians went on to complete another emphatic win, built on a blistering Gilchrist innings.

Next morning, as I sat secreted in a back corner of the hotel breakfast room to appear not-so-intrusive to the small groups of Australian players spread out through the restaurant, I became aware of a figure looming over my muesli.

'Checked your emails this morning?' Gilchrist asked, his jaunty manner disguising an underlying weariness. I blamed Warne's recent bombshell and the previous night's late finish for my tardiness in doing so.

'No drama,' he said, almost apologetically. 'But when you do, you should find a column there from me.'

I looked confused, only because I had no recollection of asking for one. Or of the Factory telling me one was due. But unlike most other paid celebrity columnists, Gilchrist was known to enjoy, and take professional pride in, his writing.

'It suddenly came to me last night, just after that stumping off Warney's final ball, that this will be the last time that people in Australia see him performing like that in one-day cricket,' he continued, a wad of newspapers rolled tightly beneath his right arm. 'So I spent the rest of the innings mulling that over, and I thought it might make an interesting column. How Warney's single-handedly changed the way one-day cricket is played. That spinners no longer just tie up an end, they're now a real attacking weapon. And I've chucked in a few personal observations about how he's achieved that.

'Just because I could,' he said, self-deprecatingly.

Then, as he strode off, he added: 'It's the usual length, 750 words or so. When I got back here after the game last night, I was still pretty hyped and couldn't sleep. So I pulled out the laptop, knocked something together and sent it off to you. Let me know what you reckon. If you think it needs a bit more work, I can probably have a go at it this afternoon. Once we get to Melbourne.'

'If you're not careful, you'll give player columns a good name,' I called after him, only partly in jest.

I returned to my room shortly after to find that a missive from the vice-captain had indeed dropped in my inbox at 2.36 a.m. As expected, it ticked every box for an insider's column – lucid, relevant and insightful. Putting the reader in the player's shoes. I flicked it straight on to the boss, with not so much as a comma altered.

The other trait that set Gilchrist apart as a columnist was that his interest in newspapers extended beyond the considerable money they throw at such arrangements. He enjoyed exploring new ways of conveying the on-field experience in words. He was aware of the opportunities a regular presence in a national newspaper provided, and took that responsibility seriously. His perspicacity and professionalism added significantly to the paper's cricket coverage, and he indicated he was interested in pursuing a role in the print media beyond his playing days. So, when his contract lapsed later in the year, the Factory shrewdly chose not to renew it. In a triumph of marketing over merit, Ricky Ponting was signed as an occasional columnist instead.

13

West Indies, March–June 2003

In the four years since I had snuck from the Caribbean under threat of lawsuit, the clement islands hadn't drifted any closer. Even though the route for Australia's 2003 tour took us the other way – through Los Angeles, New York, Trinidad and finally Guyana – it still soaked up two full days of air travel and associated waiting around. Not that I was grumbling. I had resolved to cultivate a disposition as sunny as the region's idyllic weather throughout the two-month tour, regardless of bureaucratic obstacles or empty bottles hurled my way.

The animosities of Sharjah, if not forgotten, had been glossed over in another round of managerial role shuffling. For my part, I had reignited my enthusiasm for international cricket assignments, aided in part by the harsh realisation that the alternative to touring life was life in the office. And in my case, that meant reporting on the eye-glazing winter rituals of Melbourne's suburban football. From the paper's perspective it was largely due to the series' scheduling, tacked on to Australia's successful World Cup defence. Which meant reporters who had tailed the team through an Ashes summer and then two months in South Africa had been granted a leave-pass from the West Indies so that they could reacquaint themselves with their lives. There was no such respite for the players who had been on the road since Kenya almost a year earlier. Consequently, they were not sharing my level of joviality when they landed in Guyana on a damp late-March morning.

Indeed, they made no attempt to hide their grumpiness. The fact they were able to return home after their triumph in Johannesburg barely long enough for a cursory street parade through Perth, and to pack their Test match whites, had given rise to bubbling discontent that their World Cup achievement had not been duly acknowledged, or properly celebrated.

Apart from heartfelt guarantees that my room booking would be honoured for the duration of our stay, nothing much had changed in Georgetown over intervening years. The heavy security presence pretty much everywhere was only partly due to the Gulf War that had finally kicked off in the days before we left Australia. Violent gang crime had become even more popular than before, to the extent that not long after our arrival a US diplomat was ambushed on the second tee of the city's Lusignan Golf Course by a group of gun-toting teenagers, who demanded $60 million Guyanese for his release. The street value of an international cricketer was thought to be considerably higher, so confinement once more became our mutual companion. I was therefore deputed, by the six-man travelling press corps, with coaxing Stephen Waugh – widely tipped to be undertaking his final overseas tour – to share dinner with us in the days prior to the first Test. Having been virtually impounded with the team since our arrival, most of our tour expenses were fully intact. And it was the lure of winkling some largesse from the media, rather than the media's lively company, that excited the skipper's interest when I encountered him on his way to an after-training swim.

'Yeah, that'd be good,' he said, without breaking stride. 'But it'd be best to invite the coach and the team manager as well. Just to keep everyone happy.'

Then, as I was about to negotiate the finer details, he added: 'We'll do it here, at the poolside restaurant. Tomorrow night. At eight o'clock.'

I was immediately reminded of a tale I'd heard years prior, when Waugh made a rare appearance for Bankstown in Sydney's grade competition. His rival skipper was a university student, nervous and excited about the prospect of meeting, and opposing, one of Test cricket's all-time greats. When they came together at pitch's edge for the coin toss, the novice extended his hand and introduced himself. Waugh shook it hurriedly, grunted 'G'day' and flicked a $1 bit skywards.

'Call,' he commanded, following the coin's flight.

'Heads,' stammered the intimidated youngster, unsure of how he'd so upset his hero before a ball had been bowled. It landed heads and, as the winner steeled himself to announce his intentions, Waugh barked, 'You can bat,' and bent to retrieve his investment. As the youngster stood dumbstruck, the Test captain jammed the dollar in his pocket and set off briskly, alone, towards the dressing sheds.

No sooner had they supped on the media's hospitality than the officials made their excuses and left. But Waugh stayed on for a couple of additional rum and colas, indicating he was either keen to inflate the bill or had a bone to pick. When the first round of drinks arrived, so too did the picking.

'One of the things that really shits me about the media is when you blokes write something and attribute it to "sources",' he said, directing his grievance at no particular party. 'Sources close to the team, or sources inside the Cricket Board. I reckon that's bullshit. If you're gonna say something, you should have the guts to put your name to it. Otherwise, journos could just make up anything, and say it's come from "sources".'

He leaned back, obviously spoiling for an argument. We, in turn, argued the legitimacy of anonymity in news reports. The value of whistleblowers. That some of the world's great injustices would never have been exposed if the informants had to be identified on the record. Like Watergate. Even Ranatunga-gate. Besides, journalists were bound by a code of ethics, so most would never simply manufacture quotes out of thin air in order to generate a headline. Tweak maybe. But blatant fabrication just couldn't be countenanced. This final assertion forced a derisive laugh, most notably from the skipper.

'Yeah right,' he snorted. 'All I'm saying is that we get scrutinised by you guys, and the public, for every little incident. Every word out of place. Whereas you can write whatever you want and hide behind "sources".'

'But aren't there issues that get under your skin?' I asked. 'That you'd like to speak out about but know you can't because of the job you hold?'

I only had to look into his uncompromising eyes to immediately know it was the wrong question. Or a reasonable question, just posed to the wrong person.

'Not that I can think of,' he said, draining his glass, and splintering an ice cube between his teeth. 'If I've got something to say, I'll back myself and put my name to it.'

The first Test began with the West Indies batting, but wickets in the first half-hour soon had the Australians in the ascendant. Then, without warning or explanation, the game stopped dead. Adam Gilchrist had hurled his bright orange wicketkeeping gloves onto the mottled turf, and bolted like a Jamaican sprinter for the dressing room. His confused teammates formed a huddle in the centre, unsure as to the reason for his departure, or the probability of his return. Playing cricket without a 'keeper is a bit like shooting pool on a dinner table. Not totally unfeasible, but unnecessarily time-consuming. After a few minutes of blank looks and anxious inquiries from players and officials alike, the vice-captain came bounding back through the gate and rejoined the game, revealing little apart from an occasional wince. He exchanged a few words with his captain, refitted his gauntlets, and the match continued.

It was later revealed that an impatient bout of gastric trouble was the cause of the unscheduled break. Team officials who had settled in for a quiet hour or two of newspaper reading prior to lunch told of the white flash that burst through the viewing and changing areas and hurtled into a vacant toilet cubicle, almost taking the ancient wooden door from its hinges. Racked by violent spasms, with hands clamped to his thighs and legs extended parallel to the floor, Gilchrist was reduced to a hapless vessel through which the bug furiously churned. Worried support staff gathered outside the bathroom entrance, unsure whether to summon a doctor, a plumber or a priest. The accompanying soundtrack was said to resemble the Flying Scotsman rumbling through a lake.

When it had passed, Gilchrist gathered what was left of his decorum and jogged ruefully back to the middle. He tried to paraphrase the reason for his absence to his captain, who simply folded his arms across his chest and sniffed: 'Mate, I've been playing Test cricket for seventeen years, and that's the first time I've ever seen a game stopped for a bloke to take a shit.'

Despite Guyana's own Shivnarine Chanderpaul thrashing the third-fastest century in Test history, the West Indies were confirmed as a relic of former glories by losing comfortably at Bourda. Then, with Chanderpaul a mysterious late scratching from the next Test – according to 'sources' because the West Indies Cricket Board declined to pay for his wife to accompany him on the 500-kilometre trip to Trinidad – another defeat loomed large. The holders of the Frank Worrell Trophy were effectively assured of retaining their prize after scarcely a week's cricket.

'We need you to compile a list of all the cricket trophies Australia now holds, including the Worrell, which'll be in the bag by the time the story runs on Friday,' the new boss, stealthily known around the office as the 'Bi-polar Bear' due to unpredictable mood swings, cackled as play drew to a close on day four in Trinidad.

'All of them. The Ashes. The World Cup. The one-day series they play for here in Australia every summer. To show they've won pretty much everything on offer in world cricket, but they're still only ranked number two Test team in the world. We'll do it up as a graphic and run it on the front page. It'll be bloody funny, I reckon.'

Graphics had become the new obsession for an industry fast losing ground to more visually appealing media. Not only did funky fact boxes and detailed diagrams give newspapers more of a web-page feel, they gave in-house artists something to design other than cartoons. What this graphic did not immediately explain, to me anyway, was its relevance to what was going on in the Caribbean. Or why it needed to be compiled by the person geographically situated furthest from the office. From most offices, in fact. But embracing my new-found sycophancy, I wholeheartedly agreed it was a terrific idea, and set about assembling the data upon return to my room, with its views across the sprawling Queen's Park Savannah.

After trawling the records at my disposal, phoning the Australian Cricket Board for an inventory of its Jolimont trophy cabinets, and executing a final cross-check to eradicate the sorts of errors that creep in at 3 a.m., I shunted the material to Sydney and collapsed into bed. Shortly after losing consciousness, the phone rang. I knew immediately from the cold, measured tones that the Bear had more than a sore head.

'That list you've sent is rubbish,' I was icily informed.

Trying frantically to find my toadying in the darkness, I mixed endless apologies with promises to make good the shortcomings as soon as I could work out where I was. And what they were.

'I asked for a list of the trophies they hold,' the voice continued. 'All of them. You've given me the ten or so major ones. I could have done that myself, off the top of my head. What about the bloody Standard Cup, or whatever they won in South Africa a year ago? That's not there.'

My mind raced. Every trophy ever won, and retained, by the Australian cricket team was not so much a list as an anthology. I thought of the meaningless tournaments played in places far removed from public interest. In Hong Kong, Kenya and New Zealand. And I wondered who in their right mind would keep track of those forgettable series' eventual winner, let alone what they collected for doing so. Not even the players involved bothered remembering that level of detail. But this was my new age of unquestioning compliance, no matter how puerile the request.

'I'm really sorry,' I stammered, trying not to sound too much like the verbal version of what Gilchrist had suffered in Guyana. 'I thought you were after just the main ones. The perpetual trophies and the major Test series. Misunderstanding on my part. All my fault. I'll get on to it straight away, and you should have a full list in half an hour or so. What's it there now? Around 5 p.m.? That should give you plenty of time to get it in the paper.' Somewhere between Port-of-Spain and Surry Hills, my attempt to be obliging was translated into flippancy.

'Mate, you can stop being a smart arse,' I was told bluntly. 'I've asked you for a simple list, and you can't provide it. You just don't fuckin' get it, do you? If I want something done, I want it done properly. I don't make these requests for my own amusement. If you can't cut it, just let me know and I'll have no trouble finding someone who can.'

The phone clicked dead. As did another of my synapses that registered job satisfaction. I kicked the laptop back into life, hunted down as many of the omitted details as possible in the available time, and sent through a list so lengthy it would have required its own lift-out. I lay awake until sun-up, telling myself over and over this was, after all, the world's best job. By the time I left for the cricket ground, I almost believed it.

I arrived at Barbados Airport ahead of the third Test bearing all the fake bravado of a narcotics smuggler. In the absence of any formal notification that the earlier writ had been settled, my intention was to appear above suspicion by maintaining unrelenting eye contact with immigration officers. Unfortunately, this ploy caused the uniformed passport checker to visibly recoil in her seat, doubtless fearing I was bringing in some exotic strain of strabismus. The prospect of several weeks in the classic Caribbean – the swaying palms and bleached white sands of Barbados and Antigua, as opposed to the gang crime and ugly cityscapes of Guyana and Trinidad – had hauled me from my introspection. It should also have meant a corresponding lift in team morale but, instead, their funk seemed to deepen. Some players welcomed wives, children and parents to the wider touring party. Cricket Australia regularly shelled out for these sanctioned conjugal visits as part of their collective bargaining agreement with the cricketers. It was designed to ensure their relationships survived the long stints of enforced exile. Making the most of the similar compassionate breaks afforded long-absent journalists, I would illicitly squirrel away some of my tightly monitored expenses allowance to mail the occasional postcard home. But having the WAGs and their brood along also meant the playing group now split into two distinct groups – families enjoying a seaside holiday, and solitary men waiting around idly for the cricket to start.

Physical exhaustion was also draining spirits, especially among bowlers forced to labour on pitches so devoid of life that renown d deck-decoder Jason Gillespie noted they needed 'Viagra to get it up'. The ball, apparently. So Stephen Waugh decided to get publicly stuck into West Indies cricket officials for preparing such unresponsive surfaces, and then piled into the state of the game in the Caribbean in general, claiming his team's easy wins in the first three Tests felt disappointingly hollow due to the lack of fight from the other side. And everyone, friend and foe, had a crack at Brian Lara, who didn't even turn up to the ground for most of the third Test's third day, citing a mystery illness that happened to appear just hours after he'd been seen out on the town, celebrating his thirty-fourth birthday.

It seemed everywhere I turned, grumpiness radiated back. Desperate to sustain my own productivity, I threw myself into a punishing day-and-night work routine to prove, to whom I wasn't completely sure, that I was fully committed to the job. My respite came from the recuperative pleasures of Rockley Beach, where I would wade into the gently warmed soft-blue water until it wrapped around my shoulders like velvet. It had taken a full tour and a half, but I had finally found the Caribbean's magical appeal.

The only reason I was excited to leave Barbados was the news that, due to some sort of administrative oversight, I had been booked to travel the next leg, to Antigua, in business class. Adding to my sense of entitlement was the knowledge that there were not sufficient seats in the exalted section to accommodate the players and their assorted significant others. They were all to be herded into cattle class. So, although it was a flight of barely an hour, I revelled in the disdainful looks from the Australian players as they filed past me and through the curtain to their cheap seats on the other side. But we were no more than two minutes into our ascent when an opportunistic cricketer vaulted into the vacant berth next to me.

'Don't let them know I'm supposed to be sitting back there,' Brad Hogg whispered. 'And if the hosties ask, tell 'em I've been here right from the start.'

I suspected that even cabin crew on a notoriously inept Caribbean airline would eventually notice a seventeen per cent increase in the business-class passenger manifest. But until such time as that happened, I resigned myself to an hour of the sort of 'Hogg-isms' that kept his teammates endlessly amused and utterly perplexed.

Like the time the West Australian team bus skirted Royal Randwick racecourse en route to the Sydney Cricket Ground, and Hogg pondered aloud, 'Is that where they run the Melbourne Cup?' And the pit stop outside a diner on the verge of England's M1, during which Hogg dutifully ran around collecting all the rubbish lying on the floor of the team bus, before stuffing it into a garbage bin in the parking bay. The group was many kilometres down the motorway when it became clear one of the bags he had tossed contained a soiled Australian playing uniform from that day's game. He was even more crushed when he realised the lost laundry bag was his own.

However, there was something annoyingly endearing about the one-time postal deliveryman who grew up in wheat belt country around Narrogin, south of Perth. Sporting a haircut best described as military chic, and a boundless energy which matched his child-like curiosity, he was as harmless as he was guileless. What's more, Hogg was genuinely grateful for every opportunity that came his way, and never took for granted the fleeting fame of professional sport. Which is why he combined touring life with his ongoing attempts to complete a Bachelor of Business. As we began our descent into Antigua, conversation in row four had stalled and, instead, we both studied the in-flight monitors that showed 'Time to Destination: 0:22'. Hogg turned his attention from the screen to me and mused: 'So how long 'til we land?'

I looked at him, back to the television screen, then back at the cricketer, trying to figure if there was some prank I was missing.

'Umm, twenty-two minutes, I'd reckon,' I replied. 'Just going by the TV.' He chewed over this information and I waited for the gotcha moment.

'Yeah I know,' he said, mildly agitated. 'But don't forget we were late leaving Barbados.'

The harder I looked for the logic in his reasoning, the more disturbed I became. The rest of our journey passed in silence.

Come the final Test in Antigua, the irritation that had been brewing between the rival teams through the preceding month spilled into full, unedifying view. Lara became apoplectic when a couple of Australian fielders asked aloud if the drinks cart making its way towards the middle contained 'a couple of beers for Brian'. Glenn McGrath raised the temperature further when he engaged in a violent argument with opposing batsman Ramnaresh Sarwan, who the Australian had dissed, only to become incensed when the diminutive West Indian gave back even better than he got.

Then, with the West Indies closing in on a history-making victory, local hero Ridley Jacobs was wronged by an umpire, prompting the inevitable bottles, rubbish and hysterical abuse to rain down on the field, and on the touring press. Apparently, we needed to also cop our comeuppance for being arrogant, propaganda-peddling colonial apologists, and there was no shortage of angry people seated around our open-air press box to loudly make those points. It had taken until the Test series' penultimate day, but I was somewhat comforted to rediscover that old Caribbean bile, just as I had left it.

The unpleasantness that pervaded the Tests cooled like a Leeward Islands breeze the moment the seven-match limited-overs series rolled around. Mainly because, with the Test match specialists dispensed with, Australia's World Cup-winning one-day squad was able to reconvene its truncated celebrations. That priority was obvious from the morning we arrived at our hotel in Jamaica to start the coloured-clothing games.

Upon learning that our rooms would not be ready until at least mid-afternoon, several members of the press contingent sulked off to the poolside café to find out if the kitchen might be operational at such an impertinent hour. We were greeted by a pair of chirpy Australian fast bowlers perched atop towering stools at the bar, their disposition transformed by the contents of enormous cocktail glasses that wore garnish like a Carmen Miranda headdress.

'Pina colada,' one of them announced, nodding at the glasses before them, and taking a long drag on a straw poking from the undergrowth.

'Half price before noon,' the other added, drawing a huge grin from the under-employed barman. The fact that even the journalists agreed it was a bit too early in the day to hit the sauce confirmed that the mood among the playing group was quickly shifting from pissed off to simply pissed. After more than nine months on the road, the cricketers clearly believed it was time to retire to the bar.

The fact that the Australians won the first four one-day matches to add another anonymous trophy to that never-published list was as much a testament to their ability to switch on when required as it was an indictment of their opposition. The West Indian team that had been exposed as a divided, uninterested rabble in the Tests was even less engaged in the shorter form. And nobody better characterised that indifference than their skipper.

Preparing to depart the verdant, volcanic island of St Lucia for Trinidad after the third one-dayer, our plane, with its load of restless passengers, sat motionless on the tarmac for more than fifteen minutes awaiting the arrival of a last, tardy traveller. Brian Lara finally appeared, swaggering towards the rear in search of his seat. He was conspicuous, not so much by his belated entrance, but by his attire. Not for him the grey, green and maroon polo shirt and smart business trousers of his teammates, who had skipped town on an earlier flight. Lara was decked out in a white sleeveless T-shirt, boldly displaying the leopard's head tattoo on his right bicep, frayed jeans, black leather shoes, oversized sunglasses fixed firmly in place, and a thick gold chain around his neck. He looked like he might have walked straight out of a nightclub. Which he had. He stopped in the aisle immediately between my seat, and a pair of giggling young ladies. He smiled at them, looked at me, and zeroed in on the spare seat to my left.

'How you doin'?' he greeted me, while stuffing his shoulder satchel into the locker above my head.

'Hey, you mind movin' over so I can sit where you are?' I knew it wasn't my company he sought, so I happily agreed and we strapped ourselves in. 'That's good of you, man,' he said. 'By the way, I been meanin' to ask you for a while. How you enjoyin' this trip to de Wess Indies? It's been a long time on the road for your guys.'

Our conversation continued until we touched down in Port-of-Spain, albeit with regular interruptions as he flirted across the aisle. Our discussion was largely driven by Lara, who was suspiciously happy to voice opinions on any number of subjects. They included a brutal assessment of some of his teammates ('I mean, Marlon Samuels. Wass he ever achieved to be walkin' round so cool? I say to him, "Try losin' the shades and makin' some runs"'). His passion for Trinidad's Rio-style pre-Lent mardi gras ('I don't care what the cricket schedule says, I got to be at home for Carnival'), to the stewardess from whom he ordered a couple of cans of local Trinidadian beer ('How old you reckon she is? I knew her when she was in her early twenties, if you know what I mean. And she's not lookin' any older now').

Lara nudged me in the ribs as she returned with his drinks, and he whispered something to her that rendered her wide-eyed as he handed over a fistful of faded red Trinidadian dollars. He then offered one of the beers to me.

'For you, man. Tanks for givin' up your seat. And welcome to Chrinidad,' he said, as the crack and hiss of freshly opened cans drew disapproving looks from all but the girls. As we sipped, Lara became increasingly philosophical.

'You know why I don't really trust journalists?' he asked rhetorically. ''Cos you guys always lookin' to dish some dirt. I don't mind bein' criticised for my cricket. Thass my job. But all the other stuff, the private stuff. Thass nobody's business but mine. I know what some of you media guys been getting' up to when you come to the Caribbean. And when you're on tour in other places. Why don't we read about that in the newspapers?'

I told him I agreed that the off-field proclivities he, and other cricketers, engaged in should ideally be overlooked by the press, as long as they didn't impact on players' ability to play cricket. For example, provided a birthday bash didn't stop a Test captain from turning up at the ground next day. And that he was absolutely right in suggesting media folk had no business in sanctimoniously imposing their convenient morality on how he, or others, chose to live. But I also pointed out, as diplomatically as possible given the circumstances, that he couldn't realistically expect the adulation and intrigue to switch off the moment he walked from the field.

After all, cricket afforded him a few privileges for which his adoring public forked out. The plot of land overlooking the Savannah, gifted to him by the Trinidad and Tobago Government for setting a couple of batting records in 1994, and on which his palatial home was built. Free travel on the national airline. The right to drive his luxury car in Port-of-Spain's highway lanes otherwise reserved for VIP vehicles. Receipt of his nation's highest honour, the Trinity Cross. By contrast, I ventured, journalists were just spectators with better seats. Witnesses to the news, but never accessories. The day that 30,000 people paid money to watch me type was the day I could expect public scrutiny of my private life. Which should allow me plenty of time to develop one. He mulled this over. Or possibly, behind his Stevie Wonder glasses, he had nodded off. Either way, I seized on the silence to pose one question before we hit the ground.

'So why are people here so uptight?' I asked, at which point he repositioned his glasses atop his head, revealing badly bloodshot eyes. 'Everywhere we go, people are cussing or harrumphing. Hotel staff are surly. Cab drivers always moaning. And at the cricket, as soon as things don't go their way, they start chucking stuff on to the field.'

The spirited defence I expected from the captain of the region's only unified entity didn't materialise. Instead, Lara tilted his head to one side and spoke more quietly and carefully than at any time during the trip.

'You know, thass because it means so much to them,' he said, leaning forward lest anyone overhear, his beer breath jolting me back in my seat.

'Cricket gives the West Indies its pride. When we were the best in the world, that gave West Indians something to hang on to. They can see that slippin' away. And I guess they see you, as an Australian journalist, as part of the group thass takin' from them something they really treasured. I would say, don't take it personally.' He sat back, reaffixed the shades and rested his index fingers either side of his chin.

'You want to see the real Caribbean?' he said, snapping back into character. 'I'm havin' a big party up at my house tomorrow night. Some of your guys comin' along. You know, Michael Clarke. Brett Lee. You should come too. I'll get an invitation to your hotel. You staying at the Hilton, right?'

Lara's parties ran a close second to Carnival as Trinidad's most famous tributes to hedonism. I tried to visualise the look on the cricketers' faces as I wandered through the heavy front door, and told him I would be delighted to come along, provided he cleared it with the other players first. The invitation I never expected never arrived. And the party, if it happened, wasn't mentioned by any of the Australians, or by its host.

By contrast, the bash to celebrate the World Cup win, the dual series' triumphs over the West Indies, and an imminent three-month break in the playing schedule was becoming increasingly public. Some of the Australian players had fallen so heavily off the wagon they were in danger of disappearing under the wheels. Leading into the final weekend of one-dayers on the Spice Island of Grenada, the tourists loitered aimlessly around the beachfront resort in search of ways to fill in their time. Training held no interest, especially after thieves posing as Trinidad baggage wranglers made off with a host of items including bats, shoes and sunglasses. Instead, the poolside bar offered much greater appeal.

The press watched the last few days unravel from what we thought was a safe distance. That was until, early one evening, a seriously inebriated Andrew Symonds stumbled towards the table where four of us sat, enjoying a quiet, non-intrusive dinner. Having lurched back from a toilet visit, Symonds was unable to locate the polystyrene holder he was using to prevent his beer getting warm. He walked directly to me, give or take a few lateral deviations, pointed a menacing finger, and snarled: 'Have you stolen my stubbie holder?'

Sensing this situation was potentially far more dangerous than its comic veneer suggested, I resisted the urge to laugh. And assured him I had not.

'Well someone has and I reckon it was you,' he continued, eyes glazed and body coursing with malice. 'If I find out that you did, and you've fuckin' lied to me, you're going in the pool. Remember that.' He stood there breathing heavily. And swaying.

Aware of the confrontation, one of his teammates shouted from the bar: 'Calm down, Roy. It's over here. Ya dropped it on your way to the dunny.' As he weighed up this development, we summoned the bill and then retreated to the safety of our rooms.

Even less impressed by the schoolies-style muck-up mentality that had taken hold was Australia's coach, John Buchanan. He racked his professorial brain to devise methods by which motivation could be recaptured and sustained for the final weekend. He devised a day of 'beach Olympics' that included clichéd bonding rituals, such as raft building and volleyball. He went so far as to factor in a journalists' team that would pit itself against the players and support staff. Standing on the other side of the net to a marauding Andrew Symonds did not strike me as a sensible use of my time, and I politely declined. That lack of interest was echoed by a majority of the touring party, cricketers included, and the idea was canned within a day of being floated.

So Buchanan suggested a more analytical exercise, and invited the media corps to make a formal presentation at the final team meeting where we would give frank assessments on where things had succeeded or failed during the nine-week campaign. He even urged us to make it a multimedia show, blissfully unaware that journalists are as familiar with complex computing tools such as PowerPoint and spreadsheets as they are with the phrase 'I honestly have no opinion on ...'

Our media posse convened and agreed that there was nothing to gain, and much to lose, from such an exercise. Penning a daily critique of performances in a newspaper was one thing. Standing out front of the Australian team and suggesting to Ricky Ponting that he should not reach so hard for the ball early in his innings, or that Ian Harvey should find somewhere more private than a pool deck sun lounge to sleep off a big night was tantamount to professional suicide. We voted unanimously to give it a miss and the decision was relayed to Buchanan, who was clearly surprised.

'We're all in this, you know,' he said, showing the hurt of a job applicant being punted after the first interview. 'You guys are part of the touring party, and at times like this we all need to pull together.'

'That's the misconception, right there,' I pointed out, stopping him short. 'We're not part of the touring party. We travel together, we stay at the same places, we share a nationality. But there's a line of objectivity that has to separate us. If we cross that, we're nothing more than a paid cheer squad. And the brutal truth is, it's neither here nor there to any of us journalists whether you guys win or lose. Dealing with all of you is obviously easier when you win. But to be honest, it makes for much sexier newspaper copy when you don't. And when it comes down to it, we only ever barrack for the story.'

The coach shook his head in bewilderment, but resignedly opted not to pursue it further. He walked away looking as defeated as his team, which crashed to predictable losses in each of the last three games.

The mood at Grenada's Maurice Bishop Airport, as we prepared to head home, was more upbeat than at any stage over the preceding two months. That lasted until we all gathered at the tarmac's edge, excitedly clutching boarding passes, as our twin-engine plane warmed up. Then, from the head of the line, former Test batsman turned television commentator David Hookes swivelled to face the queue that snaked behind him through the terminal, and gave us a soul-destroying double thumbs-down signal.

'Not going anywhere,' he shouted above the roar. 'Fuel pissing out the front of an engine.' He then descended into crazed laughter that wasn't contagious.

For seven hours, we all sat slumped in the terminal while a replacement plane was summoned from the United States. Those who weren't prepared to prop at the bar either tried to sleep in hard-backed plastic chairs purpose-moulded for eight-year-olds, watched evangelical daytime TV programs, kicked a tennis ball around the corridors, or returned time and again to the three duty-free shops to mull over whether they needed another souvenir T-shirt or bottle of rum punch. Or, for most of the time, stared utterly miserable through the windows, across the shimmering runway.

The delay meant no hope of meeting our respective connections in Miami. Instead, we were shunted into an overnight stay in Puerto Rico while alternative arrangements were hastily made. Soon after arriving, the press corps set out on a fact-finding mission to unearth dinner, but as we passed by a small first-floor bar in our transit hotel, we were met by a beaming Darren Lehmann who insisted we join the small group of players who had opted for European beer and Cuban cigars to see them through to our pre-dawn departure. It was, he pointed out, a fitting end to a nine-month expedition that had gone awry at pretty much every turn.

'After all,' he hooted, extending both arms as if to welcome San Juan to the fold of dubious cricket venues visited along the way, 'we're all in this together.'

14

Tri-nations Tournament, India,
October–November 2003

The dead of night doesn't exist in India. No matter the hour you cruise its highways, streets and alleys, a constant parade of souls is on the move. Sepia versions of the dazzling colours that spill from the palette of daily Indian life. Bathed in the soft glow of sodium vapour lights, or rendered ghostly pale by the harsh glare of headlamps from trucks and buses that rumble unrelenting through the night. From wherever they emerge, bound for whatever destination calls them at such unsociable hours, these apparitions shuffle noiselessly among the carpet of sleeping bodies that stretch, like victims of some unseen cataclysm, along roadsides, through railway stations and across public parks.

It was this armada of the sleepless, more so than the suffocating midnight heat, that was my overwhelming first impression of India upon finally emerging from New Delhi's international airport. The frenetic crush of travel touts and cab drivers that encircled the exit forced me into a hasty retreat to the terminal's pre-paid taxi counter in the naive hope that being allocated a cab might reduce the harassment awaiting me on the outside. The month-long limited-overs tournament I had been despatched to cover might have been deemed so peripheral by Australian cricket that none of its top-line bowlers had bothered to make the trip. But there was no such diminution of interest among Indians. For cricket, or for a cab fare.

Unlike previous assignments, my maiden visit to the subcontinent was preceded by a detailed briefing from my superiors. Unfortunately, it didn't extend to useful details about living, working or moving about one of the world's more demanding and confronting environments. Rather, it dealt exclusively and pointedly with the flashpoint issue of reporters taking advantage of the company's apparent benevolence upon returning from lengthy stints on the road. It signalled the start of a crackdown on leave days that employees were granted in lieu of paid overtime when working erratic shifts. Management suspected the paper was being shortchanged because staff were claiming to have worked longer hours than was believable. Or certainly affordable.

It was explained to me, during a lengthy homily from the paper's principal bean counter, that cricket tours were widely known to be little more than extended vacations. According to someone who had never undertaken one, they basically consisted of occasional stints in luxurious air-conditioned press boxes eating laid-on gourmet grub, interspersed with lots of lazing around costly five-star hotel pools.

'Let's face it, on the days they're not playing cricket, you're only writing a few hundred words about hamstring injuries,' was the derisive summary from the penny pincher who held open contempt for sports assignments, which apparently sucked a disproportionate sum from the editorial budget.

I couldn't quite reconcile why the newspaper would make a commercial decision to enhance its cricket coverage by having a cricket writer accompany the cricket team on cricket tours, then bitch endlessly about how much it was costing. It was rather like firing a bullet into your own foot, then screaming for tighter gun control. But it was made abundantly clear that should I return from India clutching a belief that I was owed two days off for each full week spent on the road, as per standard working arrangements in most OECD countries, I was to think again.

'What you have to do is tote up the hours you spend *actually* working, and then we'll calculate how much lieu time you're entitled to,' I was instructed.

'So, does the term "actually working" cover time spent, say, in transit?' I asked, trying to strike a balance between militant and moronic. 'For example, do I record the fourteen-hour flight from Melbourne to Delhi as a day's work? Or in terms of a normal working day, would that be considered as two?' I continued, genuinely perplexed by the novel formula.

'Well, I think we'd see that as being worth probably half a day's work,' came the reply.

Even though I had comprehensively failed senior school physics, I vaguely recalled that black holes were the only known field into which time could irretrievably vanish. I was surprised to learn overseas reporting assignments were another.

'So, fourteen hours of travelling equates to roughly four hours of work?' I hesitated, hoping to convey the impression that it was me, rather than the person on the far end of the phone, who was barking mad.

'Well you're not really producing anything for the paper while you're sitting in a plane,' I was told. 'As far as the company's concerned, it's not exactly productive time. I mean, you can't claim the time you spend commuting from home to the office as working hours.'

I contemplated this logic and wondered if Brad Hogg had been appointed to the executive staff without my knowledge.

'But if I worked in New Delhi, I probably wouldn't choose to commute from Melbourne,' I countered meekly, before I gave up and hung up.

So just months after eventually returning to my life at home I headed to India unsure of what to expect, other than oppressive heat, crushing humanity, imminent illness, testing work conditions, crippling bureaucracy and, apparently, a need to compile a detailed time and motion dossier. I also felt strangely liberated by the knowledge that I had been informally sanctioned to devote any free time that arose to indulging my own interests. Provided no company funds or minutes were involved.

Having been warned that patience is invariably the first casualty of any Indian sojourn, I wasn't the least fazed when my suitcase failed to negotiate the Singapore stopover. This was, certainly for me, familiar territory, and I bounded up to the lost luggage desk with a chirpiness rarely seen by baggage services staff.

'No need for the identification chart,' I smiled, as the clerk dragged out a limp pad of carbon-impregnated incident reports and rummaged through a torn manila folder lifted from a middle drawer. 'I've done this a couple of times before. It's a number twenty-two, in brown. With wheels and a retractable handle.'

The woman smiled, obviously impressed that I was fluent in her lingo. That kinship did not translate into a more expeditious processing of my claim form, however, which was completed, authorised, stamped, walked across to the transport police desk, reauthorised, returned to baggage services, restamped, and then filed in a leather-bound ledger.

'We will call you at hotel when your bag arrives,' the supervisor announced, her pledge sealed with a brief head wobble. I cheerily asked when that might be.

'Maybe tonight. But probably not.' Another less authoritative wobble.

As I began my billable hours early next morning, a mandatory check with the Australian team's touring media manager revealed that while there had been no torn hamstrings during the night, a number of the players shared my lack of fresh clothes. Minutes later, there was a knock at my door.

'Thought this might come in handy,' the media man said, handing me a team-issue, navy-blue polo shirt strewn with sponsors' decals and still wrapped in its protective plastic sleeve.

'So you can blend in with the rest of the lost luggage brigade,' he added. 'Sorry that Cricket Australia doesn't do an underwear range.'

I thanked him sincerely for his thoughtfulness, and inquired whether his professional expertise had already been enlisted by the notoriously demanding and insistent Indian media.

'Had quite a few calls when we arrived, then they started again before dawn this morning,' he said, jadedly. 'But the biggest problem's going to be autograph hunters. Some players said there were people knocking on their doors during the night, and I've even had a couple myself. They don't want to accept that I'm not a player, no matter how rude I eventually get.'

When a call came shortly after lunch, alerting me to my suitcase's arrival, I swept through the lavish foyer, feeling both conspicuous and fraudulent in my team top. The face of the wiry young man who stood watch over my twenty-two brown with wheels and retractable handle lit up as I approached. He could not hide his excitement at meeting someone who, from waist to neck at least, was an Australian cricketer.

'Please sir, you will sign,' he beamed, as he thrust a slip of paper and a pen at me.

'No, no,' I smiled, waving away the writing material and reaching for the retractable bit. 'I'm not a cricket player.'

'Please sir. You sign for me,' he repeated, with greater urgency. It was met with a firmer rebuff, as I once more tried to reclaim my case.

His demeanour then shifted, as did his lean frame which he positioned between me and my belongings. His beaming smile was quickly disappearing.

'Sir, you must sign,' he growled, wrapping his sinewy fingers tightly around the bag's handle. 'This is release form, and I cannot give you the luggage until you have.'

I returned to my room, unpacked the case and shoved the gratis shirt in the bottom where I pledged it would remain, undisturbed, for the tour's remainder.

The political machinations that drive Indian cricket often carry more intrigue than the games its officials administer. While Test matches tended to stay anchored in cities with modern facilities, one-day internationals were doled out like sweets to compliant children in order to secure the votes of regional cricket officials around India's tempestuous board table. Which explained why Australia's opening game of the 2003 TVS Cup triangular tournament was scheduled for a transformed hockey stadium in the northern fort city of Gwalior. A regional centre located between the world's most famous monument to love in Agra and the site of the world's worst industrial catastrophe in Bhopal.

It was also, I learned as I checked into the charmlessly rustic Sita Manor Hotel in what could be most generously described as the unpretentious quarter of town, timed to coincide with the nation's annual Diwali celebrations. The hotel's austere lobby had been further stripped back to make space on its buffed floor for a mosaic of marigolds depicting the sun, with the path to the check-in desk bordered by tiny terracotta oil lamps. The Hindu Festival of Lights, due to reach its climax on the evening before the sold-out match, coupled with the arrival in town of India's living deity, Sachin Tendulkar, had excitement in the former Mughal stronghold near boiling point.

The bus carrying Australia's cricketers arrived at the much more salubrious hotel they shared with the Indian team, just metres from the Captain Roop Singh Stadium, and instantly triggered a surge from the hundreds of locals who had waited in the baking sun for a glimpse of anyone legitimately famous. To the shock of the tourists peering out through tinted windows as the bus came to a stop, the surging mob was at once set upon by dozens of khaki-clad police officers who laid into the defenceless crowd with their *lathis* (heavy bamboo canes). The Australians then filed out of the bus and skirted around the portable metal detector that sat half-erected and inoperable in the hotel doorway, avoiding all direct contact with the throng, which continued to press forward, lest that should incite them further and result in another bashing. The combined detail of police, private security guards and armed services personnel that camped in the hotel lobby, as well as the permanent crowd of onlookers beyond it, meant players from both sides again faced virtual incarceration.

No such encumbrances existed for the media pack, as the impending festival meant we had become almost invisible to staff at our hotel. Especially when it came to the provision of luxuries such as the advertised business facilities, meals and reliable electricity supply. Eventually, I decided the best chance of solving most of these dilemmas was to flag down one of the noisy rickshaws that sputtered remorselessly along Gandhi Road, just outside our front door, and use the cricket ground's amenities. That plan came unstuck when I arrived at Roop Singh to find organisation in its press box was marginally inferior to that at Sita Manor.

I abandoned all hope of working from the ground when I attempted to set up camp on the concrete desk space I had allocated myself and found I was being assisted by a solitary worker, part of the platoon of men that swarmed through the empty grandstands attentively doing what appeared, to my untrained eye, to be bugger-all. My helper, wearing nothing more than a knee-length *dhoti* tied around his waist, a white singlet and a pair of needle-nosed pliers, then set about twitching strands of live electrical wires plucked from the row of benches in front of me. All the time he did so, he stood bare-footed in a puddle, several millimetres deep, of what had once been water. I frantically communicated, through the international languages of sign and panic, that this task could wait until match day. I did not share the view that filing stories for the sports section of a daily newspaper was a life and death vocation.

Come Diwali Saturday, the Australians trained early to avoid the worst of the sapping Madhya Pradesh heat. Once that was done, and in line with office instructions to clearly delineate work time from my time, I opted for the first available train to Agra, 120 kilometres up the line, to explore the Taj Mahal. While the process of buying a ticket required even more carbon paper, rubber stamping and head wobbling than the lost suitcase episode, it did not include helpful advice on where to position myself along the expanse of Platform 3 in order to readily find my reserved seat when the half-kilometre-long Lashkar Express groaned into Gwalior station.

As I scoured the twenty-five or more faded blue-and-white carriages for any identifiable markings that matched the details on my cloth-eared ticket, I was engulfed by a stampede of desperate travellers trying to climb aboard, by even more frantic passengers attempting to get off, and by a swarm of children with trays balanced atop their heads selling nuts, *chai*, fruit and sweets to those who remained aboard the train, able to do little else other than wave money through the metal grilles that doubled as windows.

I reasoned that by the time I deciphered which of the identical cars contained my seat, the service was likely to have chugged through Agra and be rattling its way to Delhi. So I adopted local custom, dropped my left shoulder, and barrelled through the nearest doorway as if locking down for a rugby scrum. It was difficult to tell who was more taken aback by what confronted them as the train eased out, having never really come to a complete stop. Me or my new companions.

Like most trapped in India's feudal caste system, I had ended up several classes below where I hoped to be. My ticket showed 'Air-Conditioned Chair Car'. My surroundings revealed just one of those three, and even then it was a 'car' in name alone. Its wooden bench seats were overstocked with the elderly and the very young. The more able-bodied lent against the dusty steel walls or sat squeezed into every available space on the filthy metal floor. The heat was brutal. The smell of slowly braising humanity even worse. There was more than a hundred people crammed into this fusty capsule, and every one of them had their eyes locked on the disoriented Western blow-in.

My decision to push through towards the next carriage was motivated more by need to find an air pocket than air conditioning. But all ventilation holes, as well as the gaping doorways between carriages, were occupied by startled families and groups of men whose faces depicted a mix of astonishment and dread, as if I was about to vomit on them. That may have happened had I not found a small bolthole among three men who stood sharing a bag of peanuts. They stared and crunched as I lolled against a wall, trying hopelessly to look blasé. After fifteen minutes holding that pose, I was compelled to keep walking when a young man with horrifically deformed legs and wielding a small straw broom pushed his way into our shared space and began sweeping discarded peanut husks into a hessian bag. As he did so, the litterers took it in turns to gleefully pelt him with pieces of shells and shards of nut. As much as I felt the urge to intervene on the untouchable's behalf, I sensed my involvement in a social structure I did not understand could only further lower his rock-bottom stocks. So I pushed deeper into the unknown.

Eventually, I reached a second-class sleeper cabin that provided no onward passage. As I inched my way past families huddled together on thin vinyl mattresses, I was approached by a boy aged no more than ten. He gently grabbed my wrist and alerted me to a vacant top bunk wedged against the carriage's rear wall, and not a metre below its ceiling. Soon, everyone in the vicinity was excitedly pointing to the nook and gesturing that it was mine. So, as the families below hurriedly rearranged their belongings and I succumbed to peering pressure, I slipped my right foot into a metal stirrup protruding from the bunk's nearest leg and swung myself belly first into the gap. The elegance of the manoeuvre, rather like a small plane touching down without functional landing gear, was compromised when I cracked my skull on an ancient metal fan welded to the bed head. I lay pinned in this position, attracting delighted crowds like I was a furry new zoo attraction, for almost an hour. I declined their kind offers of food and drink, not out of ingratitude, but because I could not figure a way, in my contorted state, of wriggling my hands close enough to my mouth to take on sustenance. But the warmth of their welcome and the overwhelming generosity of their spirit were obvious, even from my unnatural angle. I was tempted to continue the journey to Delhi with them until, upon nearing my destination, a group of them clambered up to extricate me and then gathered to bid me farewell, as if I was a treasured uncle.

Agra's Cantonment Station was even more overwhelming than sub-economy train travel. The tourist centre's touts are renowned as the most persistent in India. Which is a bit like being voted crankiest in the Caribbean. I had steeled myself to resist all offers of guided tours, a resolve that lasted all of three minutes when I tired of being chased, cornered and harangued like a teen heartthrob at a high school. A young man in jeans and a red T-shirt pushed to the front of the pack and got himself employed with his novel pitch: 'You know, the best way to get rid of all these pests is to hire one of us.'

I climbed into the back of his motorised rickshaw and we bounced off through Kaserat Bazaar's maze of streets, lined with souvenir stalls and artisans' workshops. Having travelled as deep into the tourism precinct as traffic was allowed, he deposited me a couple of blocks from the Taj Mahal ticket office and smiled conspiratorially when I asked how he could be found when I was ready to leave.

'Don't worry, I'll find you,' he smirked.

Once I ascertained that the entrance fee for tourists, including Agra Development Authority toll tax and Archeological Society of India levy, was roughly forty times that imposed on locals, and that my mobile phone had to be surrendered to an overweight *wallah* for apparent fear its ringing might disturb the serenity created by thousands of clicking cameras, I paused to consider which of the many dedicated entrance gates was set aside for befuddled Australians. That was when I felt a hefty nudge at my right hip. Expecting to find a clumsy pickpocket, I was instead confronted by the enormous face of an off-white Brahmin cow that poked its shiny black nose into my side. Before I had a chance to be properly startled, it nuzzled its snout in underneath my ribcage, and then effortlessly flicked its great head upwards. In the process, it took both my legs from under me and launched me briefly into the air, before I crashed down, right shoulder first, on to the dirt road.

As the dust cleared and I realised nothing other than my credibility had been damaged, I looked up to see my sacred attacker ambling towards a queue of several dozen local women, all clad in saris of varying hues and brightness, who found the whole performance side-splittingly funny. I couldn't help but laugh along with them, exhorting them to even greater hysterics. Even with my impostor's shirt safely stowed away, being the centre of attention everywhere I went was making me feel something like a cricketer.

It wasn't my Agra experience that left me decidedly fragile when I took my place in the freshly wired press box next afternoon. It had emerged during the night that my room at Sita Manor overlooked Gwalior's most popular Diwali cracker culvert, a concrete-lined laneway that amplified the rat-tat-tat-tat of penny bungers and tom thumbs to a level resembling a Baghdad shoot-out. And any thoughts that a few reflective hours at the cricket might help allay my shellshock were shelved the instant I set foot in the heaving, hysterical stadium.

The excitement that had rapidly built from the time the Australians' bus provoked a near insurrection at their hotel reached an ear-splitting crescendo when opening bowler Nathan Bracken let go the first delivery at India's Virender Sehwag. It scarcely dimmed two balls later when Sehwag was caught at slip, and then rose again to fever pitch when Australia's other new ball rookie, Brad Williams, began his spell to Tendulkar. This was unlike any comparable crowd noise I had experienced. Not the Melbourne Cricket Ground at opening bounce of an AFL grand final. Not the home straight at Flemington as the Melbourne Cup runners flashed to the finish post. Not even tour guides bellowing for business at Agra Station.

All those upswells at least contained definable beginnings and ends. They ebbed, in order to flow. In India, especially when Tendulkar is batting, there is a constant, unrelenting barrage of hollering. It's as if, by some remarkable act of orchestration, a Mexican wave of screaming has been devised. That when one over-hyped fan needs to stop shouting to suck in a lungful, the person next in line seamlessly fills the acoustic void. Delicate Australian reporters used to putting our heads down and typing in the regular quiet spells between incidents were left exhausted by the time the first drinks break was taken. The non-stop hysteria obscured the normal rhythms of the game. It was like trying to concentrate on a movie while wearing headphones that piped nothing but raucous white noise. And it only subsided below hair-pulling level after two and a half hours, when Tendulkar was finally dismissed for an even hundred. Had he carried his bat, I would have needed to be carried out.

It's difficult to comprehend the level of personal adulation Tendulkar is afforded among Indians until witnessed first-hand. Hundreds of millions compulsively follow the cricket, not to cheer the Indian team and hope their hero does well in the process. They focus exclusively on Sachin, and unashamedly expect his teammates not to hog his stage. During the Test matches against New Zealand that immediately preceded the TVS Cup, fans at the game in Mohali held up placards calling for V.V.S. Laxman to hurry up and reach his fighting rearguard century so he could immediately surrender his wicket and ensure India was forced to follow-on, and they could see Tendulkar bat in the second innings. When their wish was granted, and the Little Master was bowled for one, they packed up and left.

There was no such disenchantment in Gwalior, where Tendulkar crowned the Diwali celebrations and the crowd lingered to savour his team's victory. The garrison of security personnel deployed to ensure no fireworks were smuggled into the ground stood by impassively as spectators observed the Festival of Lights with cardboard placards helpfully handed out to wave in celebration of boundaries struck or wickets captured. As night fell, these were rolled into conical torches, held aloft and set ablaze. Shrouded by the miasma of smoke that settled on the breathless evening, and with hundreds of spectral fires glowing orange around the concrete terraces, the match took on the eerie feel of a pagan ritual.

A similar state of exultation had taken root in the press box. Initially, I attributed it to the elation that loitered in the wake of Tendulkar's century. But casting around, I realised the delirium was likely caused by more than 150 bodies that had incrementally squeezed into an enclosure designed to comfortably fit no more than fifty. Most of them appeared, by my newspaper's definition at least, to be non-working journalists. Indeed, some of them were barely functioning people. They stood, blocking the walkways, or perched on scarce desk space, intent only on attracting the attention of folks elsewhere in the crowd who needed to be impressed, or of harried staff enlisted to dispense occasional drinks and snacks to accredited reporters.

Shortly after the change of innings, a sweaty, seemingly mute young man pulled up a plastic stool to the spare corner of my allocated work space. He ignored my greeting and my mordant inquiry as to whether he had sufficient room. He was clearly not packing any of the usual tools of my trade – laptop, notebook, pen, weary cynicism. His only outward signs of animation came whenever a steward approached bearing food or drinks, and then he transformed into a frenzy of movement.

He grazed his way through pakoras, biscuits, two cups of sweet tea, a serving of dhal and a banana, and then snared a bottle of room-temperature cola from a distracted waiter, only to discover its crown seal firmly intact. He then attempted to prise the cap loose by clenching it between his upper and lower molars and biting down as he lifted the bottle haltingly towards horizontal. I shielded my eyes and flinched until I heard a horrible cracking and splintering, at which point he began furiously spitting what I expected to be chunks of enamel and bloodied gum onto my desk. Summoning the courage to look, I found he had, instead, coughed out the bottle top as well as half a dozen chunks of glass from the vessel's shattered neck.

'Where are you from?' I asked, unable to contain my curiosity.

'Agra,' he replied, positioning the soft-drink bottle carefully so he could swig with minimal risk of further facial disfiguration.

'Are you a journalist?' I continued, wildly hoping I might shame him into sitting under someone else's armpit.

'Rickshaw driver,' he said, only shifting his eyes from the game to swipe a passing wedge of cake. Then he belched softly.

I found it hard to imagine the cult of Sachin Tendulkar could boast a more fanatical chapter than Gwalior's until we reached the site of the next match against India – his hometown, known to the world as Bombay when he was born in 1973. The sound that shook an over-stocked Wankhede Stadium when Tendulkar emerged to begin his team's innings was more frightening than pulsating. It carried the ungodly roar of a tropical cyclone. It seemed simply too big for the concrete and steel grandstands battling to contain it. It rattled the press box's grotty windows and left the unprepared visiting media feeling they sat next to a jet engine that had suddenly blasted into life. The deafeningly guttural chant of 'su-chiiin … SAH-CHIN' that somehow rose above the background racket continued long after his stumps were rattled by Michael Clarke's gentle left-arm spin, having scored sixty-eight.

Away from the ground, Sachin was impossible to escape. He gazed out from billboards. Smiled his way through merry television commercials. Beamed in newspaper display advertisements, and looked decidedly less comfortable in magazine paparazzi snaps. For someone who reputedly treasured whatever snatches of privacy he could steal, it seemed incongruous that he should lend his name and face to the marketing of motor scooters, soft drinks, English football, health drinks, sporting goods, mobile telephones, and even his own eponymous chain of restaurants. Although his genius was being hailed across India before he turned sixteen, when he figured in an unbeaten partnership of 664 during a major inter-school competition, it was unclear whether Tendulkar's decision to cash in on his divine status was a pragmatic acceptance of a life already severely compromised by his popularity, or whether the promotional campaigns had actively fuelled the worship.

While Tendulkar's cricket achievements since adolescence confirm that, unlike so many modern celebrities, he indeed possesses an extraordinary talent, what remains even more revelatory is the context in which that success has been earned. No other global superstar haunting any corridor of fame can claim to have triumphed so regularly, so completely, under such a crippling weight of expectation, over such an extended length of time. Apart from a tax irregularity relating to the importation of a gleaming red Ferrari bequeathed to him by Fiat when he equalled Bradman's record of twenty-nine Test centuries in 2002, and a couple of frustrated on-field outbursts, Tendulkar's image remains one of an exemplary citizen. No drunken scandals. No extracurricular stupidity. Every over-indulged footballer or hedonistic movie star should make a couple of twenty-two-yard dashes in Sachin's shoes before wailing about how the pressures of adulation or the trappings of eminence led them astray. It's in more fields than cricket that Tendulkar can be venerated as a paragon of the possible.

Perhaps the other reason for Tendulkar's omnipresence in the Indian media is to reassure the nation's billion-plus population that he remains alive and well. Cricket duties and advertisements aside, he is rarely sighted outside his home or hotel room. A visit to the shops or a dash to the reception desk would unleash pandemonium, so he remains holed-up. Throughout our month in India, the Australian players were similarly reluctant to brave the crowds that lurked beyond the security cordons. Unless there was a chance to make money.

The rewards for flogging merchandise in a nation where access to running water is often a secondary priority to cable television had become well known to Australia's cricketers. Or certainly to their agents, as a routine flick through India's seventy-five-plus TV channels revealed. There was Ricky Ponting, dressed in his yellow limited-overs clobber, hamming alongside a Bollywood-style support cast to peddle a brand of electrical goods. In another ad, he lent his name to a company that produces Scotch whisky.

Stephen Waugh's visage was used by a multinational insurance firm, as well as his Indian-based bat maker that was also the biggest tyre manufacturer in a nation with more than a hundred million registered vehicles. Brett Lee was the face of a range of upmarket watches. Late in the series, Adam Gilchrist devoted a long day in Kolkata to shooting a commercial for a brand of motor oil. And throughout the tour, Matthew Hayden and Michael Bevan acted as ambassadors for a mass-marketed Australian beer that was desperate to secure a foothold among savvy Indian swillers. It was the same product whose Colombo bash had been so unceremoniously curtailed by Bevan's tantrum, suggesting the purveyors, if not the beverage itself, carried no residual bitterness.

Increasingly, cricketers who continued to lament the privations of touring life on the subcontinent, and the lack of free time in their schedules, held no qualms about jetting off to India at the drop of a cheque. There, they could pocket the rewards of crass commercialism without fans back home realising they'd sold out. And given the sums involved, it wasn't a difficult decision to make. At the end of the arduous 2005 England tour, I met one of the most overworked players as we checked out of our London hotel.

'Bet you can't wait to get back home to the family,' I observed, sensing he shared my exhaustion. 'Are you on this afternoon's flight?'

'Nah, I'm stopping over in Mumbai,' he said, with not a hint of reservation.

'Must be a bloody good reason to add India to this itinerary,' I joked, as I signed off my room bill.

'For barely a day's work, there's 150,000 reasons my friend,' the cricketer smiled. 'And what's better, they're US reasons.'

15

Tri-nations Tournament, India, October–November 2003 (II)

The Beatles never quite made it to Guwahati when they were ashram-hopping through India in the late '60s. In fact, not many foreign travellers do end up in the culturally and geographically distinct state of Assam. Not even those desperately trying to discover themselves, as well as the subcontinent, by straying as far as impractical from the established tourist trails.

If, as seemed initially feasible, the swarm of awestruck onlookers who crammed every available nook at Guwahati's dilapidated, isolated airstrip had hung around for thirty-five years patiently awaiting the Fab Four, they gave no demonstrable hint of feeling shortchanged when the Australian cricket team disembarked instead. In fact, they remained spookily reverent. While receptions for John, Paul, George and Ringo consisted of screaming and fainting, the terminal's unadorned corridors echoed with little more than the squelch of rubber-soled soles on buffed linoleum as Roy, Pup, George and Willo strode through.

Why Guwahati maintains a low profile, even among the global backpacker army, can be largely explained by its geography. Which is to say, it's not easily found – even for those of us privy to the resources of a media empire's travel consultants and a vastly more useful guide book. Australia's cricketers had been treated to a couple of days in the comparative luxury of Delhi to regroup after the tournament's frenetic first week or so, which had taken us from Delhi to Gwalior, back to Faridabad (in Delhi's outer northern suburbs), to Mumbai, and then finally to Pune, where a bout of tummy trouble had laid low several in the squad. India's five-star hotels do sumptuous better than most, so a couple of nights in Delhi's Taj Palace proved an essential tonic before tackling Guwahati, which every local warned us would provide the itinerary's sternest challenge. And while the players enjoyed their private fully catered viewing of the Melbourne Cup, I remained in my room scouring my rudimentary map of India in the futile hope of unearthing our destination.

'So where's our next stop?' asked Nathan Bracken, with a world-weariness that belied a one-day international career barely a dozen matches old, when we crossed paths in the lobby later that day.

'Some place called Guwahati,' I said, offering him a stick of the potentially habit-forming cardamom chewing gum I had discovered during a trawl through Mumbai's Crawford Market.

'Never heard of it. Is it far from here?' he continued, peering out through the hotel's front doors in the sanguine hope that it might, like Faridabad, be a mere bus ride away.

'No idea,' I replied. 'I can't even find it on the map.' He blinked several times in what I interpreted as astonishment but, in hindsight, was probably a reaction to the gum.

Our exchange was overheard by a well-dressed man nursing a brown leather satchel who sat alone, but attentively, on one of the foyer couches. He approached and respectfully introduced himself as a travel agent awaiting a client. He kindly offered to point out our next destination on a detailed map he extracted from the bag. Embarrassed but curious, I followed his index finger as it tracked a line from New Delhi, along the southern rim of the Himalayas, across Bangladesh's north-west and eventually settled on a spot next to the Brahmaputra River. Assam sat between Nepal to the west, Bhutan, China and Tibet to the north, Burma to the east, and Bangladesh, then the Bay of Bengal to the south. The only south Asian nation with which it didn't appear to share a border, as near as I could tell, was India.

'It's why many in Assam believe they should be a separate nation, and why they continue to fight for independence,' our learned friend assured us.

'Kind of like Perth, but with weapons,' I said, turning to Bracken, only to find he had learned enough and was already on his way to the lifts.

Our three-hour flight to India's eastern-most city yielded strikingly unhindered views of the Himalayan range, with Everest's peak clearly visible above a thick ribbon of cloud. The scene that unfolded beneath, as we descended to an airstrip set amid thick undergrowth, was not quite so breathtaking. The runway's lush green verges were littered with the rusting hulks of decommissioned military aircraft. Lokpriya Gopinath Bordoloi International Airport seemingly doubled as a scrap metal depot or it posed a more treacherous landing proposition than Kai Tak. Equally unnerving was the realisation that we were about to be deposited smack in the middle of nowhere, with only dense vegetation, flooded farmland and dead aircraft for company. Surely this was not our destination, I thought, and mentally kicked myself for not sharing my newly acquired travel intelligence with the flight crew.

The unnatural stillness of the airport was made even more surreal by the silently staring crowd that lined the corridors, dangled from mezzanine walkways, and pressed against the towering glass windows that opened on to an all-but deserted car park. Then, from nowhere, a small armada of taxis, all shapes but uniform size – diminutive – arrived to take those of us not permitted bus transport on a forty-five-minute drive through the sodden countryside and into the dirty, chaotic streets of central Guwahati.

The media's rundown guesthouse stood hardly a kilometre, yet a good fifteen-minute drive through the mire of motor and pedal traffic, from Nehru Stadium where Australia was due to play the tri-series' other team, New Zealand, two days later. The cloud of fine white dust that plumed from non-stop building work and settled on everything throughout our pension was certainly in no danger of being disturbed by lively staff. In contrast, the rival teams were billeted in the decidedly more grandiose, and fully completed, Landmark Hotel, which physically adjoined the cricket ground. While we were welcomed by indolent desk staff, the cricketers arrived to another silent vigil, this time from intrigued locals gathered twenty-deep around the hotel's locked gates.

Adam Gilchrist, who, despite being no stranger to India had been taken aback by the size of the airport welcoming committee, received an even ruder shock when he arrived in his room and rinsed off the day's travel under a lukewarm shower. With only a towel around his waist, he then threw back the heavy bedroom curtains to take in the view across the frontier city and down the vast river that stretched to the horizon like an inland sea. He had hoped to catch a final glimpse of the burnt-orange sun as it vanished into the heavy afternoon haze. Instead, he was met with the burning stare of 500 sets of eyes and a collective gasp that was audible through the single-glazing. The crowd may have remained steadfastly fixed for hours in the hope of spying an international cricketer in the flesh, but this was far more flesh than any had bargained on. The Australian vice-captain tore the shades closed, dressed in the near dark and settled in for another evening as a cricket fugitive. When he rose the next morning, he ensured he was adequately attired before again flinging aside the drapes to find that, rather than having returned to their homes, the congregation had grown noticeably.

'It was like that window scene from Monty Python's *Life of Brian*,' Gilchrist chuckled later that day. 'Except that none of them made a sound. They just stood there, and stared.'

It wasn't only the mute esteem in which they held cricketers that set the Assamese apart. Picking through the damp earthen back alleys that connected our building site to the barren cricket ground, we were treated to snapshots of basic, traditional Indian village life that somehow endured in a city of nigh on a million. The mud streets and intricate network of paths and crevices that linked them were bordered by tightly packed rows of cement, corrugated iron and plywood dwellings. Most were too tiny to contain the generations of families whose domestic life spilled onto the surrounding streets.

In the windowless front room of one such house, a man wielding a blowtorch scorched the hair from a boar that hung lifeless from the ceiling. On either side of the alley, timber boxes hardly bigger than footlockers and perched on rickety stilts threw open their street-front doors to reveal compact women stuffed into the back corners hawking a meagre assortment of fruits, nuts, floral garlands and household items. I thought it impolite to inquire if these miniature kiosks also served as their homes.

As I poked, completely enthralled, in and out of covered courtyards, and up and down musty paths, I was greeted with guarded curiosity by adults, and with wide-eyed enthusiasm by youngsters. By the time I reached the stadium, a group of more than twenty urchins had fallen into step behind me. Having connected white-skinned interloper with cricket ground and deduced travelling celebrity, the clamour for my autograph increased steadily in urgency, even though my fan club boasted not a shred of paper between them. Instead, they proffered the palms of their hands, bare arms and legs or, in the case of one enterprising lad, his younger brother's forehead.

The morning after the Australians' comfortable win secured them a berth in the tournament final in Kolkata, I spent a restless few hours strolling among Guwahati's endless stretches of fabric emporiums and tea merchants. My unease was not the result of being gawked, giggled and pointed at everywhere I turned. By then, I had become quite comfortable with my unwarranted fame. Rather, it sprang from the knowledge there was only one flight out of Assam that would get me safely to Bangalore for the next game. And the nightmarish traffic jam that was already beginning to clog the capital's streets became more impenetrable by the minute as my colleague, Jon Pierik, and I abandoned our ambling to wait nervously for the arrival of our pre-booked cab.

A small, badly dented minibus duly turned up, but had travelled no more than 500 metres through the mass before we became stuck. Our agitation was compounded by the Bollywood music that blasted from tinny speakers that swung from a length of thin wiring taped across the bus's rear window. As we crawled through the lunchtime snarl, I yelled to our driver that he was in line for a sizeable tip if he could get us to the airport in personal best time. And even more if he pulled the plug on the racket. He accepted the challenge, killed the music, beeped and bulldozed his way through the congestion and then, as clear road finally beckoned and he pushed the accelerator to the disintegrating floor, a single explosion, not unlike a concussion grenade, shook our seats, and our optimism. The reason he pumped the tabla drums 'n' sitar beats so loud was clearly to hide the fact his van was shot to bits.

We limped as far as a roadside market near Bhubneswari Mandir, barely a quarter of the way to the airport, then the vehicle's death rattle gave way to rigor mortis. As our driver repeatedly tried to kick over the lifeless ignition, a crowd quickly gathered and he shouted in Bengali at a man who immediately disappeared into a nearby laneway.

'Someone will come now to fix,' the driver explained, in a voice as unconvincing as it was unapologetic.

'Too late,' I yelled at him. 'We need another taxi … now!'

We extricated ourselves from the stricken vehicle, dragged our suitcases clear while the driver watched grumpily, and frantically tried to wave down any vehicle that looked vaguely capable of transporting two panicking journalists, with luggage, to a waiting flight. We also declined several requests for autographs. A battered black Ambassador taxi piloted by a grinning driver, whose completely bald head was similarly devoid of teeth, pulled up behind us. Our saviour leaped from his car, and immediately began a heated argument with our original cabbie.

'We don't have time for this,' I shouted, despite having no clue what 'this' related to.

As we stuffed ourselves and our possessions into the cab, it emerged that the spat was over non-payment of the minibus driver's fare. I explained to our new best friend that the stipend, plus bonus forfeited by his unreliable predecessor, would be his if we made our plane. He continued to flash his gummy smile, although he clearly understood not a single word.

We had driven barely five minutes, deep into tranquil countryside populated only by lumbering oxen and rice fields, when the ancient black car shuddered to a stop. This time we were sunk. No townsfolk gathered to gauge our predicament. The driver simply sat bolt upright and stared ahead. The only sign of a recent human presence was what appeared to be an abandoned chicken farm across the road. It had doubtless gone bust because the chickens had had to make their own way to market.

Shattered, we pulled our luggage from the latest inert vehicle and briefly debated what posed the least appalling option – walking the remaining ten kilometres to the airport and camping there until we could catch a flight anywhere. Or turning back for an indefinite stay in Guwahati. We were about to start trudging towards the former when I made an inspired rummage through the depths of my case to retrieve the one item that might deliver us a miracle. Almost instantly, a dark green military-model Jeep that was hurtling back towards town let fly a strident horn blast before it lurched into a high-speed U-turn and slid to a stop next to the dead cab. At no stage during this exercise did the Jeep's driver, or his teenage passenger, shift their gaze from my crumpled navy-blue Cricket Australia-issue shirt.

'Are you Australia cricket team?' the driver asked incredulously, his dark eyes eventually moving from the shirt to the pathetic scene around it.

'Yes we are,' I replied, trying to make myself look as strapping as possible. 'And we need to get to the airport right now. Our plane is about to leave.'

'I know,' the man shot back. 'The rest of team is there now. You must hurry. Come. I am security chief at this airport. I will take you.'

His young companion was instructed to load our baggage, and the senior man twisted around awkwardly and dusted down the back seat in readiness for his celebrated guests. As we climbed aboard, abandoned driver number two was seen to offer a brief head wobble before gently resting his forehead on the steering wheel.

The Jeep then bounced its way along the pockmarked airport road at an exhilaratingly illegal speed. Every few hundred metres, the driver would screw his head around to stare, and to unleash a Lotto-winner's smile. He broke from this routine only to bark an instruction at his offsider, who clawed helplessly at the glove box in front of him. The driver let out a strangled cry, ripped the keys from the Jeep's steering column, and tossed them casually towards the passenger seat. Our chauffeur turned and shot us a reassuring grin, while his sidekick unlocked the compartment and triumphantly produced a tattered black-bound notebook and a badly chewed ballpoint pen. He solemnly handed all three articles to the driver who, believing that eyes are as superfluous to the driving process as hands and keys, turned to face the rear seat.

'Please, I will be honoured if you could be signing your names for us,' he said deferentially.

With just minutes to make good our scheduled escape from Assam, I sought silent forgiveness for the deception I was about to perpetrate and, having searched my scrambled brain for a suitable doppelganger – *vis-à-vis* an unathletic middle-aged cricketer once able to bowl a bit of off-spin – I dashed off, with as much flourish as I could muster in the back of a buck-jumping Jeep: 'Thanks for all your help … Tim May.'

I passed the book to my colleague and then stole a glance at his contribution as I handed the artefact back to its ecstatic, and hopefully illiterate, owner. 'You saved our lives … Mark Waugh' had been scrawled on the facing page. Both men handled the book as if it were a first edition *Mahabharata*, once the Jeep had roared to a stop almost alongside the check-in desk. As we ran for the departure gate, it was being passed respectfully among a circle of uniformed officers who had swamped the proud security chief.

As is so often the way in India, the only result our fretting delivered was wasted energy. Our flight was delayed by more than an hour, which meant we missed our connection in Delhi and arrived in Bangalore after midnight. Working into the small hours over a story cobbled from interviews conducted mid-air, I wondered what the day's travel misadventures equated to in work time. That abstract query surfaced again when our subsequent flight to Kolkata required a 4 a.m. hotel check-out. But as we chugged through that city's early-morning commuter mayhem on arrival, my worry was eased by the remarkable daily ritual of an Indian metropolis waking up. Hardly an arm's length from our taxi, fully clad men and women took their morning ablutions in gutters and concrete troughs along the highway's edge. Whole communities huddled around camp stoves and open fires, oblivious to the traffic banked up alongside them. As our driver turned off the main route to tackle an ambitious short cut, a tall man who was totally naked save for a pair of makeshift sandals sprawled himself across our taxi's windscreen, almost emasculating himself on a wiper blade. His sudden appearance was far less expected than the mechanical hitch that left our cab lifeless when we reached the Royal Calcutta Turf Club. Given we could see our hotel in the near distance, we completed this aborted journey on foot.

West Bengal's capital, better known as Calcutta than Kolkata, unfortunately remains a Western by-word for slums and deprivation, though more recently for the uplifting work of its Albanian patron saint Mother Teresa. It is also palpably different to other Indian mega-cities. Not quite as dissimilar as Guwahati. But whereas Delhi is driven by politics, Mumbai is a centre of commerce and Bangalore the nation's silicone valley, Kolkata crackles with a passion and creativity befitting its reputation as an artistic and literary hub. It is also home to the most imposing stadium in all cricketdom.

My first viewing of Eden Gardens, ringed by a sprawling *maidan*, august public buildings which echo the city's past as British India's jewel, and the mighty Hooghly River whose *ghats* provide recreation, bathing and laundry facilities for thousands of Bengalis each day, came as the Australians trained on the eve of the sold-out final against India. Initially, I thought the celebrated stadium more cavernous than imperious. Apart from the colossal grandstand which housed the players' pavilion and a press box which resembled an elevated tram stop, most of the spectator space resided on gently undulating terraces which made the ground appear not so much a cauldron as an enormous saucer. It was only when I traversed those steps that I understood how it could feasibly hold up to 120,000 fans, the sort of attendance many locals, among them Kolkata's most beloved cricket son, Sourav Ganguly, expected for the Tuesday night final.

Each concrete plinth was divvied up by a series of white painted lines, uniformly spaced less than a metre apart, with each segment assigned a unique number. Indians, particularly those relegated to the cheap seats, are known as lean, lithe specimens. But even so, to squeeze the population of Hobart into such a tight configuration would require, at the very least, synchronised breathing. That explained where the huge crowd would be stacked. How they got there was revealed on the morning of the final as I negotiated a labyrinth of freshly erected bamboo cattle runs installed to funnel the hordes evenly and smoothly to the seventeen entrance gates dotting the perimeter. Those unable, or unwilling, to comprehend this system were assisted by the rows of *lathi*-wielding police, who coerced the confused into the appropriate chute by employing a sharp crack across the legs, or a jab into the ribs. The sheer volume of people stampeding towards the ground, raising columns of dust which hung lazily over the *maidan*, was mind-boggling. The collective noise they produced and maintained throughout seven and a half hours of cricket remained in my memory long after the ringing departed my ears.

Indian cricket supporters are unique in that they genuinely believe by being in the crowd, and by making their voice heard, they can alter a game's outcome. Unfortunately, those who wielded legitimate influence let the occasion get the better of them. Fielding first, the Indians dropped a remarkable nine catches in the course of fifty overs. Four of those were turfed by Laxman, who, on the same ground two years earlier, had inspired his nation's most famous Test match win over Australia by scoring an epic 281. That innings was consigned to an historical footnote through his butter-fingeredness during this energy-sapping Kolkata afternoon. And once Tendulkar was bowled for forty-five, the *maidan* again filled, this time with fans taking early leave, with a mere 70,000 or so staying behind to witness the Australians take their raucous victory celebration out onto the pitch. While the final proved a forgettable contest, the occasion lives as the most spine-tingling of my cricket-writing tenure. Though perhaps my recollections are tinged by the stunning young woman who materialised before me from the immense crowd as I made my way to the press box and, fully aware I was not a cricketer, welcomed me to Kolkata and wished me good fortune and good health for the remainder of my stay. I had not yet completed my first visit to India, and already I could not wait to return.

The Australians' victory party continued at the team hotel through the night and up until departure for the airport next afternoon. The excesses were clearly evident as the victors stumbled aboard our homeward flight. Their fellow travellers were seated and ready to go as they made their entrance with all the slick orchestration of a kindergarten concert. Far from affronted, the other passengers shared their good humour, if not their high spirits. As they stumbled through the cabin scouring lucklessly for overhead locker space, they posed for photos and scribbled indecipherable autographs. The only item that could not be stowed was a long, wooden case that Jimmy Maher wielded as if it were an assault rifle.

Having opened every locker down to row thirty without luck, and having slammed each one shut in mock outrage, Maher despairingly whined in his best north Queensland drawl: 'Can someone just make some room. We've gotta get this bloody great trophy back 'ome.' He then shook the TVS Cup, packed safely in its case, triumphantly in front of his face.

Had that stunt been pulled by a drunken player on Australian soil, the outrage would have been deafening. And instant. Talkback radio callers, serial letter writers, pious columnists. All would have fallen over themselves to lambast such boorish arrogance. In India, however, several obliging travellers jumped from their seats and began clearing space for the cargo. And when it was stored and the cricketer buckled in for his and everyone else's safety, most of the passengers, and even members of the cabin crew, erupted into a rousing round of applause.

16

Australian Summers 2003–05,
New Zealand, February–April 2005

The gentle hillock that rises above the sheltered port where ferries from Tasmania's east coast dock a dozen times a day is one of the few points on Bruny Island serviced by mobile phone signals. Local tourism authorities warn those who might become lost during a hike through the island's forests or along its steep cliffs that a mobile phone would prove as useful a survival tool as a solar-powered torch. Bruny Island is isolated technologically as well as geographically. And it was the tranquillity and seclusion offered by this wilderness retreat, which once provided safe mooring for James Cook and William Bligh, that made it the ideal antidote to the head spin of India. And perhaps the place to heal a relationship deeply and deservedly fractured by my having spent eight of the previous fifteen months in beds other than the matrimonial.

It also offered an environment in which to calmly evaluate my strategic error. Well, a couple of them really. But the most blatant stemmed from a clumsy attempt to challenge the paper's 'you're either working or you're shirking' edict as it applied to my month-long Indian mission. I tried to make it clear to my superiors that, on the subcontinent, you can chew up the best part of a mandated eight-hour day just trying to find a serviceable taxi. This, in turn, meant the log of hours I had accumulated and then presented on my return was laughable. At least, I found it funny. Though not for long.

By annotating every movement of the assignment, it wasn't difficult to see how a month away could tote up almost as many days of lieu time owed. Items like the 5.45 a.m. start for players and press when we had to beat Delhi traffic to make Faridabad in time for the game's start. A day that ended early next morning to ensure sufficient work was completed before embarking on the 1,400-kilometre trip to Mumbai. Or Bangalore's all-night gig, squeezed between the late finish to a day-nighter and the pre-dawn departure for Kolkata. Even with a capacity for maths that matched my acumen for physics, I knew it didn't take many twenty-two-hour working days to spin the overtime meter into overdrive. On a tour that extended to twenty-eight days, included twelve separate flight legs, two long-haul train journeys, and took in seven matches in as many different Indian cities, the final ledger revealed I was about 150 hours in the red. On average, five extra hours per day. Not unheard of, in light of the task. But a number the Ideas Factory welcomed in the same way a vampire greets daybreak.

So I floated what I reasoned was a fair compromise. I offered to swap my twenty days of accumulated lieu time for a two-week sabbatical. A chance to regain my bearings and re-buttress my unravelling life against the next bout of looming stress – nine weeks on the road as the Australian summer itinerary wound on. I quickly sensed it had not been received in the same spirit of bipartisanship in which it had been extended. But by the time the recriminations began, I would be incommunicado. Or so I figured. It proved another skewed judgement.

As the toy-sized hire care's automatic transmission slipped back a gear or three to tackle the gentle incline of the Island's Main Road, the sudden chirruping of my dormant mobile phone all but drowned out the tiny engine. By the time we strained to a point high enough to lock on a signal, I was aware that six messages had been left over the preceding hour. All from the same person. None of them inquiring how the repair of my marriage was progressing. I got out of the car, clambered through a rusting fence in search of higher ground as I dialled, and was frantically trying to disentangle myself from barbed wire when the Bear's voice came clearly down the line from Sydney. The ugly three-corner rip in my shirt as I yanked myself clear was nothing compared to the verbal savaging I copped as I scrabbled upwards in search of the knoll's peak. I was in unknown terrain, but the diatribe was all too familiar.

'I don't know what you think you're playing at.' Blah, blah.

'I'm getting sick and tired of doing all the work and then covering your arse.' Yeah, yeah.

'If you can't be bothered doing the job, I'll have no trouble finding someone who will.' Sure, sure. But then an addendum that even by the tortured logic I expected, was a tad conspiratorial.

'I reckon you've planned this all along,' the Bear spat. 'You knew Steve Waugh was announcing his retirement today and you wanted to make sure you weren't here so you didn't have to cover it.'

Given that 'here' referred to Sydney and my regular place of employment and domicile was 1,000 kilometres away in Melbourne, I could not immediately figure why I would have needed such an elaborate work-avoidance ruse to ensure I missed the captain's farewell announcement. Even more puzzling was the suggestion that, having worked a month without a break amid the daily adversities of India to pose as a cricket writer, I would then willingly sit on the biggest – the only – scoop of my career by somehow stumbling across prior knowledge of Waugh's decision yet leaving it unwritten while I kicked back on an inaccessible island that afforded uninterrupted views of Antarctica. With the sou'-westerly howling in from Great Bay and the stream of accusations causing a dull ache in my frontal lobe, I began a hasty retreat back down the slope to the road. Salvation lay in the flickering unreliability of the phone signal.

'You're cracking up,' I shouted ambiguously into the wind, before the phone mercifully dropped out.

If the boss interpreted that parting message in the spirit it was delivered, then I was on a fast-track to more than one painful divorce during an Australian summer that ultimately veered from disagreeable to downright silly. It began with Stephen Waugh's carefully choreographed retirement announcement in my absence, which did not so much dominate the subsequent Test series against India as totally eclipse it. From the day of his press conference, his farewell appearances took on the fervour of a nationwide testimonial. This led to the palpable discomfort of teammates who felt the man who preached the importance of team above all else had suddenly abandoned the ensemble during the encore to grab adulation as a solo artist.

In fairness to Waugh, his brash tour promoter was the mass-circulating tabloid newspaper for which he wrote a regular column. The fact that it was not the paper I worked for added significantly to the summer's torment. Borrowing from the cricket team's jargon, 'ownership' of a story had become one of digital-age journalism's favoured buzz words. Making sure your news organisation's 'brand' was perceived as the most authoritative and reliable source for any given news event. It was made abundantly clear we had surrendered 'ownership' of Waugh's final summer, and top brass at the Ideas Factory were deeply unimpressed. Just as apparent was the expectation that the next major cricket story to happen along simply had to be ours. And I was the officer on the beat, albeit comatose in a Brisbane hotel room, when that story broke.

Queensland's summer sun was already burning bright, mocking the bedside clock that showed 6.15 a.m. when the phone cut short my recuperation from the previous night's match. A voice from home informed me that David Hookes, ex-Test batsman, commentator and jet engine troubleshooter, lay critically injured in a Melbourne hospital following an overnight assault. He would not, I was assured, survive the day. Even without the encumbrance of a sleep-deprived fog, this would have been difficult news to process. Hookes and I were hardly close friends, but I had enjoyed his company over dinner and in press boxes during several overseas tours. And as coach of Victoria's cricket team, he could be relied on for an inflammatory headline on a quiet day. As this day unfolded, and I was instructed to drum up as much shock and devastation as could be prised from his former teammates and colleagues, I was dogged by a heavy, energy-sapping sadness.

That was replaced, over ensuing days as the tour caravan moved on sombrely to Sydney, by a brooding contempt for my profession, and my role within it. Journalism saves its worst *braggadocio* for swaggering roughshod over grief and sensitivities in times of tragedy. It stems from a collective misanthropy that's cultivated to recognise only the story, and to deny any human emotion that might call into question the merits of its publication. The smug refusal to be shocked, embarrassed or wrong is proudly flaunted by hard-bitten journalists, who view any tiptoeing around those confronted by life-altering trauma as professional weakness.

For days after Hookes's death, I received regular phone calls from the news desk relaying a single, unflinching command from on high. It was the newspaper's obsession to secure an exclusive interview and eyewitness account from Darren Lehmann, the deceased's great friend who was present on the fateful night. Who phoned for an ambulance from the scene, and remained at his mate's bedside until life support was withdrawn. Who, in addition to being ill with shock and stricken by inconsolable grief, was also a key witness in an ongoing police investigation.

'You can come up with as many excuses as you want,' I was told when I tendered these as reasons why I felt subjecting Lehmann to a barrage of phone calls, and having photographers stake out his home, was as insensitive as it was counter-productive. 'But the editor wants this interview. It's a cricket story and you're the cricket writer.'

Employing that logic, the lunar landing could have been covered as a travel yarn. But I assured my masters I would devote my boundless energies to the task. In reality, I left a grovelling message on Lehmann's phone, expressing sympathy for his loss and apologies for our hectoring. If he felt he wanted to talk, I added with shameless hypocrisy, I was happy to listen. The message went deservedly unacknowledged.

Darren Lehmann told his story months later, in the appropriate forum: Melbourne's Magistrates' Court. My inability, some suggested reluctance, to secure that story led to more red ink being etched on my service record. Another similar act of subversion would surely be my last. But that was a peripheral concern as the summer of 2003–04 wound down, and Ricky Ponting led his first Test touring party overseas, to Sri Lanka, a series I kept tabs on from a distance, albeit with flickering interest. Circumstances at home had taken a decisive turn for the solitary, and my more urgent need had become replacing items lost in the dissolution. A chair. A bed. The functional keepsakes of a dignified life. As well as the wherewithal to enlist a lawyer other than an antediluvian Bridgetown QC.

Therefore, when an offer to contribute a monthly column for a national cricket magazine arrived unsolicited, and while I was dutifully taking a slab of leave to reduce the debt burden I was imposing on my newspaper, I snatched at it with all the haste of a man swamped by legal costs. As I optimistically explained down the phone to the Bear, whose imprimatur I needed before I could exercise my right to write, it involved the production of 'Where Are They Now?'-style feature articles, tracking down forgotten figures from Australian cricket's past. Not only did it offer a chance to boost my bank balance while promoting *The Australian*'s masthead among a new cohort of readers, the fact that it required trawling through the past meant it would not compromise my fearless pursuit of daily news. I felt adequately prepared to debate the proposition's pros and cons with my boss. Being pinned to a wall, strafed with gunfire and stomped on caught me a fraction off guard.

'You … you … you just don't get it, do you?' the Bear stammered, so enraged he battled to translate his fury into monosyllables. 'You seriously expect me to let you do work for another publication in your spare time when you can't even do your own job anywhere near properly? I mean, our cricket coverage is a fuckin' disgrace. I could send a trained monkey to cover matches and he'd do it better. If it wasn't for my ideas, we wouldn't have anything in the paper at all.'

And on it went. Another vituperative rant that became more unpleasant with each utterance, and seemed to last considerably longer than the five minutes of real time it occupied. In terms of professional development, it was the nearest I came in twenty years of journalism to a performance review. It also raised almost as many issues as it addressed. Why had these heinous shortcomings been kept such a closely guarded secret all these months? Why was my gross ineptitude repeatedly rewarded with overseas tours and interstate assignments? Why had the paper repeatedly trumpeted the quality of its cricket coverage when, according to its overseer, it was a source of industry shame? What was I thinking by initiating this latest tirade in the first place? Absence of opportunity and a similar lack of will meant none of these thoughts were articulated. I just hung on to the receiver, and deflated.

'I wouldn't treat my worst enemy the way that you treat me,' began the final harangue. 'You need to have a bloody good think about where your career's going, 'cause I sure as hell will be.'

I slowly replaced the handset. I was fairly confident he had finished, and infinitely more certain that I was. As I canvassed my personal and professional options, a strange yearning for the camaraderie and autonomy of the cricket tour began to shine through the confusion. The players who had been so distrustful and dismissive when I first entered their world a decade earlier now took on the guise of extended family.

The redemptive properties of Brett Lee's ever-present smile which, whether genuine or not, conveyed the impression he was always pleased to see me. The schoolyard inanity of being forever tapped on the right shoulder, and spinning around to find a smirking Glenn McGrath scuttling away to the left. Learning of the latest variety of roses to bloom in Justin Langer's garden. The unreal world of cricket's roadshow had become my reality. The routines of travel provided a familiarity that the capriciousness of everyday life no longer did. Little wonder my domestic situation was a shambles. Away had become home. Home had become a transit lounge. And the prospect of being indefinitely stranded here, on my own, was suddenly terrifying.

That was why the airport gathering ahead of the Australian team's 2005 tour to New Zealand exuded something of a 'first day back at school after summer vacation' feel – the comfortingly familiar spiced by the nervous thrill of the uncharted. Eight months after it had been made clear 'touring cricket writer' was no longer included in my job description, the regime change that installed the paper's sixth sports editor in less than eight years led to it being reinstated. And with it came one final crack at making the world's best job live up to its billing.

Up until that point, I had begun to suspect my initial nostalgia for the cricket circuit was little more than misty-eyed romanticism brought on by emotional turmoil. That was until I bumped into a senior Australian player, out on an evening stroll with his wife, during the course of the 2004–05 summer. Following mutual pleasantries and general chit-chat, they generously offered me a stay at their beachside property which sat idle when cricket commitments choked their calendar.

'I've heard what's been happening, and I gather you could do with a few days' break,' I was told. 'And we'd be happy for you to use the place seeing as we can't.' Perhaps I had not imagined that, against all else, the cricket team now perversely stood as my one secure source of amity.

The first training session in New Zealand was conducted amid unusually steamy Auckland heat, in nets tucked away on playing fields behind the city's great rugby cathedral, Eden Park. The mid-February sun, coupled with knowledge that the tour opener was a light-hearted frolic framed within cricket's latest fad, the twenty-over format, meant the Australian pace bowlers left the donkey work to eager young local cricketers on loan to the touring party for the morning.

The concept of the 'net bowler' remains one of cricket's quaint anomalies. Despite it being a hugely lucrative professional sport, its best batsmen often hone their skills at practice by facing up to eager teenagers of varying ability. The teens' only payment is a bottle of sports drink, and perhaps a few happy snaps with their heroes at session's end. But it's as much a commercial necessity as a logistical one. No cricket association can afford to fly a full squad of auxiliary bowlers around the world to provide competitive training. Unfortunately, the whole exercise often proves as amateurish as it sounds – as the New Zealanders later showed when they set up an elaborate role play in the aftermath of their hefty first Test loss.

Their batsmen had been dumbfounded by Shane Warne, who landed the ball in craterous bowlers' footmarks on a worn pitch, from where it would bounce at unnatural angles or dribble along the ground. Preparing for the next encounter, the Kiwis' coaching staff took a trowel to practice pitches and excavated a series of replica potholes in roughly the places they would develop under match conditions. Then, they rounded up a handful of Wellington's most promising young leg-spinners and instructed them to bowl at the holes, while the cream of their nation's top order prepared to keep them at bay. After almost an hour, during which time not one of the lads was able to land a ball in the fake footmarks, the experiment was abandoned.

Weeks prior to this farce, the tour's inaugural training session in Auckland was equally unscientific, though decidedly more dangerous. As the roster of lads wheeled away at the relaxed Australian batsmen, tuning up for their introduction to Twenty20 cricket by slogging everything flung at them, one boy of barely fourteen put in such an effort to unsettle Damien Martyn that he entered his bowling follow-through almost doubled-over.

By the time he righted himself, Martyn had taken aim at the generous half-volley on offer, and blasted the hard white ball back at roughly the same trajectory, but three times the speed, towards its point of origin. For a half-second, the look on the young bowler's face registered the belated alarm of a grenade thrower who's held the bomb and hurled the pin. He raised both hands in a reflex protective gesture, but the sickening crack of leather on skull confirmed it was both late, and futile.

Players and support staff rushed to him as he lay prone on the grass, hands clasped to his bloodied face, moaning softly. As he was loaded into an ambulance, a huge, angry lump had already taken shape on his forehead, the distinctive stitch marks of a cricket ball seared crimson into the mauve welt. Before the lad was ferried to hospital for x-rays and brain scans, Martyn slipped him one of his cricket bats in an act of contrition and concern. The boy lay motionless on a stretcher, bat clasped to his chest like some sort of talisman. He returned to visit the team several days later, showing no ill feeling. Just a neat row of tiny replica stitch marks burned above his eyebrows.

Cricket's newest era formally arrived with the maiden Twenty20 International at Eden Park on a balmy mid-February evening in 2005. The gravitas of the moment was not lost on the participants. The New Zealanders had spent much of the summer cultivating porn-star moustaches and mutton-chop sideburns to fit with the event's 'back to the '80s' theme. They even donned the body-hugging beige uniforms that have haunted their country's sporting image since that era. The Australians appeared in a similarly gauche collection of body shirts, gold jewellery and towelling head bands. Ricky Ponting who, like most of his team, had no previous experience in the super-abbreviated form of the game, best summed up the occasion when asked if the thirty runs he plundered from a single over was a feat he had achieved previously.

'Probably not since primary school,' he replied, with disarming candour. 'I think it's difficult to play seriously.'

The novelty certainly won over the capacity crowd, which became so captivated by the non-stop action that they neglected to throw either missiles or abuse. But the usual drunken boorishness returned when the fifty-over stuff got underway in Wellington later that week. Australian fielders positioned near the boundary fence during the home team's evening innings bore the brunt from the terraces. Simon Katich almost wore a full cup of beer. Matthew Hayden was spat on. And, upon challenging one of the ineffective security officers stationed between the fence and the boundary rope to get off his collapsible stool and help clean up a pile of filth forming on the playing surface, Glenn McGrath was curtly told by the official to 'piss off'.

During the next match in Christchurch, I vacated the comparative civility of the press box and, for half an hour, joined the rabble that congregated in the open-air DB Draught Stand at the southern end of what rugby diehards still call Lancaster Park. The pleasantly warm Canterbury evening and the similarly tepid local liquor ensured the yobbo culture I hoped to observe was loud and proud by the time New Zealand's run chase began.

There are few other major sports in which the practitioners are subjected to the sort of sustained abuse that's routinely aimed at cricket's outfielders. Footballers might argue that they cop their share of sprays from the bleachers, but the perpetual movement of their game often helps remove them from the firing line. Cricket's stop-start nature means those fielding near the fence must literally stand and cop it. And it was Glenn McGrath's turn in the shooting gallery when he took up his station at third man for the opening over. The chanting was fairly standard stuff.

'McGrath's a wanker.' 'McGrath, you're a homo.' A drunken chorus bawling: 'Ooh, ahh Glenn McGrath ... Fuck off Glenn McGrath.'

From there, it became plain sad. Men dressed in nuns' habits, inebriated teenage boys wearing nothing but football shorts and body paint, adolescent girls barely able to stand but still swigging

Marlborough sauvignon blanc from small plastic bottles. All showcased their ingenuity, emboldened by the booze and egged on by the mob. McGrath mostly wore the abuse with resigned good humour. He smiled and raised his thumbs when they taunted him, politely refused their offers of alcohol, and even returned the blue plastic cigarette lighter hurled at him from two dozen rows back. But his demeanour hardened when he failed to hang on to a scorching top-edged catch that crashed into his raised hands and then ballooned over his head into the crowd.

'You fucked up, you fucked up,' they chanted, in a drone of spite and spittle. McGrath ignored them, cap jammed down hard, hands planted firmly on hips. Then someone lobbed a half-full 1.5-litre lemonade bottle at the defenceless fielder. A tennis ball flew just past his left shoulder. A near-full plastic beer bottle landed at his feet, spraying foam up his leg. He bent to pick it up, and pretended to drain its contents before tossing it on to the pile of debris he had begun assembling outside the boundary rope.

No employee should have to endure these workplace conditions. And no comparable international sport displays such a courteous tolerance for having its drawcards pelted and abused. It's difficult to imagine Tiger Woods swaying out of the path of an errant apple while lining up a putt. Or Roger Federer having to sidestep the discarded carcass of a barbecued chicken before firing a backhand winner. Perhaps officials could have enlisted Michael Kasprowicz's help in framing strategies to defuse these outbreaks of idiocy. Walking to his fielding position on the boundary in Wellington, he held his hands aloft, palms pointed at the baying horde in a gesture of appeasement.

'Hey. Hey. Hey,' the former Australian schoolboys rugby forward screamed over the howls of derision. 'If you're all abusing me at the same time, I can't make out what you're saying. So at least have the courtesy to put shit on me one at a time.' The morons found this a reasonable request, for a few minutes at least.

The guerrilla tactics did nothing to lift New Zealand's on-field fortunes. Defeat in the twenty-over game was followed by five more in the one-dayers. So lopsided were the contests, story prospects became bleak in the lead-up to the first Test in Christchurch. The sole issue of curiosity lay in whether Brett Lee, who had bowled at frightening pace in the white-ball games and sent one hapless Kiwi batsman to hospital with concussion, never to return to the one-day international arena, would win a recall to Test ranks after eighteen months on the outer.

Lee did his bit to enliven the plot, declaring that if he was overlooked again he would have to consider taking up off-spin. Or bowling left-handed. Come Test eve, all four rival members of the touring Australian press pack were stalking the team's hotel in the hunt for an inside whisper on whether the selectors would lean towards Lee or Kasprowicz. Even during our brief preparation of his pre-Test column, Ricky Ponting steadfastly refused to offer anything more definitive than 'We'll decide on the morning of the game'. Contact with other members of the squad yielded an apparently non-cooperative 'Can't help you, mate, but I'll be in touch if I hear something'.

It was late afternoon when I received a short text message from someone within the Australian camp. It read simply: 'Kasprowicz in, Lee out. But you didn't hear it from me.' At dinner that night, the four press men of the Antipodes gathered for an uneasy meal at a café on the banks of the River Avon. Each one of us feared the others had cracked the selection table's secrets. But nothing was spoken, lest anyone not in the know be tipped off. As New Zealand offered Australian journalists the cricket world's only positive time difference, there remained ample opportunity for an updated story to be hurriedly refiled to make final editions. And the solidarity of a shared professional burden only extends so far.

When the papers came out next day, three-quarters of us had it right. The dissenting voice who plumped for Lee cut a lonely, tortured figure in the press box on the Test's first morning, unable to take solace from the knowledge that all of us had occupied that chair at some stage, and would again in the future. Getting scooped remains one of daily journalism's few certainties.

Rather than dampening the clamour for Lee's return, his exclusion from the first Test only fuelled more intense speculation through the days before the second began in Wellington. It gained additional piquancy because of the prospect that, if he didn't play for Australia, he might be able to fly to Brisbane and turn out for New South Wales in the Sheffield Shield final. Given the sort of form he showed, and the work he had put in to regain fitness and purpose, it seemed nonsensical to have him sit idly by, filling the role of drinks waiter for the final two Tests.

The problem for Australia's selectors was that, even if he didn't make the starting XI, Lee was the only reserve bowler in the thirteen-man touring party. If one of the incumbent quicks was to drop down injured an hour before game time, he would be needed. Conversely, if he hung around in Wellington to see the Test start safely without him, he wouldn't arrive in Brisbane until four hours after the Shield final began, leaving his other team at a serious disadvantage.

A whisper then floated across the Tasman. The fast bowler's Sydney-based manager hinted that, by chartering a plane from Wellington as soon as Lee was free of any potential Test obligations, he could be at the 'Gabba and in a baggy blue cap by early afternoon. When this morsel reached the Ideas Factory, all sanity broke loose. The story was deemed so important it was earmarked for the paper's front page. Then, around 8 p.m. Wellington time, it was decided it also required an exclusive picture of the fast bowler, even though the newspaper's budget jugglers had ruled it too expensive to send a staff photographer on the tour. This request was delivered in the usual cheery manner by someone claiming to be 'Chief of Stuff', or suchlike, and who had obviously risen to those rarefied managerial heights that no longer supported conversational niceties.

'We need that photo of Lee within the next hour,' he blustered. 'Where is he right now?'

I explained that he was most likely having dinner somewhere in the city of around 200,000 people.

'Well, grab a photographer and get a photo of him at the restaurant.'

I cheerily pointed out that not only was I unaware where, or even if, he was dining outside the hotel, but should I somehow succeed in unearthing him we were missing someone who was able to frame and transmit a front-page quality picture of the fugitive. I was busy reassuring him I would engage a freelance snapper and set about tracking down the blond quick when my room phone rang. I asked the Chief if he minded holding and answered to a gobful from the newspaper's pictorial editor.

'Why the hell aren't you answering your mobile phone?' he roared. 'I've been trying to get you for the past five minutes and it's turned off. I had to go through the hotel switchboard. We need a photo of Brett Lee. Urgently.'

So I explained that my phone had been busy because that very same message was being relayed by someone who had just emerged from the very same editorial conference and who shared the very same Sydney office.

'Okay,' he said, without recant. 'But let me know as soon as the pic is in the can. They've drawn it in for the front page.' I then returned to the original call.

'Don't ever leave me hanging on the phone like that,' the Chief exploded. 'You reckon I've got nothing better to do at this time of night, with a bloody paper to put out.' And he hung up.

I shook my head, laughed out loud at this latest outbreak of slapstick officiousness, and then contacted agency photographer Hamish Blair, who was fortuitously travelling with the team. Further inquiries revealed Lee was indeed out at dinner with a group of teammates and would not be available for any media commitments until the following day. Self-preservation dictated I not pass that final tidbit on to my superiors. Instead, I joined Hamish in the lobby bar for a drink. Partly to share a chuckle over the newspaper's penchant for managerial hairy-chest thumping. But mainly because our best, indeed only, hope of jagging the picture was to ambush the subject as he returned to the hotel. No more than twenty minutes after we pulled up our refreshments, Lee led a group of four players through the front doors and showed little outward alarm as we dashed across the foyer to intercept him. I outlined the scenario, trying not to sound overly desperate.

'Not a problem, we can do it up in my room in a couple of minutes,' he said, breaking into that contagious grin. 'I'll even grab my guitar. Guess I should probably be strumming something bluesy, to fit with the story.' He showed a greater propensity to see through the hackneyed ways of newspapers than many people running newspapers.

Cricket Australia decided the next day that the charter flight idea was simply too complicated to be feasible. Then, as it turned out, the rain and thick fog that ensured the Test's opening day was abandoned without a ball bowled also grounded planes at Wellington Airport. Even if Lee had been cleared to leave, he would have been forced to stay. That hiatus allowed the Kiwis to escape the second Test with a draw. No such fortune was visited upon them in the final Test in Auckland, where Australia chased down a modest fourth-innings total in near darkness on the penultimate evening.

Over the course of six weeks in New Zealand, Ricky Ponting's team had not looked in remote danger of losing a match. No chink was exposed in its game plan. The Australians boasted the luxury of employing the world's most feared fast bowler of the day as a training weapon. And, as the players jetted out of Auckland a couple of days after Easter, they began a two-month holiday that would ensure they were rested, physically and mentally, for their upcoming Ashes defence in England – where they had not been defeated in a Test series for two decades. The crowning achievement of Ponting's already lustrous captaincy career sat plump and ready, waiting to be plucked.

17

One-day Series, England, June–July 2005

T he greatest Ashes series of modern times began in France – on a
deep-green agrarian field, across which the distant echo of heroic
deeds past stirred above the faint drumming of light rain. Australia's
previous success in England, in 2001, had been kick-started by a wave
of national pride and broader perspective awoken by a visit to Anzac
Cove on Turkey's Gelibolu Peninsula, as Stephen Waugh's squad made
its way to London. Four years later, Cricket Australia decided a train
and bus ride to the Somme was more in keeping with its budget. When
it came to a stand-off between culturally invaluable and commercially
viable, a Gallipoli landing was ruled too high a price. Albeit ninety
years too late.

The compromise was met with annoyance by a number of Ricky
Ponting's men, although that eased when it was pointed out that the
Australian War Memorial at Villers-Bretonneux was, in military terms,
even more significant. The site of the cemetery, starkly laid out among
rolling hills of what was, less than a century earlier, the world's killing
grounds, was arrestingly tranquil. The helter-skelter that kicked off the
team's hundred-day crusade through England, Wales and Scotland had
been anything but. Landing at Heathrow at 5.30 a.m. on a depressingly
dank Monday that suitably announced the onset of English summer,

our advance party of three journalists and a photographer collected the rented Vauxhall station wagon that would be our travelling office until mid-September. Its first outing took us via the M25 and M20 to Ashford in Kent, recently voted Britain's fourth-best place to live, and the last embarkation point for the Eurostar train service before it disappeared beneath the English Channel.

The effects of our twenty-two-hour plane journey (worth six hours of office time) and a further three in a hire car (exchange rate unknown) had not lifted when we emerged early next morning from our motor inn – a refuge for travelling salesmen, who sat gloomy and alone at dinner and breakfast – to board the train to Lille. No sooner had we checked into the twelfth-best hotel on the Boulevard Louis Pasteur than we were herded on to a media bus that whisked us an hour down the A1, through Villers-Bretonneux to the War Memorial, where we finally caught up to the cricketers.

It might have been the leaden skies and persistent mizzle. Perhaps the melancholic aura of so much youthful promise laid waste. But it might also have been a measure of travel fatigue that led to our group's trance-like shambling among the hundreds of ghostly white headstones that jutted defiantly from the precisely trimmed grass, our hands plunged deep into pockets against the rustic French chill. It was too early in the day, and too soon after arrival, to comprehend how that scale of butchery could be wrought on a landscape of such serenity. Standing sentinel over the site, a village green without a village, towered a single sandstone crucifix. And a few hundred metres from the quiet road that terminates at Fouilloy, on the south bank of the Somme, stretches a length of wall on which the roll call of the sacrificed is etched – thousands upon thousands of men, most of them younger than the cricketers, and whose experience of the world beyond home started and finished with the mud and mutilation of the Western Front.

For the half-hour or so that we stepped softly through history, barely a sound was uttered. Until the morning silence was broken by the adenoidal prattle of a London-based television journalist, who seized his moment to perform a vital 'stand up' in front of his cameraman. In television, where journalism and narcissism collide most conspicuously, no story is considered properly told until it's been watermarked with the reporter's noggin. It's the quintessence of 'ownership'.

'This was the calm before the Ashes storm,' he resonated, in an affected baritone that could have startled the fallen. It certainly grabbed the attention of the living.

'An emotional tribute by Australia's cricket heroes to their countrymen who had also given their all,' he deadpanned down the lens. 'And for some, the strain was clearly showing.'

The camera then panned from the talking head to the head of Jason Gillespie, silently bowed and with lips pursed as he walked purposefully away from the graves towards the road. A picture worth several thousand words. None of which conveyed the truth. It had been hinted to the media that the fast bowler was the only member of the touring party thought to have a direct familial connection to the Memorial. That unconfirmed information, plus the cricketer's impromptu withdrawal, was sufficient to conveniently support the TV reporter's hypothesis that Gillespie had been 'moved to tears upon finding the name of a brave relative who fought and died in France'. I knew this would be the subject of the tour's first urgent phone call once that report was broadcast in Australia, so I launched a pre-emptive strike. After he returned to take his place at the wreath-laying ceremony, I checked with the laconic fast bowler if the reason for his temporary absence was as purported.

'Nah, I wasn't even really sure whose name I was looking for,' he said, obviously aghast at suggestions he had milked the moment. 'It was apparently one of my wife's distant relatives, but that's about as much as I know. I took off because it's bloody cold out here, and the only loo in this part of France is on our bus.'

Similarly, one of the few eateries open for business in provincial Picardie on a damp Tuesday was 'Restaurant Le Kangarou', where the team took lunch after touring the Franco-Australian war museum housed within Villers-Bretonneux's L'Ecole Victoria. The school derived its name from post-war rebuilding completed thanks to donations received from schoolchildren in Victoria, and to perpetuate the town's enduring gratitude, a sign hangs in transplanted, patriotic green and gold from the fascia overlooking the quadrangle exhorting: 'Do Not

Forget Australia'. At the kangaroo café, the translation seemed to have been scrambled to 'Do Not Forget Australia's Cricketers (and officials travelling with them)'. Members of the media troupe were firmly and Frenchly rebuffed at the front door. Despite our hungry pleas to purchase as little as a baguette or a plate of *pommes frites* that we were happy to consume outside in the drizzle so as to spare the players' sensibilities and confidences, it was made pointedly clear the joint was hosting a private function. And the press was not on the guest list. Fortunately, the other enterprise in the village to recognise Tuesday lunch as a legitimate trading time was a Turkish *doner* and *pide* parlour. The owner was clearly delighted by the rush of unscheduled patrons, but diplomatically declined to say if his good humour was supplemented by a delicious historical irony.

By day three of our itinerary, we were feeling more like backpackers on a gap year spree than media professionals covering a major international sporting campaign. Having jumped another early train back to Kent to retrieve the hire car, we traversed England's south-east corner bound for our third home in as many nights – the south-coast holiday haven of Brighton. The only constant of the tour to date had been the glaring absence of cricket.

That was eventually rectified when the tourists turned out for a twenty-over game against an Invitational XI of past and present players, from England and abroad. An event that was lent a distinctly carnival air, as much by the format as by its setting. The peaceful forested grounds of Arundel Castle, with its playing field ringed by hospitality tents and lime trees, could easily have been prepared to host a jousting tournament, or a band of lyre-strumming minstrels. The cricket, when it got going, harked back to times not so distantly past. Australia's opening delivery of the tour, from Brett Lee, claimed the wicket of New Zealand's hapless captain, Stephen Fleming, only recently purged of the torment inflicted on his team at home. The Australians looked not to have skipped a beat despite their two-month estrangement from the game.

From West Sussex, we piloted the wagon to Leicester, in the middle of the Midlands, for another warm-up match and from there we retraced 150 miles to Southampton, a mere hop and skip from Arundel, for the next fixture forty-eight hours later. Whether the itinerary was fulfilling the hosts' apparent aim and making the cricketers giddy couldn't be empirically measured, mainly because insufficient cricket had been played at any of the stops to make an informed judgement. The first indication that the Australians were out of sorts surfaced eight days after we arrived, during a twenty-over twilight game against a contemporary England team at Southampton's Rose Bowl.

Ponting's men sauntered into the contest armed with the same sense of purpose they had taken into previous Twenty20 fixtures, minus the facial hair and fancy dress. Contrastingly, the home side threw itself at the opposition with all the purpose of a team that had not tasted global success in limited-overs cricket since the birth of limited-overs cricket. Overjoyed English fans lingered long after Steve Harmison claimed the final wicket, with the Australians one hundred short of their target, and their chants of 'Eeeeeasy, eeeeeasy' and 'You're not very good' drowned out the post-match presentations. Like an exuberant pup scolded for getting silly during a backyard game of fetch, the Australians seemed nonplussed by the speed with which a light-hearted romp had turned serious.

Their humour dimmed further after another loss, two days later, as Somerset thrashed the tourists' inadequate bowling to all parts of Taunton's County Ground, and some points beyond. Questions immediately began filtering through from the office in overnight emails and in early-morning phone calls. What's going on? How can a full-strength Australian team get beaten by a second-division county outfit? More inexplicably, how did they lose to England? I tried to stall the Factory's rising scepticism by pointing out that Australia's next opponent, at the start of a ten-match triangular one-day series, posed much less of a threat. In more than a hundred previous limited-overs internationals, Bangladesh had only twice defeated accepted Test-playing nations. And one of those was Pakistan in a game that elicited far more interest from anti-corruption investigators than learned cricket watchers.

The fact that the Australians' problems increased exponentially from this point can be directly attributed to Cardiff's celebrated nightlife.

A year earlier, the Welsh capital's gleaming Millennium Stadium had hosted football's FA Cup Final between the imperious Manchester United and London scrappers Millwall. Both clubs were renowned and feared for their stridently militant fans and, in the days leading into the play-off, a concerned FA official reputedly rang a senior member of Cardiff's constabulary to ensure adequate security precautions were being taken. The officer seemed more than a little sceptical.

'Well, we'll do everything we can,' he lilted. 'But I'm not sure we can guarantee the supporters' safety.'

The football executive explained that it was more likely the hardcore fans who would pose the problem. But the policeman remained equally adamant that he was more in tune with the looming scenario than the Londoner.

'I hear what you're sayin', but we can offer no guarantees that some of the football fans won't get hurt. After all, in Cardiff, Fridee night is hens' night.' As it transpired, there was a handful of confirmed arrests in the city on Cup eve. All for fighting. All of them women. And it was the siren song of the parties raging hard in bars and clubs along St Mary's Street that proved irresistible to Andrew Symonds. That he chose to enthusiastically celebrate Shane Watson's twenty-fourth birthday beyond sun-up the following day could be construed as touching. The fact that Watson and his teammates had vacated the party not long after dusk due to impending work commitments against Bangladesh next morning meant it was also stunningly misguided.

The next his colleagues saw of Symonds after their celebratory dinner was en route to pre-game breakfast on that sunny Saturday morning. He stood out, and not only because he was still wearing his civilian garb of the previous night while they were uniformly kitted out in team warm-up gear. His pose, slumped against the back wall of a lift, also indicated he was not enjoying peak fitness. He changed into his training outfit and shovelled down a greasy breakfast, but while undergoing preliminary stretching exercises at the ground, the truth leaked out. Reeking of booze, Symonds propped his right leg on a wheelie bin to extend his hamstring and, to the bewilderment of those watching, remained utterly oblivious as the support symbolically rolled away from beneath him.

His name was hastily scratched from Australia's team sheet, the official explanation being that he had suffered a 'niggle' during the warm-up. Conspiracy theories then ran rampant through the Sophia Gardens press box when Ponting fronted international television at the coin toss to announce the problem had, in those few minutes, transmogrified into the flu. Word also emerged from the TV commentary team, where Darren Lehmann was filling a guest role, that the truth lay closer to Symonds being well and truly leathered.

Lehmann then confirmed that he had received a drunken call from the Queenslander around 3 a.m., urging him to come out and join the Welsh wildlife. The ex-player wisely demurred and advised Symonds to call it a night. That counsel was ignored. Other reports then surfaced that Symonds had been seen stumbling about outside our hotel around 6 a.m., just hours before game time. The official story from the dressing room suddenly changed again. The all-rounder was now being investigated for a breach of team rules.

Faced with the unfamiliar scenario of events spinning rapidly out of their control, the Australian brains trust showed a worrying, but ominously instructive, inability to think on their feet. Ponting stuck to his prefabricated plan upon winning the toss and, despite the morning's upheaval and a damp pitch rendered lively as it sweated under the Welsh sun, opted not to immediately unleash his bowlers on the under-qualified Bangladeshis. Instead, Australia's hastily recast line-up struggled with the bat and then, as the pitch flattened out in the heat, Bangladesh cashed in on lacklustre bowling and lamentable fielding. Unlikely cricket history was made with four balls to spare, and it wasn't only the late-afternoon rays beating into the makeshift media conference room that generated heat in the post-match post-mortem.

Despite the airless conditions, Ponting sat ashen-faced. He tried manfully to defend the morning's deceptions, as well as downplay their impact on the result, and grimly promised that Symonds' punishment would be delivered swiftly and decisively. He had no choice. His humiliated and riven team's next match waited barely twelve hours away, forty miles across the mouth of the Severn River, in Bristol.

* * *

When the first call from an incredulous boss arrived just before midnight in Gloucestershire, I was slogging through the third of a slated four stories. Two hours later, on the heels of that Sunday's morning editorial conference, details of the direction that the coverage was to take had been radically redefined. By 4.30 a.m., most of those alterations had been accommodated. And by 8.30 a.m., I was staggering like an over-filled cricketer through the already festive crowd that milled about the bacon sandwich vans set up on the playing fields that abutted Bristol's County Ground. The three-and-a-half-month tour was but a fortnight old, and I was already fielding flashbacks to the final weeks of the World Cup six years earlier. The finish line was a distant haze, with more than a month to pass before the first of five Tests started. And the load of work began to press heavier when Ponting's team suffered an even heftier loss, to England, a day after the Bangladesh fiasco.

Unearthing and deciphering what was going so rapidly wrong became more taxing with each successive night of abbreviated sleep, and with every long-haul road trip. The six-hour journey diametrically across England from Bristol to Durham was a subdued affair in the media vehicle, and undoubtedly even more strained on board the Australians' luxury bus. Barbs and accusations had already been hurled within the dressing room and, as external criticism intensified, the players predictably embraced victim mode, turning swiftly against those who dared query their mettle. Plainly, it was the media's fault that their vaunted bowling attack had been abruptly rendered as ineffectual as an Indian taxi, and that one of their players had reported for duty as pissed as a cricketer.

Upon reaching Durham, both feuding factions were housed in the same Chester-le-Street hotel – a refurbished fourteenth-century fortress, whose reception desk was staffed by rosy-cheeked Geordie lasses clad shoulder to floor in heavy velvet gowns. It was as if we had wandered on to the set of a pre-Tudor period play, a mood enhanced by a popular local legend suggesting that Lumley Castle, built in the wake of the wars in neighbouring Scotland, was haunted. Not only had its first owner, Sir Ralph Lumley, been imprisoned and executed after being implicated in a plot to overthrow Henry IV, his wife was apparently slain by local priests and her body dumped in one of the property's wells. It was Lady Lily of Lumley's supposedly ghostly presence in the castle's labyrinth of stone corridors that lent an air of heightened paranoia to an already uneasy party. And in addition to medieval murder mystery, the besieged Australians found themselves central players in an episode of 'Carry-On Cricket'.

They were deemed ripe for ridicule, which was modern Fleet Street's gleeful specialty. On the day we arrived at the citadel, one of the national tabloids ran a mock-up photo of Australia's fast bowlers – McGrath, Gillespie, Lee and Kasprowicz – all clutching handbags. This prompted the appearance, at the next day's training session, of one of that paper's eager young reporters with photographer in tow, whose mission was to present a handbag to one of the pace-bowling quartet. McGrath genially declined, claiming the accessory did not match his shoes.

A day later, returning from another practice outing, I noticed a small van in our hotel car park that was unpacking an eclectic entourage, among them a scantily clad but heavily stacked young woman, a man dressed in what appeared to be a pantomime rodent's outfit, and another photographer. Sensing it was my national duty to flag the latest ambush, I phoned a warning through to the team bus that had just departed the cricket ground. The players were then discreetly deposited at one of the hotel's alternative entrances and the coach was empty when it pulled up out front.

Nonetheless, it was greeted by the page-three girl who excitedly threw off her bikini top to parade her journalistic credentials, while the rodent, revealing himself to be a cruelly disfigured kangaroo, provided accompaniment on what also masqueraded as a didgeridoo but was, in reality, a length of plastic downpipe. Although the whole sorry skit was played out in the absence of cricketers, the story ran regardless in next Sunday's edition – alongside an article about a Merseyside woman whose uncle had been recently eaten by cannibals. At least when peddling pretend news, the British press had the humility to dress it up in a rat suit and a string bikini.

Just when it seemed the entire episode could not plumb further silliness, word leaked into the British press from within Australia's inner sanctum that Shane Watson had become so scared by the Castle's paranormal inhabitant that he had vacated his room and taken up residence on the floor of Brett Lee's. It had not been an auspicious tour for Watson. Pilloried by the ground announcer at Arundel (Jason Gillespie in a cameo role) for his ankle-freezer yellow pants, he was also derided by *The Australian*'s correspondent in the wake of the Taunton humiliation for being 'all blond tips and no iceberg'. And he had arrived in Durham touting a tour bowling average of 149, a number just as likely to rouse him, screaming, from his sleep as the presence of spooks. As a result, Watson reckoned he did not sleep at all for the four nights we were in Chester-le-Street, and so checked out of the Castle functioning rather like a touring journalist.

The frost that was deepening between players and press with each tabloid revelation meant I was apprehensive about the reception that awaited when, while exploring the castle one evening, I stumbled upon a library, with its raked ceiling almost reached by enormous glass-fronted bookcases, and which doubled as the guests' lounge. Secreted in a dark corner, like a pair of escapees from Hogwarts, sat McGrath and Gillespie, huddled over imported beers and deep in conversation. Sensing what I thought was a ghostly chill, I quickly turned to retreat. But not quickly enough.

'Hey, Rambo,' McGrath called in a most un-library tone, and then waved me to their table. He was obviously unaware that the press had become the enemy.

'You ever heard of this? Dizzy reckons the hours of sleep you get before midnight are worth twice as much as those after. So, if you go to sleep at ten, and you wake up at six next morning, you've had ...' He shot a bewildered look at me then his drinking partner.

'The equivalent of ten hours,' Gillespie nodded, before leaning back in his hand-carved tub chair and taking a long drag of his beer. 'But if you went to bed at midnight and then got up at that time, you'd only feel like you'd had six,' he continued. 'Big difference.'

'You ever heard anything that stupid?' McGrath snorted. 'I mean, even for Dizzy ...' The rest of his gibe remained unspoken.

'So, using that logic,' I said, not totally sure why I would buy into such a profound metaphysical discourse, 'if you went to sleep at 8 p.m., but got up at midnight, you should feel more rested than if you had a full seven-hour kip?'

McGrath gave me a thumbs up. Gillespie gave me a scowl. And, in a trice, changed the subject.

'Saw another one of those local newspaper reporters snooping around here earlier tonight,' he said, drawing a line under the previous exchange. 'A bloke wearing a sheet. With his face painted white. Looked like that Uncle Fester from *The Addams Family*.' He took another drink.

'So how do you know he was a journo?' McGrath asked, intent on scoring more points off his mate.

'He was carrying a notebook,' Gillespie countered. 'And a tape recorder. Came in here and looked more scared than scary when I asked him what he was doing. Then he told me he was dressed up like that 'cos he was on his way to a mate's bucks show. In a castle. On his own. I told him I was about to call security and he buggered off.'

'Bloody journos,' they muttered in chorus, as I slipped away.

After nearly three weeks of tracking the one-day series from England's bottom to top, from Manchester to Birmingham, from Canterbury to London, the tournament's final ended in a gripping, if ultimately unsatisfying, dead heat at Lord's. For all the Australians' internal upheaval, and despite all the external distractions, it seemed the English could be relied on to lapse into old habits when it mattered. Against Australia, that meant losing. But they were granted another crack, courtesy of a three-match limited-overs mini-series between the Ashes rivals that had been stuffed into the schedule prior to the five Tests.

The first of these was programmed for Leeds, with the next pair, and then the opening Test, in London. In a selfless act of corporate austerity, I suggested we jettison the hire car for a couple of weeks, thereby saving our employer the $100 per night it would cost to park the thing beneath our plush London hotel, located among Kensington High Street's designer boutiques and promenading celebrities. I reasoned that traversing the capital would be much simpler by taxi and, by taking a train to and from Yorkshire for the first one-dayer, we also afforded ourselves a chance to catch up on work, perhaps even some sleep, as opposed to a couple more days spent fighting the perils of the M1.

The journey north carried an air of celebration, not only because we could balance our laptops on real tables and enjoy proper local cuisine, like railway-issue bacon butties. The entire nation was aglow, basking in that day's news that London would host the 2012 Olympics. The next day brought spirits crashing with a savagery nobody foresaw. Certainly not those of us who had willingly foregone our independent transport.

It was as I reacquainted myself with the idiosyncrasies of Headingley's press box that the first reports of an incident on the London Underground filtered through. Initially, it was thought to be a fire. Then an explosion. By change of innings it was confirmed as a series of explosions. Aimed murderously at morning commuters, on packed trains and buses. More than fifty dead and a further 700 maimed.

Suddenly, cricket was an indulgence. The game continued, but it was incidental. London was once more a city under siege. It was also where our touring party was headed as soon as stumps were drawn. Or as soon as we could fathom a way to get there. Trains weren't running because Kings Cross Station was shut down. The hire car company simply laughed when I asked about the availability of rental vehicles in Leeds. Surely, I reasoned, the whole tour must now be in question. There was no way the Australian cricket team would voluntarily bus its way into the heart of a city that had, hours earlier, been the mark of an orchestrated terrorist hit aimed at civilian targets. If the same situation had erupted in India, Sri Lanka or Kenya, the squad would have quit the field and been on a plane home before sunset. But apparently, guerrilla warfare in a fair-skinned English-speaking country was far less threatening, and faith in the security capabilities of Western democracies inestimably higher.

So barely an hour after play finished at Headingley, it was to London we returned. Six of us, with luggage, crammed into a generous colleague's Peugeot sedan. Night had fallen by the time we cruised noiselessly through the capital's northern outskirts and then into its posh inner west turned eerie wild west. Desolate streets stood devoid of pedestrians. Traffic was sparse. A few people gathered outside a cinema, one of the few businesses, along with off-licences, that remained open. The shock was palpable. Fear of follow-up attacks lurked everywhere.

We checked into our London hotel with wariness supplanting our weariness. Players lingered in the foyer to workshop reports from home that wives and families who had been preparing to join the team were already reconsidering their plans. Rumours abounded that another blast would see the tour abandoned. This was subsequently refuted by Cricket Australia, but nobody could guarantee the itinerary would run its course.

A resolution to the suspense appeared nigh, one way or another when, in the days immediately after the attacks, a red double-decker bus was abandoned outside our hotel. The lobby was cleared and guests advised to return to their quarters and take refuge in their bathrooms. The normally crammed High Street was emptied of late-afternoon shoppers. From my third-floor room overlooking the street, I had an unnervingly clear view of the bus, on the occasions that I poked my head above the concrete windowsill. Fearing it might all end there, I placed an urgent phone call – to our photographer, who was on his way back to the hotel. I outlined the situation he was about to confront, and suggested it might be prudent to employ his long lens and capture a frame of the vehicle in question, for posterity. I then grabbed my laptop and passport, and retired to the loo.

Eventually, the driver, who had apparently left his bus to grab a drink at a watering hole across the road, was found and castigated. By that time, I had resumed my internal dialogue, begun in Sharjah, which queried the need to continually put myself in the path of peril. It seemed cricket writers found themselves in the globe's trouble spots almost as regularly as war correspondents. Poolside lounges and hamstring injuries, my arse.

Concerns were being simultaneously raised at the Ideas Factory. Not about any potential for physical or psychological harm. My employers' anxiety was sparked by news the hire car had been returned, which meant parking fees had been swapped for the apparently frivolous cost of London's black taxis.

'But the amount we're saving by not having the car garaged more than covers what I'm spending each day on cabs,' I explained to the chief bean counter.

'It still seems an expensive way to get around a city that's got one of the world's most efficient public transport systems,' I was upbraided. 'I don't see why you can't use the Tube.'

I closed my eyes and breathed deeply.

'That's a fair point,' I conceded. 'I'm sure that by the time the first Test starts at Lord's, they'll have removed all the bodies, relaid the tracks, rebuilt the stations, and the Circle Line will be up and running.'

The ensuing silence made me wonder if, for the first time in seven years, I had struck a nerve. But it was just the delay down the international phone line.

'Well, you could always walk those few kilometres,' came the response. 'Hyde Park's gorgeous at this time of a London summer.'

18

Ashes Series, England,
July–September 2005

The English Ashes summer that first entranced me as an eight-year-old had arrived, and with it came a constant phantom chirruping that followed me everywhere, crowding my thoughts and further impinging on already fragmented bouts of sleep. It was not a symptom of intensifying excitement. Nor was it a by-product of stress caused by having to compete against the two, sometimes three, journalists that rival Australian newspapers had sent to bolster their touring complement, given the surge of interest back home in the Australian team's misadventures. Rather it was a direct result of increasingly desperate measures to stave off the mental breakdown hurtling at me due to all of the above.

My coping tonic consisted of weekly Friday-night blow-outs, prescribed in the knowledge that the absence of a Sunday edition of my paper meant the welcome luxury of Saturday mornings and afternoons to recover before duty again called. And while my rationale for self-medicating with lashings of vodka mixed through a potent energy drink might have been commendable in intent, it was deeply physiologically flawed. The alcohol, I fuzzily reasoned, would numb my brain to the point that I could then catch sufficient deep sleep to offset the frenzied week just passed. The cocktail of caffeine, vitamins, sugars and whatever sort of synthetic speed gave the mixer its pep would then allow me to wake from my coma feeling alert and energised. Effectively, I was trying to sprint through waist-deep mud. Unimpressed at being told to slow down at the same time it was being fuelled to speed up, my body effectively gave up in disgust and I began to resemble a somnambulant corpse.

Which was my excuse why, on the weekend before the first Test, I spent five hours hypnotised by obscure 1980s tunes blasted by a DJ through an underground bunker that doubled as a Leicester nightclub. It was only when the music stopped and I could still hear Fairlight feedback screaming off the graffiti-pasted walls that I suspected I might also have picked up a dose of industrial deafness. It was two days before I could distinguish any sound above the incessant ringing, and almost a week until I could communicate without closed captioning. While their late-series rally to win the final pair of one-day internationals meant the Australian players' buoyancy had risen to match the level of media and public interest at home, I went into my first Test match at Lord's overwrought, under the weather, and hard of hearing.

It had taken forty-six days on British (and French) soil, but when Test cricket finally arrived it came clad in its familiar English uniform. Electric-white outfits, accessorised with woollen sweaters, contrasted starkly against shamrock-green lawn and rolling grey clouds that granted sufficient bursts of sun to raise hopes, if not temperatures. Queues stretched across the Nursery Ground lawns from vans dispensing strawberry-laden crêpes, Cornish pasties and proper coffee. At the opposite end of Lord's, MCC members in their egg yolk and ketchup ties took up their positions of privilege in front of the Long Room and unpacked picnic baskets stocked with smoked salmon, fresh figs and French bubbly. The pomp and expectation stood as a stark counter-point to the brash limited-overs fixtures that had soaked up the best part of two months.

Except that when play began at half ten, it did so with a pace and belligerence that reeked of one-day cricket. Steve Harmison's second delivery of the series smashed into the point of Justin Langer's right elbow. Soon after, he slammed another into the titanium grille of Ricky Ponting's protective helmet, twisting the metal bars inward and opening a crimson swoosh below the skipper's right eye from which blood dripped onto the pitch. England had emphatically announced it was up for a fight.

Come day's end, bathed in luscious mid-summer sunshine, the home team was batting. But not especially well. Seven of their number were already out, in addition to the ten Australians who had succumbed, and the powder-blue décor of Lord's space-age media centre, purpose chosen to exude a sense of calm, was doing little to quell the buzz of disbelief that coursed through the paid observers. With at least one exception. The seven hours I had spent splitting my attention between laptop screen, crazed notes, television replays and garbled phone conversations accounted for around ninety per cent of what, I was breathlessly reassured, was the best day's Test cricket in living memory.

Not that I could recall much. Like a battery hen propped on a cheap office chair, which barely fitted the narrow alley between steep tiers of slender work benches, I watched the players trudge away from me and into the historic stone Pavilion that evening, knowing their shift was over but mine was about to begin again. After-stumps media conferences loomed, followed by hours of transcription and typing before the first phone calls from the Factory started arriving around 1 a.m. To maintain lucidity through the night, I would slap my thighs and occasionally my cheeks, willing myself to keep going like a jockey closing on the winning post. Often I typed with one eye closed, to prevent the words drifting out of focus. Occasionally, I would succumb to sleep while writing, and awake some time later with my chin cradled in the upturned palm of my left hand. And so the cycle went. For the remainder of that game. For the rest of the tour. Occasionally the pace slackened to recognisable Test match speed, only to regain its kamikaze intent. Each remarkable moment cascading into the next.

Temporary relief arrived on the fourth Lord's evening when, despite a six-hour delay to cater for England's summer rain and daytime darkness, the Australians completed a thumping win. England's best punch, Adam Gilchrist assessed, had been thrown and duly absorbed. The way ahead appeared deceptively sunny. History, I foolishly believed, had recovered its course and the Ashes would be safe in Australia's keeping by the end of Test three. Public interest would correspondingly wane. And the final month of the tour could be spent regrouping, if not rehabilitating.

It wasn't only me who nurtured that rosy view. Rather than take part in a token tour match scheduled for Worcester between the first two Tests, Gilchrist took his family to Disneyland Paris. Damien Martyn was granted a leave-pass to nobody-knew-where. And the Lord's bowling heroes – Glenn McGrath, Shane Warne and Brett Lee – spent the Worcester stint signing autographs, posing for photographs, and sampling the famous cakes.

That sense of contentment turned on a single cricket ball, placed on the turf as part of a fielding drill before play began in the second Test at Edgbaston. During a light run to warm up for the warm-up, the Australians lazily flicked a rugby ball from one to another. It was as McGrath stretched to haul in a wide pass that his full body weight landed on the ball, turning his right ankle into a right angle, with the joint's ligaments stretched so far they almost ripped in half. The man whose nine wickets had effectively determined the Lord's result was removed, face drained of colour, from the playing arena aboard a golf cart. As his teammates silently feared, Australia's fortunes then disappeared into the medical room with him.

The hobbling of Australia's best pace bowler half an hour before start time might have provided ample fodder for early editions at home, but it didn't faze Ponting, who again pushed stubbornly ahead with his scripted plan to bowl when the coin fell in his favour. That decision, built on a belief that there was residual moisture in the pitch, drew a sharp rebuke from Warne, who saw it as a major tactical blunder. It was the first detectable hiss of discontent to seep from the tourists' dressing room in weeks.

By stumps, Ponting could justifiably point to the fact that his bowlers had captured all ten English wickets. That they fell for a tick over 400 runs probably vindicated his leg-spinner. It wasn't only McGrath's lower leg that had twisted beyond recognition. With no obvious warning, the Australians found themselves confronted by an opponent recast in their own image, as the frantic tempo of Lord's only stepped up in Birmingham.

When the fourth morning dawned, the transition was all but complete. The home nation converged on Edgbaston in ecstasy, and around radios and televisions as if awaiting a Churchillian pronouncement. Australia's three least-credentialled batsmen, statistically at least, needed to pilfer more than a hundred runs from an England bowling attack that had dismembered their opponents' top order twice in the space of a weekend. The result seemed as clear as the Midlands' summer morning, and my mood was correspondingly bright having laboured through the night to chronicle the remarkable *volte-face*. The first three stories completed and sent all canvassed Australia's stunning slide. The fourth, awaiting only confirmation of the final margin, dealt with England's resurgence.

Then, with a deadline ticking ever closer, Australia's tailenders snicked, poked and bravely swung within range of their unlikely target. There often comes a point, if compiling running copy from a live sporting event, when the unfolding reality diverges irreparably from any carefully prepared script. At those times, the journalist's conundrum is whether to sit tight in the belief that it's but an aberration, and that what once appeared likely will indeed come to pass. Or to concede you've got it horribly wrong and begin furiously rewriting. For me, on that loopy final morning at Edgbaston, that defining moment arrived around thirty minutes before I was to fill a gaping hole in the paper's second edition. When Brett Lee's three boundaries in a single over reduced Australia's goal to thirty-three runs, England's remained a solitary wicket. And there had also arisen the very real chance of another dead heat.

Whatever the result, it was destined to neatly intersect with deadline. So there was no choice but to prepare three stories of roughly equal lengths dealing with all plausible contingencies. Had there been time, I would also have panicked. Instead, I started frantically creating new documents, hurriedly copying and pasting words that could transcend any outcome, and madly fashioning new introductory sections that shrieked 'Australia Wins!' Or 'England Wins!' Or 'Nobody Wins!' Juggling more screens than a bashful fan dancer, the only time I shifted attention from the laptop was when the phone rang.

'Australia's gunna win this, it's one of the greatest Tests ever played,' I was told by someone on the Sydney news desk whose cricket nous was matched only by their gift for overstatement. 'We're gunna run it on the front page. So we'll need a twenty-five-centimetre write-off from you as soon as they hit the winning runs.'

I was now beyond stressed. The need for a separate, standalone article for the news section that complemented, but not duplicated, what would appear in the sports pages raised the degree of difficulty to a level beyond my impaired cognitive functions. Instead of managing three concurrent stories, I suddenly had six on the go. I allowed myself a whimper, a quick crack across the quadriceps, then got typing. The margin had narrowed to fifteen runs. An over later, it was whittled to six.

Two nations' attention then focused on a sward in the English Midlands. The final overs of perhaps the most famous Ashes encounter transfixed households. Entire suburbs. It lives on in the memory of everyone watching, whether adhered to television or sitting, in gut-churning tension, among the spellbound crowd. Everyone except journalists working to Australian deadlines. For the last half-hour, I saw not a single delivery, not a solitary run, nor even the tragi-triumphant final act when Michael Kasprowicz lost his wicket with Australia three runs shy of victory. Two runs short of a tie. When that moment of history was finally written, my sole concern was ensuring the right version of the appropriate story was sent to its correct destination. And that I had interpreted the scoreboard correctly.

The English, as a nation, were elated. The Australians understandably disappointed, but hardly shattered. Having been pummelled for two of the Test's four days, struggled for another, and relied on occasional batsmen to carry them within a lucky boundary of success at the end, they felt that they had almost stolen an undeserved win. Gathering that evening in the first-floor bar of their Birmingham hotel, they outwardly showed no greater distress than a tour group whose complimentary drink vouchers had been revoked. They were more concerned about the pair of barely covered young girls trying desperately to make their acquaintance, obviously as part of another clumsy sting from a tabloid paper that believed the rejuvenation of Test cricket in its homeland was not a sufficiently salacious story.

* * *

Sensing my growing frailty, generous colleagues back at the Factory took up the reporting cudgels during those hours, deep in the English night, when I snatched sleep like a man overboard clutches flotsam. But the toll was beginning to show, and when I turned up to a scheduled morning chat with Ricky Ponting in our Manchester hotel, two days before the third Test, he greeted me with a gratuitous recommendation that I get a decent night's sleep.

'If you blokes win this Test, that's how I'm celebrating,' I joked feebly, before running through the obvious reasons why that was unlikely. Brett Lee in hospital with blood poisoning. Gillespie so badly out of sorts there were fears he might poison himself. And McGrath still as legless as Andrew Symonds on a Welsh weekend.

'I wouldn't count out McGrath just yet,' Ponting said with a glint. 'I've just seen him. He's walking without a limp and he'll bowl at training this afternoon.'

That session was not due to start until the day's first deadline had elapsed, so I charged back to my room and dashed off a stridently equivocal story that stopped short of labelling McGrath's recovery a miracle more worthy of Lourdes than Lord's. Just in case he failed to break out of a limp at practice. The greater challenge was keeping this exclusive nugget from my colleagues as we gathered to watch the Australians' preparations from the Members Pavilion at Old Trafford. The satisfaction I felt at getting the captain's scoop on a couple of stretched ankle ligaments gave way to sleep-deprived paranoia as my friends, now recast as bitter rivals, began to sense a story was afoot – an inkling gained from the fast bowler's selfish decision to conduct his clandestine fitness examination smack in the middle of the Test match ground in bright Lancashire sunshine.

'It's just part of his ongoing rehab for the fourth or fifth Tests,' I misinformed those colleagues peering pensively through the window as McGrath began rolling his arm over from a standing start, then progressed to trotting three or four paces.

By the time he started jogging, I voiced my suspicions that Lord Lucan was concealed among the Old Trafford ground staff. And finally, as the wounded pace bowler sent down several deliveries at three-quarter pace off his full run-up, I announced I was in receipt of a coded bomb warning, and that we must all vacate the stadium immediately. None of my colleagues turned a hair. In all, my world exclusive lasted less than three hours.

Even with McGrath among their number, the Australians soon learned that the reversal of fortunes played out at Edgbaston was no fleeting anomaly. Come the opening day of the third Test, the tourists were not just outplayed. They were violently and repeatedly mugged. Gillespie's celebrated international career was effectively terminated, such was the hammering he copped, firstly from England's newly emboldened batsmen and then from the remorseless Manchester crowd. Michael Clarke aggravated the chronic back injury that remains a legacy of a misguided childhood spent trying to prove he was a fast bowler, which left him confined to his hotel bed for three days. Adam Gilchrist's contribution was so forgettable he rated it the undisputed low point of his international playing days. And when stumps were drawn on that first evening, McGrath was so drained by the demands of his rehabilitation and then his wicketless bowling stint that he fell asleep in the dressing room while applying ice to his injured ankle.

Even though it failed to produce a result, the third Test was the pivot on which the historic series ultimately turned. For the next three days, England was confident, skilled and surging. Australia timid, hapless and floundering. Another defeat loomed for the tourists when the fourth day ended, prompting hundreds of England fans to camp in the overnight cold to secure cut-price tickets available on the final morning. All 23,000 seats were filled when the final day's play began, with a further 10,000 or so disappointed folks turned away from locked gates. Thousands more were intercepted by authorities in the heart of Manchester and told not to bother boarding the Altrincham tram to Old Trafford.

That Australia finished the day still batting was due largely to Ponting's most dogged Test innings, and ultimately to the defiance of another pair of bowlers left once more to carry the batsmen. McGrath's return brought no impact with the ball but, for the only time in his career, he saved a Test with the bat.

The repeated failure of the batting group was but one fissure opening within the touring party. The intrusion of families into the team's culture was another. Traditionalists who believed that wives and kids were publicity props to be trotted out at the annual Christmas party felt their presence on tour diluted team unity. Some even muttered it was the distraction caused by keeping company with loved ones rather than teammates, as opposed to the technical inadequacies exposed by England's mastery of reverse swing bowling, that was to blame for Australia's compounding problems. Even more destructive was the suggestion of rifts among rival cliques of players' partners. The UN's foremost peace negotiators would run screaming from a brief to reconcile warring WAGs.

Also copping their share of scrutiny was the touring party's coaching staff – for their inability, interpreted broadly as unwillingness, to help those players whose form had left them. As questions began to stockpile, the support team, led by coach John Buchanan, was accused of being more adept at formulating excuses than answers. Tellingly, the accepted solution to these multiplying woes and cancerous whispers lay in the stubborn belief among the squad, and many of its more blinkered supporters, that Australia was simply the better team. And that it was only a matter of time before that was reflected in scorebooks.

The tetchiness within became public during preparations for the fourth Test in Nottingham. Hell-bent on launching a Test career, twenty-two-year-old fast bowler Shaun Tait unleashed himself on the under-prepared Trent Bridge practice pitches, and his teammates. Up until that time, Tait had struggled to find his place in a touring party of which he was the youngest member. A card-carrying Generation Y-er hanging with a group of thirty-plus family men, Tait was known to spend occasional evenings alone in the team bus where he indulged his passion for computer games.

On Test eve, Justin Langer was his first target, trapped at the far end of a practice net as Tait let loose a month of frustration and inactivity. In the space of a single over, the youngster dropped the normally unflappable opener to his knees with a lethal full-toss that rifled into the top of Langer's left thigh. He then spreadeagled the batsman's stumps with a late-swinging yorker and finally, straining every sinew, caught his teammate with a bouncing bomb that would have done the Dambusters proud, as it reared spitefully from the unpredictable surface and smacked the batsman flush on the right forearm. For Langer, already feeling the hurt of under-performance, it was the final indignity.

'For fuck's sake, mate,' he screamed, as the rest of the training session stopped and tuned in. 'Some of us are trying to prepare for a Test match.'

He bent to retrieve the bat he had flung to the turf in disgust.

'I'm not trying to pin you,' Tait shouted back, a picture of Adelaide Hills innocence that masked the truth – confirmed to us in an interview earlier in the tour – that he had little control over where the ball was headed as it left his hand.

Despite the ire he precipitated, Tait was drafted on the morning of the Test to replace his mentor and close mate Gillespie. A replacement was also needed for McGrath, who once again failed to make it through the pre-game warm-up. This time, the problem was his right elbow, which had become inflamed due to the minute changes to his bowling action brought about by his ankle injury. It was a thumbnail sketch of the entire campaign. A problem hastily papered over invariably reappeared, nastier and more debilitating, further down the track.

Over the course of five days at Trent Bridge, the problems that had been steadily mounting since Cardiff officially formed themselves into a crisis. The Australians' pig-headed refusal to contemplate remedial work led to the bowlers delivering an unforgivable twenty-five no-balls in a single innings. On-field plans were farmed out to committee, rather than implemented through decisive leadership. The glaring batting weaknesses exposed in the previous two Tests, but brushed aside at training sessions, were exploited again, seemingly surprising no one but the Australians. And when Ponting needlessly sacrificed his wicket to an unerring throw from a substitute fielder, the Launceston street-fighter within him slipped its restraints. The red mist that had brought him undone in a Kings Cross lager pit all those years ago then accompanied him back to the dressing room, lifting long enough for him to notice the face of England coach Duncan Fletcher leering over the players' balcony, mocking the Australian skipper's misjudgement.

Ponting responded by letting fly a stream of abuse that initially shocked, but soon encouraged, the venerable Nottinghamshire members. For they knew, as did we all, that the ugly outburst signalled the moment that the Ashes effectively changed hands. The Australians, through their tortured captain, confirmed they were out of answers.

There remained one last hope to recover skills and solidarity before the final Test in London – another training exercise, dressed up as a two-day match against a group of eager youngsters posing as Essex's first XI. Sagging spirits were not lifted when we arrived at our shared accommodation, a soulless 1980s-vintage country club perched among the denuded hills outside Chelmsford, and surrounded by nothing but farm country that exhaled the rank breath of blood and bone. Either that, or the resort's effluent tanks had ruptured. Whatever the cause, it was emblematic of the Australians' predicament.

Powering through the lobby one evening, in an attempt to outrun the stench, I heard a familiar voice beckoning me from a corner table deep in the otherwise deserted lounge bar. Shane Warne was sharing a nightcap and a whine with fellow spinner Stuart MacGill. And one of them was keen to shoot the rancid breeze.

'Whadda ya make of all this?' Warne said, picking up his drink and leaning in across the table. 'This whole mess.'

The question was rendered rhetorical by his unwillingness to grant me right of reply.

'It's just horse shit, the whole thing,' he continued, replacing his drink on the bleached-pine tabletop and flicking his cigarette lighter from hand to hand. It then became clear he wasn't talking about our environs.

'We're stuck here in the middle of nowhere, playing a bullshit county game that's not doing anyone any good. We should be in London, having a few days' rest, and then hitting the practice nets for the biggest match of our careers. We need to be lean and hungry when we get to The Oval.

'Too many of our blokes just aren't pulling their weight. And the coach is the worst offender. I mean, what's he done to fix all these problems? Nothin' except leave cricket balls lying around during training drills and call a team meeting every twenty minutes. I'll tell ya now, there's a few blokes whose careers are on the line right here.' He lifted a cigarette from a packet on the table, then slipped outside to freshen the air. MacGill just continued to nod furiously in agreement.

Warne had every right to feel let down. He was the only Australian to emerge from the series with reputation intact, even enhanced. Leading wicket-taker, most accomplished batsman, sole source of inspiration and defiant counter-attack. All achieved against a backdrop of tawdry tabloid newspaper headlines and a disintegrating marriage.

Even before it got underway at The Oval, the decisive final Test bore an evangelical aura. In keeping with idiosyncratic English tradition, an event of such profound national significance demanded its own cheesy soundtrack. Curiously, the imminent return of the Ashes was assigned William Blake's spiritual call to arms 'Jerusalem', which had been set to music ninety years before the decider began on green and pleasant pasture in south London. It was sung with choral gusto before and after each day's play. At the beginning and end of every session. And it was even played on radio with a patriotic respect usually reserved for Sir Cliff Richard's annual Christmas ditty.

Fervour was also the only rational explanation for fans handing over £300 for a seat at the series climax. Regardless of who claimed the Ashes, Test cricket had already emerged as the undisputed winner. And true to my calling as a dispassionate journalist, I did not have to struggle to avoid being swept up in the excitement. Bloodshot eyes now fixed unflinchingly on the finish, I cared not so much who secured the urn just so long as somebody did. That party stepped forward late on the fifth Test's fifth day, when poor light brought a premature halt to play with no result pending. The home team's two–one series lead would stand. Which meant celebrations that stretched the length of the island were then uncorked. For all the symbolism and emotion attached to England's first Ashes success in a generation, there was something vaguely ridiculous about a dozen adult peers-in-waiting jumping up and down in unison, frosted in tickertape, in delirious worship of a trophy roughly the size of an eggcup.

The post-match media conference was packed and restless when Ponting strode in, and took his seat behind a large table buried under microphones, cables and dictaphones. In the awkward silence that habitually precedes the initial question of these events, an Australian radio news reporter decided that this was the time for hard-nosed journalists to take over from the compliant cricket media, and to pose the tough question.

'Ricky, you're the first Australian captain to lose the Ashes in England in twenty years. Are you going to resign?' he boomed.

I hurriedly rechecked my notes fearing that, amid my semi-conscious scribbling, I had imagined the preceding two months. When, but for the brush of a batting glove in Birmingham and the rearguard efforts of a couple of England tailenders in Nottingham, the Marylebone Cricket Club's sacred urn could have quite easily remained in Australia's name, if not its keeping. Ponting was initially perplexed, then annoyed.

'I don't know, mate, you tell me,' the captain shot back. 'You obviously know a lot about cricket.'

The tour had ended pretty much as it began. At the scene of a bitter ideological battle. For almost an hour after the seemingly endless media conferences, I propped myself, completely spent, against the doorway to the Australian dressing room. I knew that, given what had just been lost, there was no chance of gaining admission. But neither could I depart the ground and begin the tour's final stretch of writer's confinement until I had a column from the skipper in my keep. My hopes would lift fleetingly every time the wooden door swung open, but sink back when it yielded nothing more than team support staff stacking cricket bags in the corridor in preparation for the following day's homeward flight.

The brief glimpses I stole of the losers' camp revealed a picture not nearly as funereal as I expected. Some players sat quietly on wooden benches, the music and banter that announced the end of most Test matches noticeably absent. But with each passing luggage run, the atmosphere within seemed to warm. Several England opponents clutching bottled beer and beaming smiles filed in to share a drink and a chat, and were greeted warmly as they sought Australian autographs on various pieces of clothing and equipment. As priceless Ashes memorabilia, these would prove far more lucrative in seasons to come than any county testimonial year.

One of professional sport's dirty secrets is that the pain of losing usually hits supporters harder than players. The besotted fan delusionally believes their chosen team will succeed every time it takes the field. To entertain the alternative is a betrayal of their life's cause. But players readily accept the risk of losing is writ large in the contract of competing. As Justin Langer once philosophised, if the joy of triumph provides the game's greatest feeling, then the regret of losing must be next best. Because if you're not experiencing either of those, it means you've been reduced to nothing more consequential than a spectator.

During my catatonic wait, I tried to sketch out the series post-mortem I was to compile overnight by running the big moments, the defining contests, over in my mind. I drew a blank. I had seen so little live cricket between typing stints I may as well have been home in Melbourne. Or asleep. I made a mental note to buy a DVD box set of the 2005 Ashes series in order to catch up on the history I had missed while writing and rewriting it. That pledge will one day be redeemed.

Ponting eventually appeared, baggy green cap defiantly in place, hands jammed deep in his pockets. He indicated our meeting would be conducted in the corridor and, instead of offering any preliminary thoughts, he instead stared silently through a window that looked over remnants of the crowd being ushered through the heavy iron gates and into the Vauxhall gloaming, raucously 'Jerusaleming' their way to the nearest pub.

'So you gunna resign?' I asked, trying unconvincingly to channel the self-importance of a serious journalist. Ponting turned quickly, wearing a pained scowl, before recognising the gallows humour. If nothing else, it allowed us to establish eye contact.

'And ya reckon I'd announce that through my column?' he asked, through a grin that, until then, I suspected the plastic surgery he underwent after day one at Lord's had removed.

'As good a place as any,' I suggested. 'But maybe not tonight. I'd rather we go with the usual clichés, so I can get a head start on that sleep.'

19

Australian Summer 2005–06, One-day Tournament, New Zealand, December 2005, South Africa, February–April 2006

Four weeks after that eternal English summer, Australia's cricketers waded straight back into a seven-month, non-stop playing roster that would drag them across three continents and a pair of neighbouring islands. But not everyone who was aboard the rickety Ashes bandwagon would be along for the ride. Come the start of the home series against the West Indies, Jason Gillespie, Damien Martyn and Michael Kasprowicz had been called to account for the failure in England. Within weeks, Simon Katich and Michael Clarke joined them in the selectors' bad books. Jettisoning half the team that had failed at Edgbaston satisfied those who called for heads to roll. But selectors are more forgiving than jilted fans, and all five would soon return to Test ranks.

In the meantime, the brave new faces of Australia's cricket future were unveiled, the most prominent of which belonged to a thirty-year-old who had already notched 10,000 first-class runs. In his first three Test innings, Michael Hussey progressed from single, to double, and then triple figures, his maiden century at Hobart's Bellerive Oval triggering from him unrestrained celebrations, even though it came against a West Indian attack that never quite mustered the intensity to be lacklustre. Hussey jumped and yelped, and was still bouncing like a cheap sports bra on a treadmill when the players, with a few journalists in tow, took their post-match victory celebration to a South Hobart pub. And when the hotel closed, the party made a short walk into the city, where Ricky Ponting knew of a late-night bar where you could safely get a drink without wearing a right hook.

I made the trek in a group of one, equidistant from the small cliques of players ahead and astern, when the gallop of footsteps from behind made me instinctively flinch. An incoherent shout echoed down the empty road at the same moment a hand clamped down on my left shoulder, and Hussey fell into loping stride alongside.

'Mate, this is what it's all about,' he beamed, draping his right arm around my neck as we lock-stepped down a slight incline. As I was to learn, after a few drinks Hussey became as tactile as a blind man in a fruit shop. And he'd definitely downed a few drinks.

'I don't reckon there could be a better feeling than this, no matter how long I play for. And I know we're supposed to treat you guys with suspicion, but you've been around it a lot longer than me. So I need to ask you a favour.

'If you ever notice I'm getting a bit full of myself, or you reckon I need to be knocked down a peg or two, you've got my absolute permission to tell me to pull my head in.'

He administered another backslap, then I twisted my neck beneath his elbow to try and gauge his sincerity. His blue eyes sparkled with excitement and perhaps a couple of excess beers. But no discernible ill will.

I thanked him for the offer and promised I would share with him any concerns I harboured about his performance or his temperament. After I'd written them in the paper.

'I knew it,' he roared, ruffling my hair before he bounded off to join the group in front. 'You guys really are a pack of bastards.'

The insertion into the Australian summer of a week's worth of one-day internationals in New Zealand was welcomed like a dose of croup by all affected parties. So underwhelmed was Adam Gilchrist that he sought, and was granted, leave of absence to better invest that time at home in Perth with his family. I understood his priorities. Even though I had no such ties, having spent barely ninety days of 2005 at home, a further seven nights away offered less appeal than it did purpose. But that level of apathy did not extend across the Tasman, where New Zealand officials expressed outrage that one of world cricket's great drawcards would not be on hand to get turnstiles clicking. So Cricket Australia backed down and Gilchrist's leave ticket was revoked. This meant I was nowhere near the least enthused of the touring party that boarded an Auckland-bound flight at Sydney Airport.

However, I would – despite it still being early in the Australian summer – have taken some beating for the title of most worn out. Which was why, moments after tumbling into my seat, I also fell into a deep and deeply unattractive sleep. Woken by the arrival of the food trolley, I also noticed the companion with whom I was notionally sharing dinner was a striking, willowy brunette. Travellers' luck usually dictated I was seated alongside a morbidly obese armrest thief or Brad Hogg. But in the first slice of genuinely good fortune since my hearing returned, my allocated partner was not only glamorous and dainty, but perfectly content to remain immersed in a novel. Probably because the miniature television dangling from the bulkhead before us was as lifeless as the food. When she was forced to put down her book in order to perform a post-mortem on her meal, I seized my chance to make an impression.

'You heading home or away?' I asked as casually as is possible when trying to manoeuvre a child-sized plastic fork towards one's mouth with both elbows super-glued to one's ribcage.

'Sorry?' she shot back, clearly surprised by this outbreak of neighbourliness.

'This trip,' I persisted, undaunted by a response colder than the *cacciatore*. 'Are you heading home, or away?'

'Oh,' she smiled wanly, her alabaster complexion lightly tinged by a mix of annoyance and alarm. 'I thought you asked if I watched *Home and Away*.'

Clearly worried she faced another couple of hours shackled next to a deranged narcolept with an unhealthy fascination for television soapies, she returned to her food. The low hum of jet engines covered a long silence.

'So ... do you?' I asked eventually, reasoning there was nothing I could do to make me appear any more unhinged at that moment.

'Do I what?' she retorted, her face now radiating nothing but pain.

'Watch *Home and Away*?' I dangled my kiddie cutlery at eye level between us, partly for dramatic effect and partly in self-defence. But rather than reach for the stewardess call button, she smiled brightly and we began a conversation that continues, long after we touched down. Years of travelling had, at last, delivered something more permanent than passport stamps.

After the New Zealand hiatus, the home Test series against South Africa contained three matches, none of which the tourists won. The triangular one-day tournament that followed dragged on for more than a month, and produced the same winner. Just how those of us embarking, at summer's end, on a reciprocal six-week tour to South Africa would unearth story ideas from another nine internationals between the same two groups of cricketers would have caused considerable angst had there been time to dwell on it. But the months that followed New Year bore the unrelenting, fast-revolving door of airport shuttle runs, hotel check-ins and check-outs, cricket training and cricket matches. The simple chores of domesticity, like nurturing a new relationship and maintaining a home, were luxuries that living on the road did not support. Among the essential tasks squeezed out of my summer schedule was procurement of a travel visa for Bangladesh, where our tour was destined immediately after South Africa. It was an oversight that demanded redress as a matter of priority, once we checked into our opulent hotel in Johannesburg's showpiece shopping and tourist precinct of Sandton – an enclave carved from granite and glass that stood at least a world away from the true South Africa.

Bangladesh's sole consular outpost was located fifty kilometres from Johannesburg in the South African capital, and our only scheduled visit to Pretoria was set down for the upcoming Sunday. Diplomatic staff notoriously eschew work during working hours, so weekend access was not even worth inquiring about. My only choice was to abandon work commitments and spend hours camped at the embassy, or entrust my passport to a kindly Australian backpacker who sought to have similar paperwork finalised so he could join us on the subcontinent. To supplement my application, I also handed him an effusive official-looking letter of support from the paper's editor-in-chief who, in more than a decade of employ, I had never met, but who extolled my journalistic credentials in glowing words that read suspiciously like mine.

The trepidation I felt at surrendering my vital documents to a casual acquaintance about to board the Johannesburg–Pretoria train – notorious, even by the infamously violent city's standards, as a sure ticket to being mugged, shot, abducted, or the trifecta – was surpassed by my fear of running foul of Bangladeshi border guards upon landing in Dhaka six weeks later. The plucky courier returned safely intact at day's end, though the news he brought was not exclusively good. My visa stamp showed an issue date of 2004, already two years lapsed. And it granted me stay in Bangladesh for thirty days, provided it was presented at immigration by 23 May 2005. Roughly the same time I had been bound for the War Memorial at Villers-Bretonneux. There was no chance to rectify the errors before we left for Bangladesh, but Australian team members who had previously visited Dhaka assured me any discrepancies could be instantly sorted out at passport control with a strategically placed US greenback or two.

The opening week's events in South Africa bore the hallmarks of Ashes Mark II. A bowling machine set up for Australia's first training session at Wanderers' Stadium was rendered inoperable when a member of the ground staff disconnected its power supply in order to carry out some urgent vacuuming at the adjacent rugby club. Torrential afternoon storms on the High Veldt washed out another session and meant the tour-opening twenty-over game didn't finish until nigh on midnight. That made it a long day for the eight Australian players awoken before dawn by phone calls from hotel reception staff claiming to have anxious family members on the line. Fearing crises at home, the players agreed to take the calls only to find a local FM radio jock on the other end making, for reasons known only to him and his audience, poorly mimicked sheep noises.

Losses in the Twenty20 game and the opening pair of the five-match one-day series only heightened everyone's sense of unease and *déjà vu*. But a meritorious win in the third game at the coastal city of Port Elizabeth restored morale to the extent that the Australians cancelled their planned early flight to Durban next morning, and opted to travel at an hour more in tune with the effects of after-match celebrations. The press corps was not privy to such flexibility in our itinerary, and while it clearly contravened the touring tenet of never becoming separated from the team, time apart translated to blessed relief when we arrived at Durban's Elangeni Hotel. With its Indian Ocean frontage and a broad, sandy beach pounded by thunderous waves, it spelled 'seaside vacation'. If only for the few hours until the cricketers lobbed in, and work resumed.

That lure was partly tempered by the cheery desk staff who were only too keen to warn us about the local dangers, none of which were aquatic. Beware the half-kilometre walk across the desolate Hoy Park Sports fields to get to Kingsmead Cricket Ground, and avoid it completely come nightfall, they advised. Likewise the 'Golden Mile' section of Snell Parade, which ran past the hotel's front doors and was famous for its prostitutes and pimps, its muggers and addicts. Don't take anything more valuable than a towel if swimming, and even reconsider that accessory when strolling the wide, paved esplanade towards South Beach and Durban's seedy CBD. This counsel made such an impact that I packed nothing more than my swimmers and an old T-shirt when I braved the midday heat for a frolic in the rolling surf.

After battling the heavy swell for a full ten minutes, I slumped onto the sand to recover and became aware that the chunky African man clad in only navy-blue trunks and sprawled parallel to the breakers not fifty metres up the beach was taking considerably longer than me to regain his breath. If, indeed, he had any. From where I was collapsed, he appeared to be dead.

This layman's prognosis was proved correct when a pair of paramedics arrived, conferred as they leaned over his motionless frame, and then returned to their vehicle to retrieve the sort of silver reflecto-blanket used to wrap hypothermia sufferers, or large loaves of garlic bread. They stood guard over the lifeless figure for many minutes, talking intermittently into hand-held radios and then, convinced the corpse and its final vestige of dignity were secured, drove off leaving the package glinting in the afternoon sun. All but a few passers-by resisted the urge to lift a corner of the space-age shroud to confirm their morbid suspicions until, eventually, a couple of lethargic ambulance officers arrived and stretchered the deceased across the sand and into the back of their waiting station wagon. By that time, even the grey-headed gulls had lost interest.

I recounted this ghoulish tale to Damien Martyn and Brad Hogg, whom I encountered heading for a swim as I returned to the hotel. Their eyes widened, more so at the thought of sharing the beach with a stiff than the apparent lack of public concern for the loss of a human life in KwaZulu-Natal. Hogg looked especially disturbed.

'How did he die if he was on the beach? Was he murdered?' he asked, agog. I glanced briefly at Martyn, who simply rolled his eyes.

'Land sharks,' I replied, trying to stifle a grin.

'Land sharks? There's no such thing … is there?' Hogg said, turning beseechingly to his teammate, who made it immediately clear that the all-rounder was fighting this joust on his own.

'They're rare,' I went on, sensing the bait had been taken. 'You only get them on this stretch of the African coast. And they only come out of the sea for a few minutes at a time.'

'That's crap … isn't it?' Hogg said, desperately scanning our faces for a telltale smirk. But on cue, we had both turned and headed away from him in opposite directions. As I neared the road, I heard a distinctive Australian voice behind me urging: 'Well you can swim if you want, mate, but I'll just hang out in the beach café.'

The one-day series stood level at two games-all entering the final match in Johannesburg, where the steady momentum the Australians had built over the preceding week gave way to an avalanche. Not only did Ricky Ponting's team become the first to reach 400 runs in a fifty-over international, they set an unheard-of new mark of 434 that pretty much everyone expected would stand for years. As is history's way, it was obliterated within four hours.

In deference to this phenomenal output, the game was quickly dubbed 'the greatest one-dayer ever played', an accolade the scoresheet suggests is entirely fitting. The reality, from my press box seat on the fourth tier of the towering southern grandstand, was that it all became a bit of a yawn. A rock-hard pitch, flint-dry conditions, a reduced playing arena and even thinner atmosphere at altitude conspired to ensure that the ball flew laughable distances every time a batsman fearlessly thrust his front leg down the track and swung with impunity through, or across, the line. With the ball as likely to deviate off the straight as it was to be impeded by a fielder, the match had surrendered all pretence of a contest well before South Africa snuck home with a delivery to spare. From the outset, the bowlers were never part of the game. It was on this same inequitable premise that the Twenty20 concept was to conquer the cricket world.

In truth, the story didn't really require words, as it could be adequately told through a selection of numbers. Most compellingly the eighty-seven fours and twenty-seven sixes dotted throughout the day's hundred overs. This was fortunate because, for the first time in almost twenty years as a working journalist, I failed to hit a deadline. Even though I had spent hours trawling Sandton Mall for replacement cables, communications software and even a South African-issue mobile phone, it all counted for nothing when it most mattered. My new communications devices proved as useless as the Factory-issued hardware I had initially been sent abroad with. I then spent forty-five torturous minutes at the close of Australia's innings trying to get my words to Sydney using my locally sourced technology. History had been made but, as the second-edition presses rolled and I cussedly laid the blame at the foot of the tools I worked with and even for, it didn't make the paper. Once again I was unable to fathom why an organisation that spent such vast sums sending a reporter on a global assignment, as was regularly pointed out, would not make a commensurate investment in technology that allowed the reporter to adequately perform their principal task. Heated phone calls between me, the technicians and late-night sub-editors then bounced back and forth across the Indian Ocean. But the one I dreaded most didn't arrive until the morning's small hours, as my boss headed into the Sydney office to begin the day at morning conference.

'That was unbelievable last night,' cooed a voice that betrayed awe more than fury. 'We need to be all over it today. Reaction pieces from everyone we can get. Where that effort compares with others in one-day history. Details on how it was planned and executed. Graphics on how the day panned out ...'

I confirmed that's what had occupied me since I returned, crestfallen, to my hotel where reliable wireless internet welcomed me. And then I braced myself for a bollocking that never arrived.

'That's great,' the voice enthused. 'I'll call you back after morning conference to let you know what else we'll need.'

'Oh, by the way,' came the final observation, as I visibly flinched. 'How close did South Africa get in their chase?'

Suddenly, I didn't feel quite so far from the pace.

The start of the Test series coincided neatly with the opening of the 2006 Commonwealth Games in Melbourne, which, in turn, meant reduced space and demand for cricket stories in the paper. It also meant the yoke was partially lifted, and the workday routine of strong coffee and room service club sandwiches was replaced by more rewarding ventures, such as a ferry ride across Table Bay to Robben Island, where visiting the site of Nelson Mandela's eighteen-year incarceration put any grievances I held about confined typing stints in swank hotel rooms into perspective. It also led, as the fluffy cumulus 'table cloth' draped itself over flat-topped Table Mountain during the return ride, to a recklessly ambitious pledge among a few misguided journalists to scale Cape Town's omnipresent attraction the next day.

The trek had been known to claim the lives of unfit, under-prepared hikers, and I comfortably fitted those criteria. Setting out from a roadside stop one-third of the way up the mountain's northern flank, the first half-hour was unmitigated agony, and from there it quickly got worse. The searing pain in my quivering thighs and knotted calves was useful only to mask the burning in my chest, and the worrying throb inside my skull – symptoms that forced me to stop every fifty steps or so and stand bent over, with hands on knees, pondering how long I would have to lay sprawled on the scree path before paramedics arrived to cover me in Alfoil.

Every time I righted myself, I could see my far more energetic colleagues fading further into Platteklip Gorge above me. I regretted that my exhaustive preparation for this stunt had not extended to purchasing a bottle of water. And when a couple of barely panting Dutch pensioners breezed past during one of my rehab stints, I contemplated asking them to tell my fellow trekkers that I had strategically withdrawn; I figured I could at least manage the descent, if only by falling. However, by the time I found sufficient breath to form a sentence, they too were disappearing into the rocky canyon, and the affront of being shown up by a pair of septuagenarians in wooden hiking shoes compelled me to push on. After almost two hours of vertical hell, I staggered onto the patio that surrounds the mountain-top café, badly in need of hydration and counselling. As I wobbled my way to the rear of the cafeteria queue, I received a wave and a smile from Michael Kasprowicz, contrastingly dapper in immaculate T-shirt, jeans and shades, camped at the front of the line. He, along with Brett Lee and Shaun Tait, had taken the cable-car to the top, allowing them to enjoy the panoramic view unimpeded by the shadow of death.

'You look like you need a drink, buddy,' Kasprowicz called, prompting the entire queue to turn and take note of the sweating, shaking, gibbering cardiac-seizure-in-waiting at the back. I could only nod, before collapsing onto one of the low stone walls that snake around the summit. Minutes later, Kasprowicz appeared, triumphantly brandishing a large glass of beer that he thrust into my tremulous hand. I accepted it, along with his logic that it represented a far more suitable match for my capabilities than did physical exertion.

In the days leading into the first Test in Cape Town, South Africa's coach, Mickey Arthur, asked the Newlands curator to prepare a seamer-friendly pitch for fear of what damage Shane Warne might inflict on his batsmen given a dry surface. The groundsman duly followed orders, and Stuart Clark, in his Test debut, accepted the gift by happily scything through the home team twice with his seamers to secure an Australian win inside three days. The Cape Town result was repeated at Durban, albeit in twice as much time. When South Africa's final wicket fell late on the fifth day at Kingsmead, every Australian fielder stood clustered around the batsman – partly to apply maximum pressure and hasten the end, but also because it was so close to dusk that the tourists remained mindful of the peril of being separated from a group anywhere in Durban after dark.

Johannesburg, site of the final Test, was no safer. Indeed, any jurisdiction that permits drivers to 'ignore a robot' – or drive unpenalised through a red traffic light, as the outside world knows it – if they feel their personal safety is legitimately in peril has admitted it's given up on solving its serious crime problem. And with the same two teams that had waged battle twenty times over the preceding four months preparing for the last stanza of a series already decided, inspiration among the touring press sat about as low as it was within South Africa's dressing room, where lament had quickly replaced the euphoria of the Wanderers' miracle. Record books were scoured for some sort of tenuous news hook on which to hang one final preview article and, thankfully, they showed Justin Langer was set to play his hundredth Test. Even better news for those of us needing help to frame a sentence, let alone a fresh idea, Langer had long been one of cricket's more thoughtful and engaging characters.

Over the course of a dozen years, from the time we shared our debut Test in vastly differing roles in a famous match against the West Indies in Adelaide, Langer seemed to be forever scrabbling to justify his place. If not to selectors and teammates then certainly to critics. Perhaps because, in a sport that unashamedly worships aesthetes and purists, Langer was a scrapper, as well as a contradiction. Committed to his trade beyond the point of obsession, he was also a fanatical pugilist, who lovingly tended his roses at home, and whose bent for philosophy as well as overt patriotism made him an oddball hybrid of Zen Buddhism and Rocky Balboa.

As Australia's 2005 Ashes campaign lurched fully into crisis in Nottingham, I was approached to pen an appraisal of what ailed the tourists, from an Australian perspective, for publication in the following morning's edition of *The Times*. The hastily drafted article outlined a raft of shortcomings in the Australians' preparation, in their acumen, and in their willingness to honestly self-critique. It concluded that the only area in which they had excelled was in blaming their failings on anyone, indeed everyone, bar themselves. The assessment was deliberately caustic, in the knowledge that few, if any, members of

Ricky Ponting's team would read an English newspaper. Certainly not one as venerable as *The Times*. But on the final morning of the Test, I emerged from my hotel room bound for the breakfast room at the same moment the opening batsman in the adjoining room was headed for the team bus.

'Saw your piece in *The Times* this morning,' Langer said as he caught me up in the corridor. He glanced around furtively to satisfy himself nobody was peeking through partially opened doors, or eavesdropping near the lift well.

'Don't let anyone know I told you this – and if you do I'll deny it – but I agree. Absolutely. You got it spot on.' He patted me twice on the shoulder and then slipped into a waiting lift.

He was no less candid in the days before his hundredth Test, charting a way past the standard 'tell us your career highlight/lowlight/most admired/disliked opponent' questions to articulate the toll a career in the uncompromising world of professional sport can take on an individual's character.

'Maybe ten or twelve years of international cricket makes you a bit hard,' he reflected, as he lounged on a two-seater settee in the Australians' team room at the Sandton hotel. 'To play a hundred Test matches you've got to be hard mentally, so you probably have a few less emotions and you sometimes feel it around your family and friends. I got so caught up in the outcomes, so fiercely determined to do well that I forgot about the most important thing, which was the relaxing.'

As it turned out, his milestone match was, if not his most forgettable, then certainly his least remembered. Cracked by a frightful blow on the back of the skull as he attempted to evade the first ball he faced, Langer withdrew from the field with severe concussion and spent most of the next three days in his hotel room with curtains drawn and watched over by his parents, who had flown from Perth expecting a quite different occasion. He returned to Wanderers on the final morning, when Australia's last two fit batsmen were at the crease, needing twenty runs for a clean-sweep win.

Under strict medical orders not to take the field again, Langer decided he could not, in good conscience, stand idly if groggily by and watch his team narrowly defeated without at least presenting himself for duty. And so, with his teammates transfixed as Lee and Kasprowicz once again edged their way towards unlikely success, Langer silently padded up and appeared at the rear of the dressing room, like Ned Kelly staggering out of the morning mist and gunsmoke that enshrouded the Glenrowan Inn. Like the outlaw's, his was a purely symbolic act. The win was achieved without him, and Ponting was saved the unpleasantness of physically restraining his close mate from risking his long-term health for the sake of a cricket game.

The final night in Johannesburg marked both the end of a slog and the impending dawn of an even tougher one. A month in Bangladesh, the final act in a production that had spanned the best part of a year, excited neither players nor media. So, to dull the thoughts of the workload ahead, those of us pushing on to the Islamic republic, accompanied by others in the touring media party preparing to head home, chose to hit the town. Or the township, as it transpired. Invited by a young United Cricket Board of South Africa employee to join his family for dinner at their Soweto home, we were treated like visiting celebrities and bestowed with gifts of grilled chicken, pasta, salads and home-made cakes, the likes of which one never sees on room service menus. Just as heart-warming were the tales of township life, and the front-row accounts of the transformation it had undergone in the decade or so since apartheid was dismantled.

Some of us had undertaken a package tour of Soweto earlier in our stay, which offered an airbrushed itinerary that incorporated sites pivotal in the 1976 uprising, as well as powerful monuments to the struggle – the Hector Pieterson Museum, the homes of Mandela and Desmond Tutu, and freshly painted community facilities. But we were curious to see more, so we rustled together a few rand and convinced our driver to take us deeper into the heart of Orlando East, one of the thirty or more settlements that made up the South-West Township. It revealed a starkly different picture. Galvanised iron shacks thrown together as tightly as any Indian slum. The skeletons of inner-spring mattresses that served as front fences. Tardis-like portaloos in communal yards as a nod to first-world amenities. Children, barefoot and sporting blinding smiles, played on the dirt streets. Adults stared watchfully from behind wrought ironwork that reinforced their homes' tiny front windows.

At an impromptu market, a man with a tomahawk hacked flesh from one of a collection of goats' heads, lifted fresh from a blood-soaked chopping block. A pile of other indeterminate body parts lay spread out on a plastic sheet stretched over the dusty ground awaiting the arrival of discerning customers. Nearby, under the protection of a tarpaulin stretched between the branches of a roadside tree, a barber plied his trade. Makeshift stalls dispensed the latest local harvest – ears of corn, ripe mangoes, fresh-cut and shallow-fried potato chips. The recurrent feature of most of these enduring scenes was the unbridled warmth and generosity exuded by almost everyone we met. It led us to question our own preconceptions, as well as Soweto's well-known reputation for violence and crime.

Our return visit, on the tour's final evening, yielded an even more revealing glimpse of the true South Africa. After dinner, we visited our young host's favourite bar, deep in a part of Soweto we could never hope to find again. Five of us, packed into his two-door SUV, pulled up outside the single-storey shop front, alongside a collection of sensible four-cylinder vehicles, which indicated a sagacious clientele. When we entered the front room, with its bare concrete floor, basic laminated tables and unadorned bar, the fifty or so patrons stared in stunned silence.

It provided a beginner's guide to how so many black South Africans might have felt for so long as outcasts in their own country. Like a scene from a Wild West saloon, conversation, music and time all stopped until the agitated bar manager bustled from behind the counter and guided us into a windowless back room that housed a handful of uncovered tables and a wall-mounted television showing a European football game. We were told it would be best for all if we stayed put until he gauged the regulars' mood. We remained in our private quarters for half an hour, the only interaction with the locals being occasional visits from the barman hauling a galvanised metal bucket filled with ice and stubbies of beer. Eventually, he poked his head through the doorway and told us it was okay to emerge.

Initially, we were treated with suspicion, and from a safe distance. But curiosity soon replaced misgiving, once word spread that we were

Australians bearing nothing more provocative than an unhealthy interest in the obscure sport of cricket. The young crowd was far more interested in football, and the World Cup that was bound for southern Africa in four years' time. One bold young girl, who introduced herself as Patience, invited all of us to be special guests at the coming weekend's youth group prayer retreat. She found our excuse, that we would be in the Islamic Republic of Bangladesh, unconvincingly and unnecessarily elaborate.

We did, however, accept a welcome offer to head to a neighbourhood dance party, happening a few kilometres away in another unlabelled part of Soweto. The wisdom of a quartet of white faces wandering into a suburban street event post-midnight, where every other patron was the colour of the hour, was blithely glossed over until we reached a bank of trestle tables that led to the entrance gate. There, we confronted a sign hung between the lengths of cyclone wire enclosing a barely lit open space housing a stage, several drinks stalls, and a row of portable toilets. The banner read simply: 'This is a Community Event. Please Respect it by Leaving your Weapons at Home.'

The only way we could have been more conspicuous was if we chose to flaunt our Caucasian dance prowess. As it was, we simply stood around and got used to being stared at. The only people who approached us were inquisitive rather than hostile. Most merely smiled shyly. One or two even took discreet photos. By 4 a.m. we had seen enough precociously talented young local dancers and musicians to feel woefully inadequate as well as unmistakably alien, and we returned to our hotel through the deserted mean streets of central Johannesburg. During the trip, our host repeatedly reassured us we were safe in his car. But his nervous obsession with checking his mirrors, locking all doors, and staying as close as practical to the centre of main roads – while also pushing carefully through intersections where the robots glowed ruby – suggested his bravado was thoughtfully manufactured for our delicate peace of mind.

20

Bangladesh, April 2006

Shane Warne had divested himself of his official travel blazer and corporate tie, and was stuffing them into the locker above his business-class seat as I hauled aboard our Dubai-bound flight.

'Looking forward to Bangladesh, Rambo?' he boomed, more to irritate his already grumpy teammates than pose a genuine query.

'I hear our hotel's a real cracker,' he continued as I squeezed past. 'More like a resort.'

Even though the Bangladesh itinerary had been pared to its absolute minimum – a couple of Tests, three one-dayers and nothing either side or in between – it still failed to register anything other than annoyance among most members of the touring party. Even my previous enthusiasm for the subcontinent had been tempered by tiredness and the knowledge that, as the final leg of a prolonged stint on the road, it would prove tough-going. So as the travelling Australian press contingent – myself and snapper Hamish Blair – settled into our seats set so far back as to be beneath the jet's tail fin, we immediately dispensed with another of the intractable rules of touring life. The one that decrees alcohol shouldn't be consumed beyond a tipple during work travel, even if your employer deems air miles are not to be mistaken for hard yards. Instead, we decided eight hours of gin and tonic was essential preparation for whatever awaited us in the Ganges–Brahmaputra delta. Shortly before our late-night arrival in the Emirate, we hazily decided to sneak in one final round. Our stewardess disagreed, suggesting we would be better served organising ourselves into some sort of condition for disembarkation. Besides, she added in a flat Australian accent, we had successfully drained the rear galley of gin.

'But we're on our way to Bangladesh,' Hamish slurred, in a pitch that hovered between desperate and plain drunk. She remained unmoved.

'For a month,' he added plaintively.

She looked, horror-struck, into his glazed eyes, then at me, before leaning forward to whisper: 'Oh you poor bastards, I'll grab a bottle from the front.'

With just fifteen minutes to make our connecting flight, and a further four hours of air travel in which to try and sober up, I fronted immigration at Dhaka's Zhia International Airport like someone who should be denied entry on appearance, irrespective of my paperwork's legitimacy. As the players were whisked to a waiting bus, I stood, exhausted, dishevelled and stinkingly hungover in the stifling arrivals queue otherwise made up of Arab, Russian and Indian businessmen, all dressed like models from a cut-price fashion catalogue.

I fingered the $US10 notes turning rapidly soggy in my pocket, and told myself anyone caught trying to sneak into Bangladesh using illegal documents was more likely to be subjected to psychological evaluation than imprisonment. That logic was abandoned when the moustachioed passport policeman scrutinising my bona fides summoned his supervisor. Despite invoking the name of the cricket team, producing my dog-eared letter of commendation, and adopting the haughty air, if not the outward look, of an influential first-world journalist, there was no way they were going to allow a solitary overseas visitor to sneak illegally into a country that millions would risk their last breath to leave.

Lengthy discussions among gangs of stony-faced uniformed men ensued, punctuated by even longer bursts of no activity whatsoever. I waited and sweated, slumped against a concrete wall, and eventually sprawled out on the floor. Unsure if deportation would land me at home in Melbourne, in Dubai, or back in South Africa, I resorted to the only viable stunt short of hostage taking. With laptop unpacked and a restive audience of Bengali bureaucrats watching on, I began animatedly hammering at the keyboard as if composing an urgent memo. A hastily convened conference followed, after which the most senior officer squatted next to me and cautiously inquired what on earth I was doing.

'Writing a story for my newspaper back in Australia,' I answered, as frostily as the sticky air would allow.

'Big newspaper. Many readers. All over the world. I'm writing that people should never come to Bangladesh. Visitors not welcome.' The fact he did not burst out laughing confirmed my hunch that none of my captors knew of my publication, much less its limited readership and influence. But my punt on them at least understanding the ramifications of adverse global media coverage paid off when my passport was returned without explanation and I was waved urgently through to where my suitcase, and Bangladesh, awaited.

In the back seat of a small sedan with busted suspension that proclaimed itself a taxi, I remained awake due to the driver's uncanny ability to hit potholes on the heavily pitted roadway whenever I began to doze, thereby slamming my head against the semi-opaque window, which was not quite dirty enough to block out affronting scenes of daily Dhaka life. People bathed in filthy waist-deep puddles. Steep roadside gutters, designed to cope with the regular flood surges, stood clogged with limbless beggars beseeching alms from passers-by. Children and mange-ridden dogs picked hungrily through piles of rotting debris, and entire communities huddled beneath sheets of plastic stretched over abandoned building sites. Not that anyone in the honking, formless traffic snarl gave a second glance. These were curiosities only to the unaccustomed eye.

Just taking it in required energy I simply couldn't summon. The lack of sleep, the excess of booze, the airport fracas and the subcontinent's overwhelming suffocation meant I couldn't wait to get to my hotel room. Until I got to my hotel room. The smell that assailed me on opening the door was mouldering cardboard with undertones of dank pet. I instantly regretted that my expansive list of pre-departure inoculations had not included kennel cough.

The view from the third floor told me that, even if the grime-coated windows could be forced open, any breeze they admitted would only compound my suffering. I looked out on a pair of deserted swimming pools, ringed by equally under-used banks of sun lounges. High-backed cane chairs and glass-topped tables sat carefully arranged but just as abandoned beneath a couple of concrete colonnades, the roofs of which hosted thriving plots of spindly weeds. Beyond the hotel's boundary, marked by a row of potted palms, lay a soupy black swamp.

Dhaka's main sporting venue, the Bangabandhu National Stadium, sat barely five kilometres from our hotel. It was also, during the Australian Test team's historic first visit, out of action because it was hosting the inaugural Asian Football Confederation Cup. The cricket was therefore scheduled for the revamped Narayanganj Osmani Stadium at Fatullah, twenty kilometres south of central Dhaka as the vulture flies. Unfortunately, travelling that distance through Bangladeshi traffic was as straightforward as walking diametrically across Place de l'Etoile. Trucks, buses, motorised and pedal rickshaws, and barefooted blokes hauling wooden carts all competed for precious little road space. And all of them, save for the brave foot traffic, did so with horns habitually blaring, as if honking would magically open up a hole in the mayhem.

To negotiate this twice-daily trauma, Hamish and I enlisted the services of Jalal, a wise and unflappable taxi driver of many years but considerably fewer words. Jalal also sported an auxiliary thumb, complete with nail, jutting from just below the bottom joint of the first digit on his right hand. In some cultures, this is considered extremely lucky. On the desperate streets of downtown Dhaka, where the full range of human disfigurement is forever in your face, it rated barely a sideways look.

No sooner would our vehicle stop at choked city intersections than it was besieged by harrowing figures that emerged from road's edge. Like Munch's discarded preliminary drafts for *The Scream*, they draped themselves across the car, scratched at the windows, and pushed their most ghastly deformities up against the glass in a despairing quest for cash. Australia's High Commissioner to Bangladesh subsequently explained that the most conspicuous of the beggars haunting Dhaka's main thoroughfares were manipulated by pimps who pocketed a bulk of any forthcoming charity. Not that it made the experience any less confronting.

We came to recognise the leads in this macabre cast. A man propped up by a set of bamboo crutches swung his malformed legs repeatedly against the passenger side doors. A skeletal woman draped in a black shroud tapped her yellowing talons on the window, then mimed pained eating motions. Her companion, of indeterminate age and gender with an enormous grey growth covering the place the left eye should have been, pressed the fleshy lump hard up against the glass while making a low, wailing sound. After several days of this routine, it became clear this person was blind and was led into the becalmed traffic by the emaciated woman. Throughout this gruesome pantomime, Jalal maintained a monastic silence, staring fixedly ahead and passing neither comment nor judgement.

Although an elevated bus and a police escort spared the players these glimpses of reality, their enthusiasm for the assignment was only dwindling further. Still suffering the effects of the taxing South African schedule and subsequent long-haul travel, their pre-Test training session was little more than a familiarisation visit and gave the impression that merely showing up would suffice for victory. Memories of Cardiff 2005 apparently endured for the home team only. The Australian squad's sole focus was the unprecedented five-month break that beckoned after Bangladesh.

Their unrest was heightened by the stringent security arrangements that turned the hotel into a virtual barracks, and left most of its guests feeling they were under house arrest. Armed police guarded all entrances, and bomb squads swept every approaching vehicle. A police command post was set up in the foyer, and everyone entering the lobby was subjected to airport-style screening. But none of those measures could stop an assailant already embedded. During the Australians' final pre-Test strategy meeting, the doors of their team room swung open and a young man in heavily starched housekeeping tunic barged in brandishing a covered silver serving dish. His eyes flashed about the room, bringing planning to a halt and paranoia to a spike.

'Mister Varraneh?' he said, his head twitching from one panic-etched face to the next. 'Mister Varraneh?' Only when he was challenged and disarmed by the team's security officer did it emerge he bore nothing more lethal than the toasted cheese sandwich Warne had forgotten he ordered an hour earlier.

More valid fears surfaced during the Test. Members of Bangladesh's elite armed response unit, heavily muscled young men clad in their distinctive livery of black combat gear and ebony bandanas, maintained an intimidating presence throughout the Fatullah Stadium. And during a quiet moment in the game, someone in the Australian dressing room noticed that one of the marksmen had lifted his high-powered rifle to his shoulder and was training it on an unidentified player in the middle. Amid wide-eyed terror, the security man again sprang into action, this time throwing himself at the would-be assassin and forcing him to drop his weapon. The indignant officer was then grilled, through an interpreter, as to his murderous intentions, only to reveal he had become so enthralled by the game that he employed the gun's telescopic sight to gain a clearer view.

Not all local law enforcement officers were so phlegmatic. The most hectic sections of Dhaka's hopelessly overpopulated road system were controlled by traffic police armed with, and not reluctant to use, whistles and thick cane *lathis*. The whistles alerted inattentive drivers to the perils of ignoring instructions. The *lathis* were that peril. Buses, trucks, family cars, rickshaws and bicycles – none were exempt from a violent crack across a rear panel, or a shoulderblade, if the traffic enforcer felt the urge.

It was the commuting that proved as draining as any element of the maddeningly long days. The early and rapid onset of subcontinental dusk meant play began at 9 a.m., which required a hotel departure before 7 a.m. An hour considered so unholy by the kitchen staff they obligingly packed little cardboard boxes of breakfast treats – sweet buns, hard-boiled eggs, peelable fruit and bottled water – for players, officials and press to eat while in transit. We always grabbed a couple of spares to share with our new friends, who eagerly awaited our arrival at various city intersections. The return journey was just as painstaking, though more productive because it was spent transcribing that evening's media conferences and filing story updates, through the South African phone that worked far more effectively in Dhaka traffic than anywhere in its country of purchase. If only other essentials were so reliable.

Electricity supplies were as capricious as expected in a resource-poor nation of 150 million that sits, like a flightless duck, in the middle of the world's largest river delta system. Power to the hotel would regularly snap off, then roar back into life just as the absence of air conditioning drove guests gasping out to the mosquito-ridden pool deck. But the darkness that greeted us after day three at Fatullah suggested a far more substantial black-out. Every window in the compound, save for the soft glow of candle light coming from the lobby, portrayed a depressing blackness. Front door security procedures stretched no further than a torch beam in the face of arrivals to ascertain if they were friend or *faux*. The Australians' mood, as gloomy as the spookily silent hotel due to their parlous position in the Test match, bordered on outright hostility when they were told that a limited room service menu was the only foreseeable dinner option. That was quickly ruled an unacceptable risk by the team physiotherapist, who graphically explained to all of us the dangers that lurked in eating unrefrigerated under-cooked Bangladeshi food.

After groping my way up the fusty stairwell, I stood at my window contemplating the glamour of touring life and watching a crowd of shadowy figures slowly assemble around the outdoor settings below. I discerned the telltale frames of several cricketers and, by the time I joined the gathering, disgruntlement at their predicament and their environment threatened to spill over into a full-scale mutiny. In truth, the only one of us with a legitimate grievance was Stuart MacGill, who had earlier received tragic news about a friend in Australia.

MacGill made little effort to hide his distaste for the blokey, boofhead culture that bonds male sporting outfits. Once, as twelfth man in a Test match outside Australia, he pointedly sat with his back to the game while reading a book. On a previous tour to the subcontinent, instead of baked beans and Vegemite, MacGill packed an emergency stash of olives, lavash bread and a nicely rounded Rhône Valley *syrah*, or suchlike. And he was virtually alone among international cricketers in often seeking out the company of journalists for a meal or a drink, believing they offered a fresh, if not especially incisive, take on the world.

On this night, as he shared a table in the dark with Hamish and me, the initial conversation centred on one of his pet subjects – 1980s pop music. I knew from a previous encounter in a Brisbane hotel that I was dangerously out of my league. On that occasion, I had foolishly reeled off a list of song titles dredged from the catacombs of my memory, and challenged him to name the even more obscure artists responsible for them. He dismissed each poser with the same gleeful disdain he showed for bogan rituals. The Icicle Works. Netherworld Dancing Toys. The Young Homebuyers. Cowed in defeat, I retreated to my hotel room where, minutes later, a text message lit up my phone.

'Nice try, but that's just a taste of what's in store,' MacGill taunted. 'You're in the big league now. And that was only ROUND ONE.'

Scarred by that experience, I shifted poolside talk to the shop that Hamish and I had found in Dhaka's most upmarket mall that sold freshly pirated DVDs for $US1 a copy, and the collective stash of duty-free grog we had stockpiled on our way out of Johannesburg, in case of emergency. We agreed that moment was now upon us, and promptly adjourned to Hamish's room to watch bootlegged movies on his long-life battery-run laptop. And to drown another challenging day in hard liquor mixed with room-temperature soft drinks.

Over the next six hours, the photographer and I knocked a sizeable dent in our jumbo bottle of Tanqueray Ten, while the leg-spinner performed an even more impressive demolition of his bourbon flagon. We barely noticed the electricity's return around 10 p.m., and when the wee hours arrived talk had turned to the Test, in which one of us would be playing a key role just a few hours later.

'I've written that Bangladesh is the only team that can win it from here,' I announced, with a conceit soaked in juniper juice. 'They're already 280 in front, got five second-innings wickets in hand, and only need to make another seventy or so then you blokes are stuffed. You've got no choice but to chase whatever target they set, 'cos if you play for a draw, you'll get pilloried by blokes like me. And if you go after the runs the way you batted in the first innings, you'll get bowled out.'

I mentally congratulated myself on prosecuting a case so adequately, given our level of inebriation.

'You're an idiot,' MacGill laughed, foreshadowing a rebuttal born more of unflappable self-belief than arrogance. 'We'll win this, and the stuff you've written will make you look like a goose. It's a psychological battle from here, and the Banglas will be thinking how well they've done to get into this position. That'll soon morph into a fear of squandering their big chance.

'You see, being in front is new to them, and you need mental strength to push home that sort of advantage. As soon as they start doubting their ability to pull it off, they'll fall over. It's like a staring contest. And we know what it takes to make the other mob blink.'

With that, he lurched off into the night, leaving me feeling more than a little queasy about what had already rolled off presses around Australia under my name. That thought continued to nag, even through throbbing head pain, as Jalal inched us towards Fatullah not much later in the morning. My only solace came from the knowledge that I did not have to bowl for my country, in draining humidity, at the crucial stage of a Test match.

As it turned out, neither did MacGill. The Bangladeshis more than blinked. They flat-out panicked and lost their final five wickets for twenty-four runs in less than an hour. That left the Australians almost two full days to score a touch over 300, against nervous bowlers and an opponent in shock at having meekly surrendered such an unassailable position. MacGill's forecast win arrived, for the loss of seven wickets, soon after lunch on the final day.

When I saw him in the lobby, as I queued to check out on Good Friday morning, he simply winked and kept walking. I was too tired to feel chastened, having worked through until 2 a.m. to have the full Test wash-up filed before our mid-morning flight to Chittagong, only to receive a 6.45 a.m. call from the boss suggesting we take an alternative tack. Which required most of it be rewritten. The bits that couldn't be finished in the back of Jalal's taxi were completed, fittingly given the quality of the product, in a foul public toilet while waiting to board a plane to Bangladesh's second-largest city.

Chittagong might be the gateway to the world's longest stretch of natural sandy beach, but the sub-Himalayan Riviera it ain't. Our drive into the centre of town from the airport, where a bold mural tells of the brutal revolutionary struggle that delivered an independent Bangladesh out of East Pakistan, carried us along the west bank of the Karnaphuli River, and past oil tankers anchored just metres from a sticky black shoreline. Wedged between the inky water and the narrow coastal road were makeshift huts, thrown together from whatever building scraps lay nearby – sheets of steel and corrugated iron, bamboo poles and palm fronds.

Amid the poverty and squalor, the Peninsula Hotel was an unexpected surprise, with its newly appointed rooms and even a hand-painted hard-boiled egg decorated in Easter patterns placed outside each guest's door. Although it was lunchtime, my only interest was sleep, and I flopped onto the bed just as a bolt of pain shot from the base of my spine to the bottom of my skull. It was accompanied by a sound something like a watermelon being lobbed on top of a wardrobe.

When feeling returned to my upper body, I peeled back the bedding to find a thin layer of coarse brown hair loosely woven into a mat, a few centimetres in thickness. Reception staff seemed suspiciously prepared when I phoned to report the theft of my mattress, and they cheerily guaranteed I would find the coconut fibre replacement just as comfortable. I abandoned all notions of a nap and opted instead for a stroll around my new neighbourhood. This was also cut short when I was accosted by a dirt-encased man wearing nothing but a pair of black flip-flops, several strands of high-tension wire around his throat, and a crazed grin. By evening, the sunset lent a gentle orange haze to the skyline. A *muezzin*'s call to prayer wafted mellifluously across the city, and flickering specks of golden light stretched all the way out to the void that was the Bay of Bengal. At that moment, I could stand with eyes closed and imagine I was somewhere exotic and luxurious. Upon lying down, it was painfully clear I was still in Chittagong.

The port city of three million is best known as home to the world's biggest ship-breaking operation. Each year, 100,000-tonne foreign-registered steel giants are driven at full tilt onto a stretch of debris-strewn coast, where they are picked apart by crews of poorly paid, under-equipped workers. This enterprise, I was reliably told, remained strictly off-limits to prying foreigners following concerns raised by Amnesty International about unacceptable death tolls at the site, and the environmental damage it wrought. But Chittagong was soon to gain additional notoriety.

On the opening morning of the second Test, an elderly newspaper photographer from the Bengali daily *Prothom Alo* instructed his taxi driver to ferry him as close as possible to the ground's entrance gates, to lessen the distance he had to lug his heavy camera equipment. This apparently breached the Chittagong police's security protocols and, despite him waving valid media accreditation and an authorised parking permit, the photographer was thrown to the ground, kicked, punched and belted with the butt of a police rifle. Not surprisingly, his Bangladeshi press colleagues felt this treatment a touch heavy-handed and, as players from both teams completed their pre-match warm-ups to the teeth-gnashing strains of the national cricket anthem ('Bangla-deeesh, Bungla-deeesh, Bungla-deeeeeeesh'), the local media staged a protest sit-in alongside the Test pitch.

A truce was eventually brokered, and the match began ten minutes late. But when the still-aggrieved journalists and photographers confronted senior police during the lunch break and demanded the offending officers be stood down and an apology issued, all civility was abandoned. The armed and angry police laid siege to the defenceless media pack, and the grass between the press box and the boundary rope became the scene of a rolling brawl in which around fifty members of the fourth estate were hit with fists, boots, *lathis* and rifles. One television station employee suffered such severe head injuries he was carried unconscious from the field and flown to hospital in Dhaka, where he remained in an induced coma for days.

Fearing for their lives, the remaining local media representatives sprinted the length of the field and stormed the players' pavilion. Both teams, oblivious to the brutality at the far end, were taking lunch when the gang charged through the dining room and barricaded themselves into a small office that had been occupied by the match referee, Jeff Crowe. Calm was eventually restored, and play resumed. But the Bangladesh Sports Journalists Association voted to boycott all further coverage of the Test. And what should have been a triumphant celebration for Chittagong became a showpiece of international embarrassment.

The violent outburst that marred the next day was more arbitrary, but no less devastating. Shortly before lunch, the defiant silence of the all-but-empty press box was broken by a bellicose rumble from the north. The sky turned the colour of surrounding ditch water and the scattering of locals among the small crowd dashed for more substantial shelter minutes before a mini-typhoon unleashed itself on Chittagong's Divisional Stadium.

Blinding rain and squalls that blew in several directions at once turned the terrace shelters, lovingly built from bamboo scaffolding and topped by festive swathes of striped bunting, into twisted pieces of abstract sculpture. Metal name plates were torn from the flimsy scoreboard and flung like playing cards across the flooded outfield, while ground staff were tossed about like paratroopers caught in a jet stream as they tried to lay billowing protective covers over the pitch. The event itself lasted scarcely five minutes but put paid to the day's play. When we returned, under cloudless skies the following morning, no evidence of the destruction could be seen. The colourful canopies had been rebuilt. The scoreboard had been reassembled, in nearly correct configuration. And the pitch and outfield appeared as pristine as they were on day one. Bangladeshis' resilience and spirit, hewn from living in nature's tantrum room, regularly rises, shiningly, above the nation's ferment of deprivation and disadvantage.

These dual calamities were then rendered conventional by the bizarre event for which the second Test remains known. Sent out to protect Australia's true batsmen when a wicket fell late on the first evening, Jason Gillespie weathered the tempest to be unbeaten on twenty-eight after day two. At the close of the next day, he had posted an unprecedented and inconceivable century. And when Ponting declared his team's innings closed midway through day four, the man who described himself 'a walking defensive shot' was not out 201. It assured him a noteworthy place in cricket's voluminous records and at trivia nights as the only nightwatchman in 130 years of Test matches to score a double century.

'It's a fairytale really,' Gillespie reflected that evening, already foreseeing he would never again play for his country. 'Hansel and Gretel, and Dizzy's double-hundred are one and the same.'

Hope that the Test's final day, with Bangladesh four wickets down and 200 short of forcing Australia back to the crease, would be wrapped up clinically and without incident was doused before we left the hotel. As we waited for our commissioned driver, concierge staff told us no transport was available for anyone other than teams and to officials assigned police escorts because of a snap general strike across Chittagong. Nobody could adequately explain why it was called, other than to point out that they were a regular occurrence. And that no driver was prepared to flout the ban for fear of being attacked by militant gangs known to hurl rocks and bricks at any vehicles on the road, and drag occupants out for a savage beating.

Predictably, the impasse could only be broken with a large wad of local currency, production of which led to a brave chauffeur magically appearing in his dented van. Throughout the ten-kilometre drive along empty roads, as we all scoured side streets and doorways like an armoured car patrol in Baghdad's red zone, a managerial voice sneering 'cricket tours' and 'five-star hotel pools' floated back to me as a repressed memory. That taunt returned even louder as our driver bundled us out at the stadium and, as he prepared to speed off, assured us we had no chance of securing a ride back to the hotel at day's end.

After Australia duly achieved its clean sweep, media conferences were completed and the players were safely returned to our accommodation, I approached the affable but ineffectual Bangladesh Cricket Board media liaison officer who happily confirmed that those members of the press who had not bailed out of the game on day one needed to organise their own escape through the danger. I was about to rehash my airport threats about global coverage and international shame when it dawned on me that nothing I wrote or said could be more damning than what already seemed to plague Chittagong. So I slumped, more defeated than distraught, against the front tyre of the nicest vehicle at the ground and began transcribing interviews under the blazing sun while silently hoping for some benevolent soul to return to the car and offer me a lift. I was more excited than at any previous moment of our tour when the match umpires and referee appeared to claim the van that acted as my backrest. They laughed long at my plight but agreed to ferry me back through the combat zone. No sooner had I burst into the apparent safety of the hotel lobby than I ran into Michael Hussey, whose glass-overflowing positivism helped ease my truculence.

'You coming to tonight's party?' he asked, referring to the post-match players' celebration that had been foregone amid the haste to flee the stadium, and was to be reconvened around the hotel's rooftop swimming pool later in the afternoon. It was the equivalent of the dressing-room bash from which journalists were perennially and explicitly barred.

Wary that this was an unsanctioned invitation, I told him it was unlikely. But as I stewed over the uncomfortable prospect of yet another night propped on the plywood watching illegal movies, I decided to check the offer's authenticity. The team manager sounded surprised, but said he would run it past several senior players. An hour later, I received a call to say Australian cricket's equivalent of a papal conclave had returned a verdict, and I was in.

This was no lavish, long table dinner. Just a dozen blokes in cargo shorts, casual T-shirts, and, for the sentimental few, baggy green Test caps. They sat on plastic stackable chairs strewn around a small kidney-shaped pool that had been drained of water to reduce the mosquito problem and the potential for mishaps. The ambience blared through Warne's MP3 dock. INXS, Noiseworks, Hunters and Collectors. The overworked anthems of Australia's sporting monoculture. They drowned out the traffic noise from fifteen storeys below, and cans of Australian beer smuggled in courtesy of a shrewd sponsor spilled, with flagrant disregard for local sensitivities, from a couple of bright orange Eskies. I turned up with the remains of my duty-free gin to avoid later accusations that I stole the stars' grog.

Mindful of my probationary status, I occupied a seat on the periphery, quietly nattering to those unfussed by my presence about the past year that had carried us from England, to Australia, New Zealand, South Africa and, finally, a Chittagong rooftop. And about what might lie ahead. With no certified Test tours scheduled until early 2008, it was clear that a number were now contemplating the end of the road. Or, at least, the end of life on it. And so, as the sun went down and the music cranked up, the gathering took on the distinct whiff of a wake.

The old hands – Warne, Gilchrist, Hayden and MacGill – cast a wistful eye, like graduates taking one last look around the old campus. Those safe in the knowledge that their careers would roll on – Ponting,

Hussey, Symonds and Clarke – backslapped and chiacked like mates in a front bar. Gillespie, his back aching from nine and a half hours spent hunched over a bat, stretched out contentedly on a chair and annoyed anyone who wandered past by introducing conversation with 'So, mate, how do you deal with nerves when you're getting close to a double hund ... oh that's right, you've never been there.' And Brett Lee, who had earlier conceded he was bereft of petrol and 'only operating on fumes', had already retired to the bed he had fitted with extra foam padding and was living up to his claim that he could 'sleep for Australia' should it become a competitive pastime.

Slinking quietly into the background, and feeling almost as at home as the journalist, were those expected to carry the team's formidable legacy into the future. Phil Jaques and Dan Cullen had tasted Test cricket in Bangladesh, while Mitchell Johnson, James Hopes, Mark Cosgrove and Brett Dorey had recently arrived to help reinvigorate the one-day team. I studied them across the empty pool, noting their shy self-consciousness. They clearly felt they did not yet belong, and were intimidated by those who did. As the takeaway pizzas arrived, it was Warne who moved to bridge the disconnect.

'Do you know these blokes?' he said by way of introduction, having summoned me into the midst of the newcomers who were clearly underwhelmed by my arrival.

'You'll learn not to trust the press, but Rambo's one of the good guys,' Warne continued, offering me a slice of tepid pizza from a box made soggy by grease and humidity. 'Otherwise, we'd have chucked him in the pool by now.' He laughed as he wandered off to scavenge more supper.

I assumed his punchline was a joke, until it nearly became the fate of a couple of Australian tourists who snuck unnoticed into the group as the celebration neared its peak. Welcomed initially for bravely venturing to Chittagong in support of the cricket team, they overplayed their hand when one of them snatched a Test cap and brashly cavorted among the players. For one senior team member, it was a breach too far.

'You don't put one of those on your head unless you've been chosen to play Test cricket for Australia, pal,' he snarled, his eyes betraying a level of late-night testiness I was familiarly wary of.

273

'So take it off now. And fuck off out of here.' He then took a couple of halting steps towards the stunned travellers, who wisely departed with their admiration for their national cricket team demonstrably soured.

Shortly after, my cue to withdraw arrived when a couple of members of the touring party started hurling plastic chairs from the roof and into the night, where they clattered and bounced onto the private residences of outraged neighbours below. I figured that if I was not witness to this hooliganism then I was under no compulsion to report it. More a work minimisation strategy than a moral stance.

Reclined on my slab, I sifted back through the day, the tour and its underlying messages. Like the players eyeing imminent retirement, I had to accept that life on the road was starting to appear as unappealing as it was unsustainable. Changes to my circumstances meant the benefits of staying home now significantly outweighed the reasons for running away. The impending arrival of Australian cricket's new era also meant nurturing a fresh set of relationships, and cultivating access to a different group, most of whom I had never seen play and who, from a selfish media perspective, seemed neither interested nor interesting. Then again, that may have simply reflected my ebbing enthusiasm nearing the end of a gruelling, protracted stint.

But the most troubling realisation sprang from Warne's off-hand endorsement. Being rated 'one of the good guys' meant, bluntly, that I had failed in the job. Journalists who maintain the players' approval are surely those who pander to their celebrity. The ones who brush aside incidents like late-night furniture redistribution, and are unwilling to pose the tough questions. Reporters who hold them to account and write without fear in full knowledge that they're likely to front the subject of their scathing appraisals over breakfast don't win friends, but something far more estimable. Grudging respect. In the space of a minute, Warne had confirmed what had long bothered me. I was an uncritical critic. A writer, not a journalist. This cosiness was reaffirmed next morning when, following up a conversation from the previous night, I phoned the team manager to check if there was any chance of sneaking along with the Australians' sanctioned visit to the shipbreaking yards. Once again, I was told the okay of senior players was required. So I tracked down the vice-captain, who gave his blessing.

'But we'll be travelling on the team bus, and that's a whole different issue,' Gilchrist added. 'You'll need to check with Punter to make sure he's okay with that.'

Several touring journalists then gathered hopefully at the door of the bus awaiting Ponting's arrival. As he pushed through the crowd being loosely held back by security staff, I asked if we could follow him aboard. The request clearly caught him off guard but, after I pledged we would keep strictly to the back rows and out of listening range of his team, he agreed, albeit with a hesitation that suggested it defied his better judgement. After almost a decade of travelling alongside Australia's cricketers, I was allowed to travel with them in the holiest of holies. The final Rubicon had been crossed. The circle that began on a steamy Hong Kong evening had been completed.

Half an hour into our drive to Jahanabad on the city's north coast, the subtle change in wares being dispensed from roadside stalls confirmed we were close to our destination. Instead of nuts, rice and dry biscuits, vendors were flogging industrial ovens, emergency life boats, gleaming toilet bowls (BYO sewerage system) and even the occasional ship's compass and steering wheel.

The bus turned off the highway and eased down a dirt path, past a makeshift village, and pulled up at a padlocked, blue wrought-iron gate, behind which the maligned community gathered in excited anticipation, rather than defiant suspicion. The site's beaming commandant then guided us past crude workers' huts fashioned from asbestos sheets and canvas, and piles of rusting scrap iron artfully stacked as if by tsunami, out to a post-apocalyptic landscape that stretched across the tidal flats.

Standing sentry through the acrid smoke haze was the River Styx's abandoned merchant fleet. These once proud cape-sized citadels of the sea were being slowly wrenched apart by teams of men, some barely teenagers, armed with nothing more heavy duty than oxy-cutting gear and sturdy ropes. The objects of their potentially fatal labours lay scattered across the oil-stained mud. Lengths of double-hulled bulk carriers sliced up like meatloaf. Dismembered sections of bow, stern and propeller shaft listing forlornly in the sludge, excised and cast aside to allow access to the more valuable steel and other goodies within the ships' bellies. Line after line of desolate carcasses. Far from their registered homes in Panama, China and Russia, these beached hulks would wait stranded for months until they were stripped to their final rivet. Unlike loved ones who appear strangely diminished post-mortem, these massive structures seemed even more imposing in death.

Our host then invited us up to his office with its panoramic view out over the hellish operation. There, as he served a refreshing round of coconut water and his children posed for photographs with the cricketers, he told us that most of the inevitable on-site deaths were caused by falling debris, or by explosions tripped by workers oxy-cutting into live gas lines. A risk that a pay packet of around $US1 a day apparently justified.

The one-day series passed without incident, upset or highlight. Eager to finally experience a Bangladesh that extended past misery and exploitation, Hamish and I used a spare day back in the capital to explore Old Dhaka, where the city of twelve million people is at its most intense and intriguing. At Sadarghat, we hired a river taxi pilot to pole us out across the soot-grey waters of the Buriganga, and in among the rusting, recommissioned ferries that brought bananas, coconuts and watermelons from further up river. Then we lost ourselves, and hours, in the mazes of covered bazaars and the heaving peloton of cycle rickshaws, the only form of transport suited to the strangled, narrow streets, with its jangling accompaniment of a million bicycle bells arguing in unison. I was uplifted to leave Bangladesh with evocative, inspiring images of Old Dhaka and its thriving market quarter in memory's forefront. But, on balance, I was simply pleased to leave Bangladesh and return, at last, to a home I had hardly frequented since departing for England eleven months earlier.

21

ICC Champions Trophy, India, October–November 2006

The Ashes summer of 2006–07 loomed as the most breathlessly awaited, persistently previewed cricket event since … well, since the previous Ashes series. But before avenging the hurt and the ignominy heaped on them while surrendering the urn in England, the Australians had an opportunity to claim the other major cricket prize conspicuously absent from Jolimont's glass display cases – the ICC Champions Trophy. Which is why most of the nation's best players tuned up for the biggest Test campaign of their careers by dawdling through a handful of one-day internationals spread over four yawning weeks in far-flung outposts across India.

October is a notoriously dire month for Australia's sports editors. The regional football codes have packed up and the footballers headed to sun-soaked resorts offshore to revel in their international anonymity. Cricket season has only just emerged from dormancy, and is not yet capable of generating sufficient news or interest to assume the column space left vacant by the winter sports. And coverage of the only other show in town – Melbourne's horse racing Spring Carnival – is hampered by the inability of its drawcards to speak.

So someone had to accompany the cricketers on their return to the subcontinent. If not in deference to the game's second-most important limited-overs tournament, then at least to provide exhaustive daily commentary on how Ricky Ponting's lads were shaping up for their Ashes quest. And as that someone once more packed his battered brown suitcase, I figured it would prove a defining experience. Despite the challenges posed by Bangladesh, I remained an unabashed fan of India – its culture, its chaos, and especially its people. The world's friendliest and most generous, bar none. And if a month there could not revive my waning want to pursue the life of a touring cricket writer, then the cause was lost.

Even though it was getting on for 3 a.m. when I arrived at my hotel in New Delhi's financial and commercial hub, Connaught Place, the wonderfully familiar trappings of India had turned out to welcome me. The impossible crush of taxi drivers outside the airport doors. That sharp, metallic tang of brackish water that catches your breath as it ponds, unseen, beneath cracked and crumbling footpaths. And, when I got to my room, I was greeted by the heady fragrance of industrial-strength cleaners infused with discreet undertones of naphthalene and ghee. There was also the potentially lethal bowl of complimentary fruit, strategically positioned to divert attention from the list of preposterous direct-dial telephone charges. And propped against it, a polite note on crisp white card from the duty manager advising guests to firmly close all windows and don button-down shirts, long pants and covered shoes if straying beyond the hotel's confines around dawn or dusk. Dengue fever was loose in the capital, and those were the infected mosquitoes' preferred dining hours.

The eccentricities that make India so endlessly fascinating continued to unfold before me like a vaudeville show when I set out next morning on the five-kilometre walk to where the cricketers were staying. I paused to watch a gentleman attempting to measure the distance between two apparently random points outside an office building using nothing more scientific than a thin strand of binding twine. Every time he secured one end beneath a discarded broken brick, and pulled the opposite end taut to secure an accurate reading, the affixed end would jolt loose and flail uselessly in the breeze. He would then reposition it beneath the brick and repeat the process, which produced the same result. What lifted the whole episode beyond absurd was the presence of half a dozen other quizzical bystanders, all watching intently with arms folded across chests or squatting patiently, with not a soul offering to help the exasperated surveyor by holding down one end of his string. No sooner had I resumed my amble than I was joined by a small girl, aged around seven or eight, wearing a tattered garment that had, at one stage in its difficult life, been a smart floral dress. She skipped along barefoot beside me, occasionally looking expectantly up through chocolate-brown eyes, while flashing a smile that revealed a set of perfectly aligned teeth. Having made me aware of her presence, she began her well-rehearsed street banter.

'Hello sir, can you help me?' Skip, skip, hop.

'Hello sir, can you help me?' Skip, skip, skip.

This continued almost the length of the block when, aware that her routine did not look like squeezing any cash from a hard-hearted tourist, she delved deeper into her repertoire. Dashing ahead, and turning to face me as my pace slowed, she clasped her hands in front of her waist. Without shifting her gaze from mine, she lifted her arms back over head, fingers still intertwined and, as they reached down beyond her hips, she crouched at the knees, rested both sets of knuckles on the footpath, and executed a little jump, at which point her conjoined hands passed beneath her feet. She then stood triumphantly to attention with her hands returned to their starting position, roughly where the waistband of her dress would have hung, had it not long ago perished.

'Now that's genuinely impressive,' I said, fishing a fifty rupee note from my pocket. Not understanding a word I'd said, she scrunched the magenta and grey bill bearing the Mahatma's kindly countenance into her grimy hand and skipped off along one of Delhi's wide, leafy boulevards before disappearing into the Saturday afternoon traffic.

Global media empires are not immune from the dwindling revenue streams that are inexorably driving newspapers the way of thylacines and watchable commercial television. It was therefore quite rightly deemed wasteful for a cricket reporter from a budget-challenged broadsheet to be enjoying the same $US500 a night residential comforts lavished on touring cricketers. However, the physical disconnect between me and the team also removed a vital capillary of information flow. No brief encounters outside the lift doors. No snippets of gossip in the breakfast room, or chance observations of indiscretions in the lobby. It meant interactions with players and coaching staff were restricted to breaks during training and scheduled media events that had become so scripted they were lucky to produce a usable quote, much less a pithy yarn. I also suspected that the physical separation, coupled with a typically cumbersome playing schedule – which meant the Australians were in India for almost two weeks before their first competitive match – might create a news vacuum the Ideas Factory would feel driven to fill. So it came as no great surprise when, shortly before dawn on our second morning in New Delhi, I was awoken by an urgent phone call from the boss.

The UK's *Sunday Times* was set to break a huge international story, I was assured, that demanded urgent and comprehensive reaction from Ricky Ponting, from the top echelons of Cricket Australia, and from anyone else in the touring party willing to contribute their thoughts. Barely conscious and groping for a light switch, I couldn't think of anyone likely to fit that final category at 6 a.m. And when further details of this 'world exclusive' were relayed down the phone, I became even more sceptical.

An anonymous informant claiming to be a family friend of one of the London Underground suicide bombers had revealed details of a plot to kill the Australian and England cricket teams by spreading sarin gas in their respective change rooms during the 2005 Edgbaston Test. The story included no credible corroboration from authorities or witnesses, and one of south Asia's leading terrorist experts quickly dismissed the claim's veracity. But on a slow October Sunday morning, when a front-page 'splash' was harder to come by than personal space on the subcontinent, those trifling concerns were happily ignored. And when I wondered aloud whether it had been, indeed, the world's most evil terrorist network rather than a hapless member of the Australian coaching staff that had masterminded planting a ball beneath McGrath's foot in the hour before that same Test began, I was told to get up, smarten up and start making phone calls.

Upon reaching Mumbai, where the Australians were to begin a full week's preparation ahead of their first tournament match against an as-yet-unknown opponent, I found myself even further removed from the players' accommodation. Which proved an unmitigated delight, with the walk that consumed almost an hour in the mornings on my way to conduct daily interviews, and even longer when returning to type them up, affording moments infinitely more captivating than the cricket clichés that awaited me at either end.

Heading north towards Colaba, I would negotiate wave after wave of colourfully clad reed-thin women effortlessly balancing water jugs, or sacks of fruit, rice or vegetables, atop their heads as they returned from nearby markets to the Ambedkar Nagar settlement, one of the many slums estimated to house up to half of Mumbai's eighteen million inhabitants. Occupying a square kilometre of marsh-fronted wasteland facing on to the Arabian Sea, and just a few hundred metres from my hotel, it was also suspected of being the source of a cholera outbreak reported on the day of our arrival.

My routine came also to include a morning wander past the trendy shops and bazaars of Shahid Bhagat Singh Road. Or the flotilla of flat-bottomed dories and sparsely stocked stalls at another slum colony opposite Bhadwar Park. Or, depending on the strength of my constitution, Mumbai's frantic Sassoon Docks fish market. The return leg would incorporate a more leisurely stroll. Among spirited cricket matches being fought out on the Oval Maidan, beneath the imposing stone edifice of the Bombay High Court, and through the Colaba Causeway street markets that flogged anything from digital cameras to antique gramophones. As engaging as these daily distractions were, they could not paper over the inescapable professional reality that nothing of interest was taking place. Not to a national newspaper, anyway. We were marooned in the middle of a cricket tournament that, from an Australian perspective at least, provided no cricket.

Consequently, the antithesis of news is what readers of the paper were served in the days counting down to the national team's first match in Mumbai. An absence of meaningful alternatives meant space was given to probing insights, which included career-shaping advice Nathan Bracken received from his mother-in-law, Lenore ('just relax and play cricket'), shortly after he had lost his Cricket Australia playing contract. Explosive revelations that Brett Lee had been offered a leading role in a Bollywood feature film by no lesser star than Amitabh Bachchan, and that the fast bowler was considering acting as a profession after cricket. Topping all was the dazzling explanation of the various aerodynamic factors at play to make a cricket ball reverse swing, courtesy of bowling coach Troy Cooley, who was credited with plotting the downfall of Australia's batting when he worked with England during the previous Ashes campaign.

According to the 1,030-word treatise that the paper ran in its entirety, it requires a bowler capable of generating speeds above 120 kilometres per hour while holding the ball's seam at an angle of around twenty degrees to the batsman and imparting backspin of roughly eleven revolutions per second. At which point the air flowing over the smooth side of the ball separates earlier due to a pressure imbalance, causing it to swing away from the shiny side. Or something like that. By the time it reached its inane conclusion, even its author had lost interest.

Australia's tournament eventually got underway in the genteel surrounds of Mumbai's historic Brabourne Stadium. The home of the esteemed Cricket Club of India, with its private tennis, swimming and yoga facilities, its forty-five art-deco influenced suites for paying guests, and its wide, airy porticoes opening directly on to a manicured playing surface that, on non-cricket days, hosted tall wicker chairs and afternoon tea settings that whispered 'last days of the Raj'. The Australians' opponents were the Champions Trophy holders, the West Indies, who had been forced to suffer the indignity of qualifying for the event's main draw by taking part in a pre-tournament tournament, alongside Sri Lanka, Zimbabwe and Bangladesh. A sort of 'best of the worst' appetiser, as only the ICC would consider serving up.

Then, after such a protracted preamble, an unexpected initial loss to Brian Lara's men in the opening game had all of us suddenly eyeing an early flight home, should the Australians fail in either of their two remaining group matches. Which meant the next game, against England in the famed Pink City of Jaipur, finally promised something worthwhile to write about. But events dictated it was something even more arresting than the impending Ashes that provided the material.

Casual conversations with usually imperturbable colleagues among the vast Indian press corps revealed a number of them weren't making the 1,200-kilometre trip from Mumbai to the Rajasthani capital because of security fears. This was a response to threats made by the Hindu nationalist group Shiv Sena to disrupt an earlier game in Jaipur, as well as the timing of the match between the Ashes rivals that was scheduled for Diwali Saturday. The clearly rattled press men pointed to the terrorist bombing of Mumbai's rail networks, just weeks prior to the tournament beginning, which had left almost 200 dead.

'Diwali's a fireworks festival, you know, and I can't imagine what sort of home-made devices and rockets might be smuggled into the ground for such a big game,' a veteran reporter for one of India's most influential newspapers told me as we left the post-match media conference at Brabourne.

'The Indian authorities carried out an investigation after the July bombings here, and one of their explicit findings was that all security agencies should be on the highest alert during Diwali. And Shiv Sena are already threatening to do something before the tournament's over. That's the reason I'll be watching your game safely on the television in my hotel room. And for what it's worth, I'd reconsider going to Jaipur at all if I was you.'

Having successfully outwitted dengue fever, cholera and terminal under-employment since arriving on the subcontinent, the Australians reasoned that a handful of extremists shouldn't pose too great a threat. And if the team was travelling, I was obliged to follow. Further mollification came with news that a tight security cordon would be thrown around Jaipur for the entire Diwali weekend. It included troopers from India's elite Central Industrial Security Force, normally charged with guarding installations such as nuclear power plants, supplemented by members of the battle-hardened elite internal security detail the Contingents of the Central Police Force, which was regularly involved in fighting insurgents at flashpoints including Kashmir. Even more reassuring was the International Cricket Council's contribution of $US700,000 to help bolster the tournament's security detail, and which extended to the deployment of 'spotters' at all stadium entrances to identify 'anti-nationals' likely to be more intent on sabotaging than supporting. I figured it couldn't be too hard to detect someone packing a laser-guided surface-to-air missile along with their sparklers, their cardboard placards and their supper, so it was to Jaipur I headed.

Besides, the threat of organised violence had become as much a part of an overseas cricket tour as collecting taxi receipts and filing lost luggage reports. Whether it was the furtive gangs of Nairobi, the ruthless suicide bombers of London's Underground, the thuggish brutality of Chittagong's police or the criminal negligence of Caribbean hotel operators, there weren't many places around the world where an outbreak of cricket wasn't accompanied by personal risk. So the prospect of a few over-muscled fireworks was not going to prevent me from using every spare minute of our three days in Jaipur to lap up its myriad, and spectacular, attractions.

I took the opportunity to wander through the historic commercial heart of Aatish Market and Tripolia Bazaar with their hawkish sellers and belligerent street monkeys. Past the awe-inspiring red sandstone façade of the Hawa Mahal, and even paid a flying visit to the imposing Amber Fort that rises spectacularly above the main highway to Delhi. Throughout all these ventures, the only time I legitimately feared for my safety was on the trip back to Jaipur from the fort when, approaching the Palace of Jal Mahal, which seems to magically levitate on the surface of Man Sagar Lake, my driver took both hands from the steering wheel, turned to present me with one of the ubiquitous feedback forms that anyone providing a public service in India is desperate to have completed, and narrowly avoided driving up the back end of an elephant that straddled both lanes as we rounded a bend. Eighteen months later, a series of nine bombs synchronised to detonate across Jaipur within fifteen minutes, and all strategically planted near historic monuments and across the old city's crowded markets to maximise their impact, killed sixty-three and injured more than 200.

Australia's comfortable win over England in Jaipur meant their hopes of snaring the Champions Trophy after four barren attempts were revived. But no sooner had the tournament belatedly burst into life than it slumped back into its torpor. We travelled further north, to under the shadow of the Himalayas, for a further eight days of waiting, this time in Chandigarh, before Australia's final group match against India at nearby Mohali. With its strictly planned Le Corbusier-designed arrangement of forty-six suburban sectors, and its network of public parks and wide avenues, Chandigarh stands as the Canberra of the Punjab. It certainly shared a similar love of bureaucracy. Upon clearing the airport, I squeezed into a rattling taxi and was told, as we turned on to the main road, that should I require use of the vehicle's air conditioning, I would incur an immediate technology levy of one hundred rupees.

Another week to fill between cricket outings taxed more than my ingenuity. The crazy work requirements of previous tours seemed almost preferable to lengthy, unproductive stints in far-off places. Despite carefully constructing daily perambulations from my lodgings in Sector 10 to the team's digs in Sector 17 so they traversed varied routes, the repetitive nothingness slowly sapped my energy and eroded my flickering motivation. I stretched work out to occupy as many excess hours as bearable and, in between, I wandered Leisure Valley's undulating copses of shrubs and woodland, or enjoyed the perfumed blooms and soothing water features of the city's celebrated Rose Garden. I half-heartedly planned day trips to nearby places of interest – Shimla's restorative Hill Station and Sikhism's Golden Temple at Amritsar. Even the theatrical daily ceremonies at the Wagah border with Pakistan. But all of them required extended separation from the cricket team, and I could not risk the one major story of the assignment exploding in my absence. As a result, each day trapped in Chandigarh bled aimlessly into the next. A mounting heaviness began to settle within. If I was to be marking time, I would rather be doing it with those whose company I craved.

In the years since Ricky Ponting had succeeded Adam Gilchrist as the newspaper's man on the inside, he had been cooperative and accessible when it came to preparing his occasional column, if not especially forthcoming. His most obvious limitation was a devout unwillingness to say anything but the obvious. Drafting the 750 or so words to appear under his name yielded no deeper insights than he would regularly reveal at media conferences. He answered any questions put to him honestly and in good humour. But not once in the time I acted as his ghost did he arrive for one of our brief meetings enthusing 'I've got a great idea for a column' or 'This is an issue that I really want to take a stance on'. The closest he came to floating a topic was in the days before a Test in Perth as we sat on the grandstand seats outside the players' dressing room at the WACA Ground. He had with him a new cricket bat, freshly arrived from his contracted supplier, and, as I non-expertly inspected the pristine blade, he launched into an animated dissertation about the science of bat selection.

'I pretty much know if it's a bat I'll want to use just by looking at the face,' Ponting said, as he relieved me of the unblemished lump of bleached willow like it was a sleeping infant.

'You see here,' he continued, tracing his right index finger along its smooth surface, from the splice almost to the toe. 'There's a faint pink strip running all the way down. The wood on the inside of that strip is a little bit softer, and so has a bit more give to it. It's almost like a springboard effect. So I always look for a bat that's got that pink grain running close to the outside edge. That way, it's got more flexibility in the middle of the blade.'

I looked at him as he ran his hirsute hands lightly across the tool of his trade, as if divining its latent power.

'We should do that as a column one day,' I ventured. 'How you go about selecting the perfect cricket bat. People like to read about that sort of insider stuff. It gives them a bit of a glimpse of what you guys do behind the scenes.'

'Nah,' he smiled mischievously. 'People'd think I was some sort of cricket tragic.'

It was the same smile he wore when he sat down across the table from me, *café latte* in hand, in the lobby restaurant of the Taj Chandigarh. Any hopes I held of the tour's news void being filled by a hard-hitting first-person account of what consumed the man about to embark on a career-defining Ashes campaign were snuffed out with his greeting.

'So, what have you got for me today?' he grinned, referring to the column he once more expected me to conceive, draft, edit and send.

My immediate reaction was that this might just be the time to explain to the skipper that perhaps it was his turn to start playing a few shots. That he needed to appreciate he was being paid more for a dozen or so columns each year than I drew in annual salary and, as a result, he should be coming to me with the occasional theme that he wanted to cover. He should also be made aware that other cricket folk with whom I had ghost-written paid columns – Gilchrist, Sunil Gavaskar, Michael Slater, David Lloyd – all began the process with at least the kernel of an idea. Sometimes, as Gilchrist showed, significantly more. But this diatribe took shape in my head and went no further. He was, after all, the captain of Australia, whereas I was on the road to becoming an ex-cricket writer who knew from experience that little was gained by airing petty grievances.

So I trotted out half a dozen uninspired questions, he bunted back as many trite answers, and I returned to my hotel to manufacture it into another predictable space filler that enticed as many readers as it enlightened. When it was done, I forwarded a copy to Cricket Australia for their mandatory pre-publication approval, and another to Ponting's private email address for his consideration. His employer gave it a tick within half an hour, so I sent it directly to mine for typesetting. But, as was the case with all those that came before and after, Ponting remained inscrutably silent.

His team's victory over India at Mohali was celebrated with deserved vigour. The party among the press pack was less enthusiastic when it was confirmed that the result consigned Australia to a semi-final against New Zealand, three days later. In Mohali. Even the schedule now conspired to hold us hostage in Chandigarh. The day after the India match, desperate for any diversion to fill the cricketless days, I extended my wandering to include the mysterious Rock Garden that sprawls several square kilometres on the edge of Sector 1.

I was intrigued as much by the story of its genesis as I was by its attractions. The creation of a one-time public servant and self-taught sculptor Nek Chand, its display pieces were initially fashioned from discarded industrial and household items, and the entire project was so secretive it went undetected by neighbours and local authorities for almost twenty years – as large-scale theme parks being built next door are wont to do. When it was eventually discovered, many in Chandigarh demanded it be torn down. Now, it stands as the geometrically precise city's monument to *laissez-faire*.

Entering the Rock Garden is a bit like disappearing through the back of a cupboard into Narnia – a labyrinth of interconnected waterfalls, courtyards and display spaces, many of them populated by armies of tiny figures covered with mosaic tiles. There are Gaudi-esque landscapes around which narrow earthen paths weave and switch back. Every bend reveals a new vista of Chand's strange world, made even more surreal on the dull, grey afternoon I visited by the ethereal presence of groups of Indian women in their stunningly coloured saris, floating from space to space and exchanging animated whispers.

After two hours exploring this parallel world, I arrived at its most extraordinary scene – a semi-circular cloister of grey stone walls into which were hewn a dozen symmetrically spaced arches. From hooks chiselled into the stone above each arch dangled a simple wooden swing, suspended by lengths of thick chain. And on each of these swings sat a pair of teenage girls, all dressed identically in flowing white *salwar kameez* and matching *dupattas*. Each wore their long black hair tied in a single plait which snaked down their back. In silence broken only by the straining creak of the chains, and the occasional flutter of fabric on the breeze, they swung back and forth in metronomic rhythm. As I stood, speechless, in the courtyard's centre, not one of them showed any hint of self-consciousness or curiosity. They just continued swinging, ever higher, legs outstretched and eyes fixed, alternately on the cobbled ground below or up at the solemn sky. I checked for cameras, fearing I had unwittingly wandered onto the set of a Greenaway movie.

A bench seat on a terrace that ringed the secret garden seemed purpose-sent for a bout of quiet contemplation. Against the hypnotic backdrop of this hushed retreat, I set myself to deconstructing how exactly the world's best job had all but lost its lustre. Like tracking down the faulty filament in a string of Christmas lights, I needed to identify which elements of 'working for a serious newspaper, travelling the world watching cricket' had broken down. Then it might simply be a matter of replacing the dud part, and the glow would return.

There was no doubt broadsheet journalism offered a freedom and diversity few careers could match, even at a newspaper that took little as seriously as itself. But the fact remains that news is a discretionary purchase product, little different to deodorant or Bran Flakes, and the challenge, increasingly, is finding ways to manufacture, package and sell it in profitable volumes. That's led to a fundamental shift in the way news is covered. No longer do editors convene late afternoon to sift through the events of the day and arrange them throughout a paper for maximum impact. Nowadays, the stories that generate most interest, that provoke the strongest responses, are instantly measured by the number of online hits they register. By knowing where readers' eyes and preferences are trained, editorial conferences have become the place where the day's stories are pre-emptively written. The modern reporters' task is then to assemble the words that justify the premise. Here's the headline, give me a story to fit beneath it. Increasingly, the tail wagged the dogma.

As for the travel component, there was no question it opened up new worlds. But it was equally clear it was not the real world. Hotel turn-down services, and those little grey airline breakfast sausages that, along with cockroaches, will alone survive nuclear holocaust, might embellish a fulfilling life, but can never replace it. And while packing a bag and leaving everyday behind might offer a quick fix to whatever ails, the hollow call of the road can also prove destructively convenient. There comes a time when the only hope for making things work at home is being there. Clearly, therefore, I was to rely on the game of cricket's magnetic appeal to restore my ardour for the job. Another knife-edged Ashes series might just save more than some players' careers.

Surprising nobody, the Australians breezed past New Zealand in the semi-final, which meant our group then travelled back to Mumbai, where it all began, for the final. At Brabourne Stadium. Against the West Indies. And precisely one month after we had gathered in India, during which time the Australian team had completed just four days of international cricket, the sport's global media gathered in the Cricket Club of India's sweltering open-air press box as Ricky Ponting chased another gilded piece of history.

Despite the West Indies' ballistic start which produced eighty runs in the first ten overs, they were bowled out for a limp 138. A heavy post-monsoonal downpour early in Australia's pursuit briefly raised the unnerving prospect of extending accommodation bookings and rescheduling flights. But the storm passed, and the Australians finally got their hands on the elusive prize late on what had become a pleasantly cool, still Mumbai evening. I worked through the night to properly document the occasion, and roused myself later in the morning to phone the Factory and make sure I was cleared for take-off.

'I thought you'd already be on the way home by now,' the boss said, by way of hello.

'Plane leaves tonight at 11,' I said. 'But I've got a thirteen-hour lay-over in Singapore, so I won't be back in Melbourne until Wednesday night. The price you pay for booking budget flights, I guess.'

'Bloody hell,' he spluttered. 'The Poms play their first tour match here on Friday and we need to crank up our coverage. How soon after you get home can you jump on a plane to Brisbane?'

22

Ashes Series, Australia, November 2006–February 2007

It was when I piled soiled laundry into a calico bag bearing the Jaipur Sheraton logo, and tossed it into the corridor outside my bedroom door in Melbourne that I suspected the need to wean myself from life on the road had become critical. It sat there for several hours before it dawned that, during those rare stints at home, I was the housekeeping staff. That belief galvanised further when, before leaving for Brisbane, I was briefed on the latest budget-enforced squeeze on perks available to employees whose work took them out of the office and away from their daily lives. The edict decreed that hotel breakfast had been bracketed alongside bottled water from the in-room refrigerator and phone calls to loved ones as luxury items that a global media empire had no business recompensing. And so, my usual luggage stuffing routine extended to include a box of cereal, a plastic bowl and a spoon. Living out of a suitcase for months at a time was, in itself, a challenge. Eating from one was just demeaning.

The scene at the Australian squad's main training session ahead of the first Test confirmed we were entering the most anticipated summer since the invention of the bikini. Rather than a collection of pimply trundlers and cricket balls scattered like land mines awaiting some pyrrhic fielding drill, practice stretched out like a war game over Brisbane Grammar's sprawling playing fields. Centre wicket work for the fast bowlers and top-order batsmen. Specialist nets work for the spinners. A trestle table was laid at a ten-degree angle across the popping crease of one pitch, where a bowling machine fired balls regularly into its chipped surface, from which they skewed off as replicated gully catches to an eagerly waiting Matthew Hayden. At each station hovered a media pack, the equal of anything previously seen at an Australian rehearsal. Reporters, feature writers, broadcasters, camera crews, bloggers, hangers-on, and the pathologically nosey. All craning for some morsel that nobody else had noticed. And all left to make do with nothing more revelatory than the bleeding obvious. From the outset of the series, media outnumbered stories on a daily ratio of roughly fifty to one.

When it finally arrived, the opening act of the Ashes summer – played out before an expectant full house on a steamy Brisbane Thursday morning – proved as shambolic as it was symbolic. Backed by a soaring crescendo, England's Steve Harmison bounded in from the 'Gabba's Stanley Street end, arms and legs flailing like a freshly potted lobster, and speared the series' first delivery diagonally across the pitch. So far wide of Justin Langer's bat that it landed directly in the hands of Andrew Flintoff at second slip. A mix of gloating roars, agonised groans and hysterical laughter swamped the stadium. Harmison smiled sheepishly before turning to walk back for another go. Langer squinted into the sunlight to reassure himself he wasn't the victim of some elaborate hoax. And Flintoff nonchalantly flicked the hard lacquered ball to a nearby fielder and then stood, with hands on hips, whistling softly – like the perpetrator of a minor offence when the plod arrived. Nothing to see here, he silently pleaded. Sadly, from England's perspective, that remained the case for the next three months.

As many had feared, the summer suffered severely from 'New Year's Eve Paradox', whereby the amount of expectant energy invested is inversely proportional to the level of satisfaction derived. The other New Year's Eve truism is that, for a fleeting period – roughly ages sixteen to twenty-one – it tantalises as life's social highlight because it's when the whole world is out and going crazy. From then on, it is to be avoided at all costs because the whole world is out and going crazy. Using that logic, and having played a part in whipping up the frenzy that grew steadily over the months leading to that anti-climactic first minute, I immediately began pouring scorn on the one-sided contest, as if to prove that I had not, for a moment, been fooled by the all hype.

'It's all very admirable to bowl *to* your set field,' I sneered, by way of introduction to my first-day report.

'It's quite another thing to bowl *at* them.' From there, I became more jaundiced and condescending with every England failure. Which, in turn, mounted by the hour.

Trounced in Brisbane, the tourists were then ritually humiliated at their next outing in Adelaide. Not for the entire Test, but certainly when it mattered. After dominating the first four days, the English capitulation on the fifth carried an unmistakable whiff of Dhaka eight months earlier. England's batsmen needed only to stay put for a couple of sessions to secure a stalemate, but under the glare of a baking Adelaide sun and a ruthlessly driven opponent, they too blinked. Hard and often. Like the Bangladeshis, England's self-belief simply evaporated when the game was in the balance, and took months to reconstitute.

The Australians' diligent observation and evaluation of their quarry had paid dividends. During the long, empty pauses that punctuated the Champions Trophy in India, they studied England's matches and noticed that, as a captain of limited experience, Flintoff occasionally lost the plot. That his teammates in the field sometimes struggled to gain his attention as he became immersed in his own issues, and that his strategies were regularly found to be an over or three adrift of the match's pace. This fanatical zeal for success sprang directly from the Australians' previous loss in England. Personally and professionally affronted by their failures in that campaign, the core of Australia's senior cricketers pledged to settle for nothing less than utter demolition of their Ashes rival.

Anyone who did not share that commitment risked ostracism, as Damien Martyn found. Martyn had always struggled with the scrutiny that accompanied life as an international cricketer, and fought a long-running personal battle with the media that, he believed, existed solely to persecute him. A couple of modest scores leading into the final day in Adelaide meant he went to the wicket that afternoon demoted one place in the batting order, and with his team straining against the odds for a win, battling thoughts of self-doubt and self-destruction. His response was to bat like a man with no cares and even less responsibility. He faced four balls, charging feverishly at the third to launch it to the mid-off fence. The next, he leaned back lazily and aimed a backyard waft that lobbed straight to a catcher at point.

This was precisely what his teammates, through their infamous pre-series boot camp in Queensland's sub-tropical forests and their subsequent single-minded training exercises, had sought to eradicate. The elevation of personal needs above the team's demands. By opting to pull the easy oar and leave the hard work to others, rather than find a way through his mental clutter, Martyn had broken trust and lost respect. It was during the post-match celebrations, after Martyn had shared drinks with a couple of England players in the Australian dressing room, that Matthew Hayden decided he should point out a few home truths to his long-time mate. The next day, without consultation or explanation, Martyn walked away from cricket for good.

At least that development provided something other than England's conspicuous inadequacies to write about, heading into the third Test in Perth. But the Australians' woe was soon forgotten as the tourists were again hammered, and the Ashes were decided with the summer just eighteen days old. The prospect of filling vast swathes of newsprint across the Christmas–New Year silly season with coverage of what was now a sporting contest in concept only hung heavily over the media pack as we travelled back across the continent for Melbourne's Boxing Day Test. That was when Shane Warne, the Patron Saint of the Slow News Day, answered our collective prayers.

The media conference he called five days before the Test to confirm his retirement from international cricket at series' end was – unlike the ill-fated 'woin' that had disappeared without trace in the wake of the doping furore – vintage Warne. Regular Thursday afternoon television programming was suspended to accommodate a live feed of the event from the Melbourne Cricket Ground, introduced with suitable solemnity by a deadpan Richie Benaud, who reassured the nation that it was entering a time of celebration, rather than mourning.

The MCG's grand Members Dining Room was filled with row upon row of chairs, in anticipation of the sort of turnout normally seen at White House press briefings. By the time the show was due to start, all seats were filled and almost as many media folk were forced into standing-room places in the wings or behind a bank of television cameras. A Cricket Australia official gravely cautioned that questions relating to Warne's turbulent personal life were strictly off limits, and we all dutifully complied. Given this might be the last genuine news yarn of the summer, we couldn't risk having the talent clam up or storm out, as had happened at conferences past. But we needn't have worried. Warne took the best part of an hour to explain his ten-second announcement.

The storm of hagiography it unleashed in the next day's media was countered in many quarters by the rehashing of Warne's countless character flaws, irrespective of the censorship he had sought to impose. But the most compelling analysis came not from windy social commentators or outraged morals campaigners, but from the teammates and opponents who witnessed first-hand Warne taking cricket's most complex art to never-before-seen, or even foreseen, levels. As Ricky Ponting explained with trademark economy the following day, 'a lot of people don't realise how difficult it is to bowl leg spin'.

That was Warne's undisputed genius. More so than infatuating or infuriating the public. It was a talent built on a remarkably powerful right wrist, fingers that resembled a brace of uncooked pork sausages, and an ability to impart so much energy on the ball that it audibly hummed its way towards batsmen. More often than not, it also spun furiously on an axis that ensured it would land unerringly on its seam, thereby gaining maximum purchase off the pitch. But dealing with his spitting leg break, or wrong-un, or flipper, or slider, or zooter, or whatever new delivery Warne had dreamed up, was but one question in a searching exam for the world's batsmen.

The first challenge for those who faced up was to make sure they focused on playing the ball, not the legend. And Warne, who often understood his opponents' psychology far better than his own, knew how to make that distinction as difficult as possible. He would cultivate uncertainty by merely standing at the top of his run-up, staring at his prey and distractedly fizzing the ball from one giant mitt to the other, as if unsure of how to set about his task. But it was total bluff. Warne could manipulate batsmen around the crease like avatars in a video game. Switching the direction of his attack from around the wicket, to over the wicket. Close to the stumps. Wide of the crease. Spearing the ball in at the toes. Floating it invitingly wide. Every iteration meticulously planned and flawlessly executed to manoeuvre the batsman's stance and defence to a point where vulnerabilities opened up.

Having marshalled his fielders into position, like a pernickety interior designer fussing over throw cushions, to further heighten the sense of strangulation felt by batsmen, he would regularly begin his run-up only to suddenly stop, forcing another break in his opponent's concentration. A raised palm, similarly disingenuous to a tennis baseliner apologising for a net cord, a couple of waddled steps, and it would begin again. A mosey up to the crease, a grunt as the right arm imparted the wizardry, then just the ominous whirring of the ball that allowed it to drift appreciably in its arc, making it even trickier to nullify.

For batsmen who could withstand the staring and the waiting, who could discern and combat the variations, who could see a gap in the field and execute the appropriate stroke to exploit it, there still remained the mental battle that came with survival. The ceaseless chatter. The goading and the gamesmanship. All shamelessly designed to unsettle and unhinge. For some, such as England's Ian Bell in his first Ashes Test at Lord's in 2005, it eventually culminated in complete mental shutdown. Unsure whether to play or to leave, to defend or to score, to appear relaxed or watchful, to deny the close catchers or take a risk, Bell simply neglected to do anything other than look dumbfounded and then, when the ball thudded straight into his pads and the umpire's finger rose, crestfallen.

In addition to distilling some of Warne's press conference verbiage into bite-sized newspaper morsels, I was instructed to glean the captain's reflections in one of his columns. Ponting's agent warned me the skipper was otherwise occupied for the afternoon – attending signing sessions to promote the release of the latest in his series of *Captain's Diaries*, an even more lucrative outlet for his thoughts. But I tracked him to a central Melbourne bookshop, joined the queue as the lone fan not clutching a copy for inscription, and hoped – with deadline fast approaching – that he might find a few spare minutes in which I could earn him another fistful of cash. Conscious of not depriving paying customers of moments with their hero, I suggested via a shorthand conversation that we conduct our chat at signing session's end. When the last autograph was scrawled, the store manager whisked Ponting into a locked office, the door of which was guarded by a uniformed security guard who heard my entreaty for access and then advised me to scram. Midway through a pointless appeal to his compassion, I caught sight of Ponting being led to a waiting car on the other side of the shop's front window.

I dashed from the store, rapped on the passenger's-side glass as the vehicle pulled away from the kerb, and convinced the seemingly perplexed skipper that I should ride with him to his next appointment. Or at least as far as it took him to dictate a handful of thoughts about Warne into my voice recorder. Seven minutes later, I alighted from the car as it idled in late-afternoon gridlock, and frantically began searching for a cab that could get me back to my laptop so I could get his words into the paper.

With the Ashes won, those Australian players haunted by the 2005 disappointment felt a wrong had been righted, a burden lifted, and a new era beckoned. Following Martyn and Warne into retirement were coach John Buchanan, Justin Langer and Glenn McGrath, who pointedly refused Ponting's offer for him to bat at number three on the final day of the Sydney Test, with its accompanying chance to score the winning runs should one of the openers stumble in pursuit of their token victory target.

'I either bat at number one, or number eleven,' he told his chastened skipper.

Of all these announcements, it was Langer's farewell press conference that carried, for me, the greatest resonance. As blue collar as Warne's conference was grandiose, it was conducted in a windowless converted football change room beneath the SCG's Bradman Stand. There, Langer revealed the conflicting emotions that accompanied his eventual acceptance that he had, at age thirty-six, reached the end of his working life in a job he had coveted from the time he was old enough to nurture ambition.

'It's not just a game to me,' he explained, with a sincerity born of someone who had wrung every last drop from their God-given talent. 'It's been the vehicle for me to learn how to handle success, failure and criticism. How to fight back from adversity. I've learned about mateship and about leadership. And hopefully, I've forged a strong character.'

In the end, he revealed, he had become 'ground down' by incessant media speculation as to whether he merited a place in the team. Since being pole-axed in Johannesburg, those calls had broadened to incorporate his advancing years, the greying hue of Australian cricket, and the apparent need to infuse fresh blood into the Test team, even though a comparable replacement remained years in the future.

'I've endured it for a long time, and maybe I'd like to let that go as well, and put a smile back on my face,' he said.

As he strode back out into the sunlight to finalise preparations for his last Test, his words stayed with me, bouncing off the bunker's concrete walls like it was a Leicester nightclub. As part of the media pack at Mascot Airport a day earlier that had hounded Langer as if he were a hit-run driver outside a district court in the hope of securing a definitive statement on his playing future, I too had cause for introspection. If I were to apply the same harsh criteria to my own professional performance that I imposed on others, I must also surely be approaching my use-by date. My recent form had been patchy, if not downright poor. I'd not broken a story since ... well, I'd plain not broken a story. The occasional embargo, at best. My enthusiasm had been similarly 'ground down' by those who passed judgement from comfortable detachment. And as my chosen profession rapidly evolved, I found myself regularly at odds with the new era's demands. I left the SCG that afternoon thinking perhaps I should pen a scathing article in which I called for my own sacking. It was also New Year's Day 2007, and I felt a resolution coming on.

*   *   *

Barely had the acclamation accompanying Australia's five–nil clean sweep dulled to a patriotic holler than the interminable limited-overs tri-series swung into life. A month of one-day internationals was preceded by a Twenty20 fixture that produced yet another crushing England loss, and a predictably contrived call from the Ideas Factory to turn another morning-conference thought bubble into a story of national importance. Or at least, one of importance to the national paper.

'I was watching that twenty-over game in the office last night, and it struck me that every time I looked up, somebody was hitting another six,' a member of the brains trust marvelled down the phone.

'So, we need a piece explaining why so many sixes are hit in modern cricket, especially in Twenty20 matches. With the games getting shorter, they seem to be belting the ball further.'

I tried to tactfully suggest that the answer to that query was contained in the question, but obediently vowed to get on the case as soon as I checked back into my own apartment. The thought of another reverse-swing-style physics lesson that examined cricket bat technology, shrinking playing field dimensions, and the complex relationship between needing to score at the fastest possible rate when facing fewer and fewer deliveries made my temples throb. But there was more to come.

As the summer loitered towards its uninspired finish, the only outcome less surprising than Australian victories was the regular outbreaks of spectator idiocy at one-day games – to the extent that cricket and law enforcement authorities conspired to outlaw the Mexican Wave from the Melbourne Cricket Ground. That sort of pronouncement was guaranteed to send blue-rinse tabloid current-affairs programs into apoplexy, railing about 'Fun Police', the 'Nanny State', and the infringement of Australians' civil right to behave like prized dickheads at international sporting events. All buttons the serious broadsheet was not averse to pushing. Fully occupied with the two first-edition stories I needed to file during the change of innings of another tawdry fifty-over encounter between Australia and New Zealand, the call from the Factory was not a welcome distraction.

'The editor wants a piece for the front about fans' reaction to the Mexican Wave ban,' the directive came, with its standard implied threat that it was a request from the very top. 'We've sent a photographer along to get some pics, so you'll need to get out among the crowd and conduct some vox pops.'

Vox pops were the tool newspapers employed, prior to the explosion of social media, to show a connectedness with their readers. They purported to capture the vibe of the street. Letters to the editor from the semi-literate. And a chore most first-year newspaper cadets considered undignified. So I opted for what any frazzled reporter with deadlines to hit and priorities to juggle might be driven to contemplate. I dismissively typed out a selection of fabricated quotes that addressed all the stereotyped opinions I knew the paper was after, attributed them to a set of equally bogus names, and filed them without a second thought. It was only next morning, when all 600 nonsense words appeared as sent on page three, that it dawned I had reached an irredeemable low.

After two decades as a journalist, I had finally subscribed to public perceptions of the profession, and published an unabashed lie. Not through malice, or to push an agenda. But simply because I was tired, under pressure, and fed up. Fed up with having to comply with meritless story ideas hatched in the office over a morning muffin. Fed up with an increasingly simplistic news agenda that recognised only two basic premises from which those ideas should be constructed – campaign or conflict. Fed up dealing with people who would sooner hold a grudge than a conversation. But above all, I'd grown heartily sick of the inconsequential, sardonic tripe I was churning out under my own name. Most dispiritingly, I had fallen for the modern media trap of masquerading opinion as news. Not informed or keenly sought opinion. Just spiteful, lazy sniping that revealed more about my own mindset than the events I was supposed to document.

Opinion has proliferated to become journalism's base commodity, freely traded between the news, business, sports and features pages. 'Opinion section' now describes the entire newspaper. Reporters employ opinion because it's easy. It requires minimal research, means conjecture and controversy can be stirred through otherwise banal events, and, by definition, can't be wrong. But like a gateway drug, it eventually leads to an incapability to write straight news. And from there, it's free-fall until you hit the blog – the pub conversation for those who are too socially inert to buy a round.

In trying to redress the slight of being 'one of the good guys', I had instead joined the snide brigade. By describing the sight of rotund Mark Cosgrove in Australian one-day colours as 'a slowly-melting mound of pistachio and zabaglione gelati', I had skipped fearless criticism and descended straight into character assassination. And when England's batsmen produced their most spineless performance of an insipid tour in the traditional Australia Day one-dayer at Adelaide Oval that summer, I launched an indignant rant that compensated for its total lack of perspective with a quadruple helping of hysteria.

'In the era of reality television and interactive audience polls, the time has surely come for England's cricketers to be voted off this island,' I fulminated in print.

'Yesterday's submission … stunk of a team that has as little pride as it does character, of a group of professional sportsmen as bereft of skills as they are drained of confidence, and of a collective that is counting the minutes until the first available flight home.

'In the interests of those spectators being tricked into handing over precious cash on the premise of being entertained … that flight is Virgin Atlantic VS201 and it departs Sydney for London at 3.50 p.m. today.'

I could, in grand journalistic tradition, have then claimed it was my stinging critique that jolted Andrew Flintoff's team to inexplicably rally and win four of its next five games, including the best-of-three finals series against their Ashes foes in straight sets. But that would have overstated the newspaper's influence and papered over my deeply jaundiced mindset. As it turned out, the sudden radical departure from the summer's script didn't stop me shrieking from the sidelines. As rain threatened to prematurely end Australia's headlong charge towards defeat in the second final, thereby raising the prospect of yet another day of cricket being tacked on to the schedule, I trashed the last remaining rule of accepted sports journalism by openly barracking in the press box. For England. The possibility of them failing to win before the rain arrived drove me to the verge of tears. The trauma associated with sitting through another one-day game made it abundantly clear to me that all three elements of the world's best job description were irretrievably busted. Year-round and worldwide exposure to the game had finally cured me of my childhood obsession for cricket. As a result, I decided over the course of that evening that the end had come.

The storm cleared, mercy prevailed and, shortly before 11 p.m., England emerged triumphant. It was well after midnight when I departed an empty SCG, the wet bitumen roads of Moore Park reflecting bright moonlight as I hunted for a taxi that proved as elusive as that major global scoop I had unsuccessfully sought for a decade. I was in no doubt I would miss the camaraderie of the cricketers, most of whom, once the initial suspicion subsided, provided enjoyable company as well as moments of professional and personal support during a decade of shared ventures. Even tougher would be leaving behind the rapport built with a worldwide fraternity of cricket writers, in the main a thoroughly entertaining collective of incredibly diligent professionals with whom I shared so many memorable moments that transcended our ultimately meaningless competitive jousts. After all, few journalists reflect on the content of past stories, which provide currency for a day but are largely forgotten the next. However, memories of forged friendships and mutual experiences remain vivid for life. I also knew I would never again enjoy such a privileged lifestyle, one that carried me from the breathtaking vista above Guyana's Kaieteur Falls to the floor beneath the Tobago Cays' translucent waters. From dune bashing and a Bedouin feast in the Arabian Desert to an audience with Archbishop and Laureate Desmond Tutu. All loosely in the name of work.

It was, by any measure, an extraordinary job. On many occasions, perhaps even the world's best. But after more than sixty Test matches and a couple of hundred one-day internationals spread across twenty countries, the end-of-day taxi haul back to an empty hotel room was a novelty that had well and truly passed. What's more, in a matter of days Ricky Ponting's team would be in New Zealand, en route to the Caribbean where it would spend two months defending the World Cup. Regardless of the individuals in tow, the carnival relentlessly rolled on.

I filed my resignation by email and it was accepted without question. During the follow-up phone call – conducted in haste because the boss was required at an editorial conference to plan the next day's edition – it was agreed it would become effective from the following day. So I grasped the fleeting opportunity to launch into my carefully rehearsed valedictory speech.

'And I just want to say thanks to everyone there for the past ten years,' I began. 'It really has been a …'

But the line was already dead.

Acknowledgements

Like so many of those compelling newspaper lifestyle columns, the idea for this text sprang from a Saturday-night dinner-party conversation. The fact that it took five years to progress from discussion to completion is due entirely to my tardiness. And if not for the belief and persistence of the idea's author – my agent, Jacinta di Mase – it would not have materialised at all.

Numerous others have played a significant role – knowingly or otherwise – in the preparation and production of this book. In addition to the players and team officials who allowed me to poke around their business on a daily basis, there were the infinitely patient sub-editors, who ensured my copy was mostly fit for publication, and a number of terrific news- and sports-desk colleagues, who helped countless days transcend the burden of impending deadline. I also owe a significant debt to many of my fellow cricket writers and photographers – from across Australia and around the world – who provided friendship, counsel and comic relief over many a lengthy assignment. In particular, I remain profoundly grateful to Mike Coward and Malcolm Conn, with whom I shared a decade of hugely rewarding summers. I remain in awe of their professionalism, talent and generosity, and treasure their friendship.

As a first-time author, I am thankful for the guidance and wisdom of everyone at ABC Books and HarperCollins – in particular, Helen Littleton for her enthusiasm and vision, and Mary Rennie and John Mapps for their expertise in refining the manuscript.

There is no doubt this project would not have progressed beyond a pre-dessert hypothetical if it weren't for the patience and understanding of everyone at home. I thank Tim, Jane and Abbie for excusing my habitual evening retreat to the keyboard, where I became immersed in bouts of isolationist typing, which seemed to stretch far longer than most of the events I was attempting to recapture. And nobody has been more instrumental in the entire process than Pam, whose love, support, kindness and proof-reading talents are embedded in every page.

Finally, I want to thank my sisters, Cathryn and Fiona, who suffered through my childhood delusions of cricketing adequacy and have been ever-willing to help reassemble the pieces at those times when adult ambitions proved equally illusory. Above all, I am indebted to my mother, Beverley, whose quiet courage and unwavering faith has for so long provided a source of inspiration as well as pride.